D1283177

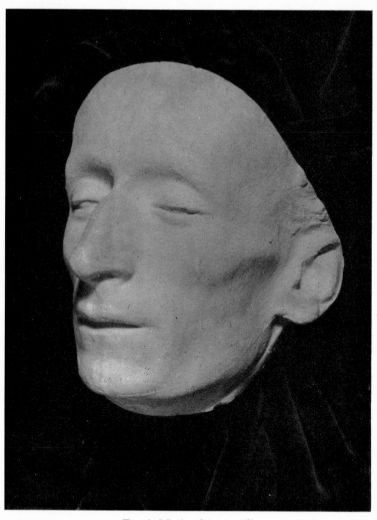

Death Mask of Leopardi

Giacomo Leopardi

Selected Prose and Poetry

Edited, translated, and introduced by
IRIS ORIGO and JOHN HEATH-STUBBS

London
OXFORD UNIVERSITY PRESS
TORONTO   MELBOURNE
1966

Oxford University Press, Ely House, London W.1

GLASGOW NEW YORK TORONTO MELBOURNE WELLINGTON
CAPE TOWN SALISBURY IBADAN NAIROBI LUSAKA ADDIS ABABA
BOMBAY CALCUTTA MADRAS KARACHI LAHORE DACCA
KUALA LUMPUR HONG KONG

The translations in this volume are based on
the Mondadori editions of the *Poesie e Prose*
and of the *Zibaldone* edited by Francesco
Flora, and on the Le Monnier edition of the
Epistolario edited by Francesco Moroncini.

Printed in Great Britain by
Richard Clay (The Chaucer Press), Ltd, Bungay, Suffolk

CONTENTS

II. POETRY

Translated by John Heath-Stubbs

The facsimile facing p. 210 is taken from
the original in the Biblioteca Nazionale,
Naples

Introduction:
Leopardi as Poetic Thinker

Leopardi was born, in 1798, ten years later than Byron, six years later than Shelley, and three years later than Keats. The year in which he died, 1837, also saw the deaths of Pushkin and of Heine. This chronology will serve to place him in that general movement of European literature which we may term Romanticism in the broad sense of that word. The qualification is necessary because the word Romanticism is employed in relation to continental literatures, including the Italian, in a more specialized way, to indicate a type of sensibility which draws its inspiration from the Gothic, the exotic, and the extravagant. In this sense, Leopardi is not a Romantic. He is indeed a Classicist. His poetry seeks its models in those Greek and Roman authors of whom he possessed a profound and scholarly knowledge. But one has only to think of the work of Keats, and of much else in the English Romantic tradition, and of such poets as Hölderlin in Germany, to realize that a nostalgia for the clear light and the pure forms of the antique world could itself be a feature of Romanticism.

Characteristic of the whole movement was the poets' recognition of their alienation. As the nineteenth century dawned, this was borne in upon them by the new currents of political, philosophical, and scientific thought. Everywhere the old patterns of society were in the melting-pot, and long-established ideas were being challenged. The poets could no longer be certain of their role in society, nor sure of their audience. They were therefore forced to rely more and more on particular inspiration, fitful and transient though it might turn out to be, and less and less on exterior sanction and occasion. Since the traditional forms of religious belief seemed largely to have lost their significance, the poets constructed their own systems, taking their symbols from revived mythologies, or from their experience of erotic passion or of natural beauty. This found a fairly superficial expression in the self-dramatization of such a poet as Byron, a profounder one in Wordworth's pursuit of a solitary communion with nature, or Keats's contemplation of sensuous beauty. But Leopardi, perhaps more than any of his contemporaries, goes farthest in the exploration of his own alienation. It is this which makes him in some ways a more modern figure than they, a precursor of the existentialist thought of our own age.

All Leopardi's work presents at one and the same time both a remarkable unity and a curious duality. He is, as we have said, at once a Romantic and a Classicist. He is even, indeed, an anti-Romantic. There is both the lyrical poet of the *Canti* and the hard dry prose writer of the *Operette Morali*. Yet the poems of the former and the dialogues of the latter frequently deal with common themes and complement and comment upon one another. In his verse Leopardi often handles many of those subjects which preoccupied the Romantic poets in general. The English reader may particularly be struck by the number of times in which his poetry suggests that of Wordsworth. This may seem a paradox, since Wordsworth is one of the most joyful of poets, and Leopardi the saddest. Yet it is nevertheless the case. For example, 'Memories' presents a close parallel to 'Tintern Abbey' both in its theme and in its structure. In each poem a scene is contemplated for what it now is and also in terms of the poet's memory of it at an earlier period of his life. Wordsworth's poem reaches its final note of hope in his invocation to his sister Dorothy. She is still in communion with that natural beauty with which Wordsworth himself will lose touch. Leopardi's ends with his despairing lament for the lost Nerina. The one poem might almost be considered as an inversion or mirror-image of the other. Again, Leopardi's Sylvia and Wordsworth's Lucy are parallel figures, not only pathetic images of girls who died young but symbols of something more essential which the poet himself has lost for ever. Among poems I have not translated here, 'Il Risorgimento' examines the central Romantic dilemma of the poet's relation to his own inspiration. So also do Wordsworth's ode on 'Intimations of Immortality' and Coleridge's 'Dejection'. Wordsworth and Leopardi were, as far as I know, entirely unaware of one another's existence. But the fact that two poets so utterly different in background and in temperament should so strikingly approach each other shows to what an extent common experience underlay the European poetry of their day.

The Greek affiliations of Leopardi's poetry bring it into relation with other widely current preoccupations of his age. He is more truly a Hellenist than Shelley or Keats. We should think rather of André Chénier in France and of Landor in England. The latter was resident in Italy during Leopardi's lifetime, and it is rather surprising that he nowhere in his writings refers to the Italian poet. For these two have more in common than their Hellenism and their employment of the dialogue form (with, in each case, a debt to Lucian). Both are aristocrats; both seem to have held a kind of Roman republicanism as their political ideal, and possessed a contempt for the mob, as well as for the more vaporous enthusiasms of their age. When Nietzsche singled out these two, with Heine and Mérimée, as the four greatest prose writers of the nineteenth century, he divined in them more in common than their stylistic purity.

In his poem 'To the Spring' Leopardi laments the loss to modern man of that mythopoeic view of the world whereby the Greeks were able to humanize the natural scene, and to feel at home in the universe. Thus also Keats lamented, and Wordsworth, that he could not hope to hear old Triton blow his wreathèd horn. Thus also Schiller in his famous ode 'The Gods of Greece'. But above all it was Hölderlin who was driven by the same nostalgia to seek to reconcile his Hellenistic neo-paganism with the Protestant Christianity of his upbringing, before he was driven into the abyss of insanity. At one period of his life Leopardi made some approach to a similar attempt at a synthesis. From an early age he had been in revolt against the grim and life-denying Catholic pietism of his mother. But in later years he drafted fragments of an ode to Christ, and to the Virgin, in which he sought to re-habilitate these images in terms of his own subjective and Romantic myth-making. But such a solution, if it might be a solution, was not for him. His universe remains, as for his own Brutus, one in which human anguish has not dimmed the stars.

For Leopardi is not only the child of the Romantic move-ment, but also of the Enlightenment. The *Operette Morali* are essentially a product of the rationalism of the eighteenth century. Like the prose of Schopenhauer, the coincidence of whose thought with Leopardi's has often been pointed out, they are in the tradition of the French moralists of the pre-ceding age—La Rochefoucauld, for example. Behind this tradition stands the figure of Pascal. Leopardi's English disciple, James Thomson (the poet of 'The City of Dreadful Night'), devoted an interesting essay to a comparison of the nineteenth-century Italian and the seventeenth-century Frenchman. Of Leopardi it might indeed be said, as Bau-delaire said of Pascal, that he carried his gulf with him wherever he went. Both possessed that terrifying experience of the empty interstellar spaces which finds expression early in Leopardi with 'The Infinite', one of his best-known poems. For a religious mind like Pascal's this experience may be a preliminary stage towards a mystical purgation. For a mind rendered incapable by temperament or upbringing of enter-ing into such a state, it can only erect a backcloth of total despair against which the human drama is enacted. More-over, Leopardi's universe is perhaps vaster and in a sense more terrifying than Pascal's. The universe of Newton had expanded into that of La Place, for whom God was an un-necessary hypothesis. Thus in 'The Broom' Leopardi speaks not only of the stellar universe as we know it, but also of the galaxies which lie beyond it. This vision is only just beginning to be accommodated to the general educated consciousness in our own day. Even more remarkably, in his 'Dialogue between Copernicus and the Sun' he anticipates, however playfully, what is in effect the modern theory of relativity.

These observations may serve to suggest that Leopardi's pessimism has a wider significance than has sometimes been recognized. It has too often been treated as a merely subjective romantic melancholy which had its roots in the pathetic circumstances of his life. Not, of course, that a consideration of these is irrelevant to an understanding of Leopardi's work. It does not require much acquaintance with modern psychology to see that the child's failure to love and to be loved by his mother led to the man's projecting that maternal figure upon an indifferent or even hostile nature. It is the image of this indifferent nature which manifests itself in the colossal figure, like an Easter Island statue, which confronts the wanderer in the 'Dialogue between Nature and an Icelander'. Sometimes, indeed, Leopardi does suggest that there is a Power behind the phenomena of the universe, but an actively malignant one. As well as the poems he planned to Christ and the Virgin he drafted one to Ahrimanes, the Power of Evil in the dualistic system of Zoroastrian religion. That it remained unwritten is significant. A Satanist no less than a Christian answer would for him have been an over-simplification. It is here only that Leopardi comes near to the Byronic type of Romanticism, which in general he held in low esteem.

The characteristic setting of Leopardi's poetry is landscape transfigured by moonlight. One may surmise that his weak eyes and the fear of that scorn to which his deformed figure exposed him, gave him a preference for nocturnal excursions. But the moon, throughout Leopardi's poetry, is a recurrent symbol for that beauty which so poignantly touches the darkness of human existence. This beauty is mutable and transient. In his early fragment, 'The Dream',

Leopardi imagines that the moon might fall from the sky; while in his last poem, said to have been composed upon his death-bed, the moon finally sets for him, leaving total darkness behind. So it is also with Nerina and Sylvia, idealized figures of young girls loved at a distance, whose early death symbolizes for Leopardi the passing of youth and hope. In a later poem, 'On the Portrait of a Beautiful Lady, carved on her Sepulchral Monument', Leopardi momentarily seems to suggest a quasi-Platonic view—that mortal beauty is a ray cast by an eternal splendour. But the poem ends with a paradox and a question mark.

For Leopardi the perpetual condition of man's existence is *noia*. This is a difficult word to translate effectively. It may literally be rendered 'boredom' or 'tedium'. But in Leopardi's writings it assumes the quality almost of a metaphysical absolute which these words scarcely suggest. The French *ennui*, its etymological equivalent, gives a better idea of its scope, and it can be related to the use of the word 'spleen' by English writers of the eighteenth century, and also by Baudelaire. From this condition man is momentarily liberated by the exercise of his imagination and his intellect. Thereby he apprehends the ideas of beauty, of virtue, and of love. But these are seen in the end to be mere illusions. Sappho dies an outcast from beauty, and Brutus cursing virtue; while in the most terrible of his poems, 'To Himself', Leopardi records the passing of love, the last illusion.

It is from the apprehension of these ideas, however, that Leopardi's poetry takes its life; the fact that they are seen to be illusions gives it its peculiar lyrical poignancy. In the prose *Operette Morali*, which Leopardi speaks of as if they were (what they scarcely can be said to be) systematic philosophy, he embarks on the task of liberating man by demolishing his delusions one by one. For Leopardi, the ultimate wisdom to be gleaned from experience is that men, fully conscious of their condition—that they are in a universe without God, where neither Nature nor Destiny is on their side—may learn to be more humane, in the solidarity of suffering. This is the moral of 'The Broom', his longest and most ambitious poem, where Mount Vesuvius stands as the symbol for the destructive potency in nature, and the insecurity of man's lot. In this poem Leopardi pours scorn upon the nascent optimistic philosophy of Progress. It so happened that the year in which Leopardi died ('as if unable to bear the prospect', as Ford Madox Ford put it) saw, in England, the opening of the Victorian era, in which this optimism was to be dominant. In another late poem, his 'Palinodia', Leopardi ironically parodies Virgil's Messianic Eclogue in celebrating the new Golden Age which England and her machines are to bring about. I have not translated this poem, but its equivalent in prose is to be found in the 'Dialogue between Tristan and a Friend'.

The duality and the paradox then remain. To some, Leopardi's aristocratic humanism will seem sterile and reactionary; but to others he will appear the most essentially modern and clear-sighted, as well as one of the greatest, of the poets of his time. It is too facile to dismiss his work, as it sometimes has been dismissed, as merely the product of a sick body and a sick mind. It is of the nature of poetic insight to transcend such things. In reading his poetry we cannot fail to be moved by the pathos of Leopardi the unloved hunchback. But the impression which finally remains is rather of the gentleness and dignity of spirit which shines through all his bitterness and scorn of life.

JOHN HEATH-STUBBS

I. *Prose*

Translated by Iris Origo

1. Gens Leoparda

When, at the age of twenty-seven, Leopardi was setting down some fragmentary notes for an autobiography,[1] he wrote that he intended to call it *The Story of a Soul*.

I am beginning to write my Life, without knowing whether I shall ever do anything which may make men wish to know about my character, my habits, and the events of my life. Indeed, though I always used to hold the opposite opinion, I now feel certain that I am not likely to leave any durable trace of myself on earth. And just for this reason I have decided to start by describing my life, for although I am only twenty-seven and therefore young in body, yet I observe that my spirit has not only used up its youth, but has advanced a long way into old age, from which one cannot turn back, so that I consider that my life may reasonably be considered nearly over, nothing being left to complete it but death. . . .

I have called this work *The Story of a Soul*, because I do not intend to describe anything else, and indeed have no other material, for so far I have experienced no great changes of fortune, nor any other events that are unusual or worth mentioning.

This was true, and remained so until the poet's death at the age of thirty-nine. The only story worth telling about Leopardi is that of his inner life, and for this he himself has supplied as much material as any biographer could desire. For reasons of space, this selection from his work can only be an introduction, for English-speaking readers, to his prose and poetry, and an attempt to show how closely they are related. Perhaps readers may also find here, if not a full self-portrait, at least an etching of the unhappy and disillusioned invalid who was one of the greatest Italian poets, and

[1] Written in 1825 but not published until after Leopardi's death, in the *Scritti vari inediti dalle carte napolitane*.

B

who, to use his own phrase, 'in depicting his despair and total disenchantment, drew the colours from his own heart'.

All that we shall try to do is to set the stage upon which this interior drama was performed.

'Of my birth I will only say', Leopardi wrote, 'that I was born of a noble family in an ignoble Italian city', to which he also referred as a prison, a den, a cave, an inferno, and 'the deadest and most ignorant city of the Marches, which is the most ignorant and uncivilized province of Italy'.[1]

These remarks were not entirely fair. Recanati—standing on a low hill some fifteen miles from the Adriatic—is like a good many other provincial Italian hill-towns. One long winding street stretches along the crest of the hill; tall shuttered palaces, of stone or faded brick, face each other in a stateliness which has lost its splendour. Through the wide arches of their doorways one may catch a glimpse of an inner court or a desiccated palm-tree, a pillared balustrade or a spunge-stone fountain. The main square has a tall watch-tower, to look out for pirates; the churches are numerous, and many of them old, distinguished by a Romanesque portal or a Renaissance façade. In winter, the narrow streets are dark and the north wind bites sharply, so that Leopardi would wrap his wide black cape over his head, while the little boys jeered at him, and even in summer the great rooms of the *palazzi*—carefully shuttered against any damage by the sun—often preserve something of the dank chill which caused the poet to work with a woollen rug over his knees and shoulders. But the town is not all that Leopardi saw, nor is it all that he has described. When the narrow side-streets suddenly come to an end, they frame a view of an astounding beauty: hillsides of olive-trees and vines falling sharply down towards the east to the Adriatic, and to the west, fold upon fold of blue mountain-ranges, stretching up to the mountains of the Abruzzi and the Maiella. 'Le vie dorate e gli orti'—they were at the poet's door, and much as he

---

[1] *Poesie e Prose*, II, p. 685: *Storia di un'anima.*

might rail against his city in his youth, it was to these streets, and to the hill above them, that his thoughts turned when he had gone away. For the truth was that he belonged to Recanati. He had written that it was a sepulchre, 'in which the dead are happier than the living'; yet hardly had he got to Rome than he told his brother that life in a big city was only tolerable if a man could 'build himself a little town within a great one'. When he was living in Bologna, he would walk upon the hills, 'seeking nothing but memories of Recanati'; when he published his *Canti* in Florence, he put the name of his birthplace upon the title-page; and when he felt his strength failing, he wrote to a friend that he would go back to Recanati, 'since I wish to die at home'.

The 'noble family' to which he belonged—*gens Leoparda*—was a very typical one of the nineteenth-century 'noblesse de province' in the States of the Church: its family tree showed, from generation to generation, few men of outstanding merit or talent, but a long line of worthy magistrates or city priors, bishops and canons and Knights of Malta, and, among the women, a large number of nuns. The poet's father, Conte Monaldo, prided himself on his ancestry, his palace, and his city—and that, he considered, was enough. 'One's patriotism is not due', he wrote in his autobiography, 'to the whole nation, nor even to the State; one's true country is only the morsel of earth on which one is born and spends one's life. That alone should arouse any interest in its citizens.' Moreover, he greatly preferred, for his own part, to be a large frog in a small pond. 'Being very proud', he wrote, 'of my unfettered personal independence, I neither desire nor require a great town. I would always prefer a hut, a book, and an onion on a mountain-top, to a subordinate position in Rome.' From the age of eighteen, he dressed from head to foot in black, with knee breeches, and in later years prided himself on being the last man in Italy habitually to wear a sword, and to be clothed 'in a noble and decorous manner'. 'With a sword by one's side,' he wrote, 'and always in full dress, it is not possible to fall very low. . . .

Dress', he advised, 'with dignity, be select in your company, greet everyone courteously, give a few pence to beggars, and you will be respected always and everywhere.'[1]

To Conte Monaldo, as to many other aristocrats of the Papal States, the invasion of their territory by the troops of the French Republic in 1796 partook of the nature of sacrilege, and he was among the first to join the solemn procession of the population and clergy of Recanati which made its way to the neighbouring church of Loreto, to implore the Madonna's aid against the invaders. And when, in the following spring, Napoleon himself rode through Recanati on his way to Rome, surrounded by guards with their hands at the trigger of their muskets, the Count refused even to look out from behind his shuttered windows, 'thinking it too great an honour for such a blackguard, that a gentleman should rise to see him pass'.

The pages of Conte Monaldo's autobiography tell us a great deal about the education of a Catholic provincial nobleman of his time—a way of life which he saw little necessity to change, when the time came for him to bring up his own sons. Born in Recanati on 11 August 1776, Monaldo lost his father at the age of five and spent his childhood in the Palazzo Leopardi 'in perfect harmony' with his mother, his great-uncle, four uncles, several brothers, and no less than four priests—'not imagining that any family could live otherwise'. Of his chief preceptor, Don Giuseppe Torres—a Jesuit from Vera Cruz—he did indeed admit that, by forcing him to learn all his lessons by heart, he had been 'the assassin of my studies', but he also wrote that he owed him 'my manners, my principles, and my whole formation as a Christian and an honest man', and it was no doubt these considerations that later on caused him to entrust to Don Giuseppe the education of his own sons. At eighteen Monaldo—although officially the head of the family and responsible for the management of the estate—was still forbidden by his mother to go out without his preceptor, and

[1] *Autobiografia di Monaldo Leopardi*, ed. A. Avoli.

when the time came for him to take a wife (after an unfortunate earlier affair of the heart) he chose Adelaide Antici, a member of a family which had already eight times intermarried with the Leopardis. Oddly enough—though not for this reason—his mother disapproved of this match; Monaldo knelt down and kissed her hand, but held to his decision—and subsequently, as he himself wrote, 'endured for a whole lifetime the severe punishment for this error'. 'I was unmoved by the tears that my mother shed at my feet, and I have been terribly punished. The arsenals of the Divine wrath are inexhaustible: woe betide those sons who dare to provoke them. My wife's character and mine are as diverse as the earth is from the sky. Every married man knows what that means, and let the unmarried beware of finding it out.'[1]

In another passage Conte Monaldo described his wife as both 'a divine blessing and a divine chastisement'. Certainly she was a woman of character. When, about six years after their marriage, Monaldo's imprudent investments and debts were about to ruin the whole family, his wife assumed complete control of the situation. She summoned a family council, laid bare all the facts, persuaded Monaldo to resign the management of the estate, and became the undisputed mistress of the household, with her husband turned into 'her penniless and restricted ward'.

The only pleasures left to him were the formation of his library and the revival of a 'poetic Academy', whose members called themselves *I Disuguali Placidi*—literally, the Placidly Diverse, or those who agree to disagree. Though a bigoted and reactionary aristocrat, he was also subject to sudden inconsistencies and disarming generosities. He once took off his trousers to give them to a half-naked beggar; he admitted that even in people of very superior minds (such as himself) a small corner is left for childishness; he attacked, on occasion, the clergy with vehemence and humour; he liked books and, for all his failure to understand them,

[1] *Autobiografia di Monaldo Leopardi.*

dearly loved his children. But when he differed from his wife with regard to their education, it was her word that was law. 'My father', wrote Paolina, 'has a good heart and is really fond of us, but he lacks the courage to face Mama's sulks for even the slightest cause.'[1] Monaldo himself confirmed it. 'If I dared to conceal from my wife the reason for a single sigh, she would take my letters out of my pocket, sue me, raise an uproar through the whole town.'

On the day when the management of family affairs passed into Contessa Adelaide's hands, she decided that everything should be sacrificed to the prestige of *casa Leopardi*. She sold all her jewels; she deprived her husband and children of any pocket-money; she even measured, 'with a little wooden hoop', the size of the eggs brought by the peasant women as part of the owner's dues; she cut down every pleasure and luxury. She reproved her servants so coldly and harshly that Giacomo would run away, so as not to hear her. She herself always wore, for economy's sake, clothes that never varied in cut or fashion: a straight gown with short skirts and high peasant's boots, but with a wide jabot to mark that she was not dressed 'à la guillotine', and she was equally concerned with regard to the clothes of her husband and children. Even Conte Monaldo, when he wished for a little money to buy books or to give in charity, was forced to sell a barrel of wine or a sack of wheat behind his wife's back. ('Thus,' he remarked, 'I used to steal from myself.') But year after year, *scudo* by *scudo*, the family fortune was built up again, and, whatever the sacrifices at home, outward decorum was observed in the sight of Recanati: the great rooms of Palazzo Leopardi still remained open and the household was not diminished by a single coachman, footman, or priest. Similarly, in the conduct of Contessa Adelaide's spiritual life, she admitted no relaxation. She was possessed by two ruling passions—or perhaps it might be said by one alone, which had a double face: the laying up of coin—temporal for this world and spiritual for the next.

[1] Paolina Leopardi, *Lettere a Marianna ed Anna Brighenti*, ed. E. Costa.

'She is an utter excess of Christian perfection,' wrote her daughter Paolina, 'you cannot imagine the severity with which she regulates every detail of our family life. Dear Marianna, I wish you could spend just one day in our house, to realize how it is possible to lead an existence that is bodiless, soulless, lifeless.'[1]

Certainly the early years of the Leopardi children—Giacomo, Carlo, and Pietruccio, and their only sister, Paolina—were overshadowed by the domination of their mother and her deliberate shaping of both their bodies and their souls. In illness she alone nursed them; their bedrooms could only be reached through hers; and when, at the age of six, Giacomo went to make his first Confession, she went with him to church and did not even move out of earshot of the Confessional. Conte Monaldo's vigilance was hardly less assiduous. At meals Giacomo sat beside his father, who cut up every mouthful that his son ate and continued to do so until the young man was twenty-seven. (It is hardly surprising that in the *Zibaldone* Giacomo should have expatiated on the pleasures of eating alone, and called himself μονοφάγος.) Yet Monaldo considered himself not only a tender, but an enlightened father. When his children were vaccinated—a daring innovation—he sent all the way to Genoa for the vaccine and kept in his diary a daily record of their progress, and he also put up swings and parallel bars for them in the garden. But of dancing, riding, or the use of weapons, he equally disapproved—'since these exercises are partly immoral and partly dangerous, and should never be allowed in a wise and Christian education'.

A further description of his parents can be left to Leopardi himself.

I have known intimately a mother who was not in the least superstitious, but most orthodox and scrupulous in her Christian faith and practice. Not only did she deny pity to those parents who lost their children in infancy, but regarded them with a

---

[1] Antona-Traversi, *Paolina Leopardi*, p. 11.

deep and sincere envy, inasmuch as those children, escaping all perils, had flown to heaven, while their parents had been freed from the burden of supporting them. Finding herself more than once in danger of losing an infant child, she did not pray to God to let it die, since our faith does not permit this, but she did in fact rejoice; and when she saw her husband weeping and lamenting, she retired into herself, with real and obvious displeasure. She was indeed scrupulous in her care of the poor patients, but in her heart she hoped that it would be of no avail, and went so far as to confess that her only dread, in questioning the doctor, was to hear of some improvement. When she saw the signs of death approaching, she felt a deep happiness, which she only attempted to conceal from those who disapproved of it; and the day of their death, if it came, was for her a happy and cheerful one, nor could she understand how her husband could be so foolish as to lament it. She considered beauty a true misfortune, and seeing her children ugly or deformed, gave thanks to God, not stoically, but from her heart. She did not in any way attempt to help them to conceal their defects, but rather required that, in view of them, they should renounce life entirely, from their early youth. If they rebelled, or attempted to follow their own bent, and succeeded even to a slight degree, she was displeased, and did everything she could, both in her comments and opinions, to make them less successful (this both with her ugly and her handsome children). She never neglected an opportunity of pointing out their faults to them, and the consequences to which they must lead, with a fierce and pitiless veracity. In these and in similar matters the shortcomings of her children were a consolation to her, and she dwelt by preference with them on what she had heard said to their disfavour. All this to free them from danger to their soul! She felt infinite compassion for sinners, but very little for any physical or temporal misfortune, unless her own nature sometimes got the better of her. The most pitiable illnesses or the death of young people who had died in the flower of their youth, with every hope before them—causing the greatest anguish to their family and to everyone else—did not move her at all. For she said that it was not the fact of death that mattered, but only its manner; and she would therefore earnestly inquire if they had made a good death, according to our faith, and if they had shown resignation during their illness. And she spoke of these tragedies with a stony coldness. This woman was by nature extremely sensitive, and had been brought to this by religion alone. What is this, if not barbarism?[1]

Many years later, in his *Pensieri*, the author of this portrait also set down his comments on his relationship with his father, prefacing them with the remark that there is hardly an instance in history of a great man whose father did not die while he was still a child.

... Paternal power, in every law-abiding country, brings about a kind of children's slavery, more stringent, because it is domestic, and more oppressive than any law, and which—however much it may be tempered by law or custom or the quality of individuals—can never fail to produce a most damaging effect: a sentimental bond which a man, so long as his father is alive, carries about with him perpetually. ... I mean a feeling of subjection and dependence, and of not being his own master, indeed of not being, so to speak, even a whole person, but only a part and member of someone else, with even a name that belongs to another man, rather than to himself. This feeling, which affects most deeply those who would naturally be the most talented, since they are the quickest, the most sensitive and the most alive to the truth about their own condition—can hardly be combined, I will not say with great deeds, but even with any plans of greatness.[2]

And finally—again in the *Zibaldone*—there is yet another comment on Leopardi's early years:

The most beautiful and fortunate age of man, and the only one which can today be happy, childhood, is so tormented in a thousand ways by anxieties, fears, and the labours of education and instruction, that a grown-up man, even in the midst of all the unhappiness caused by his knowledge of the truth, the

[1] *Zibaldone*, I, pp. 308–11. The character of Contessa Adelaide was never to suffer change. A few years after Giacomo's death in Naples, a great admirer of his work, Filippo Zamboni, went to Recanati, 'on a pilgrimage' to his friend's house—and there met his mother, 'majestic, austere, with snow-white hair'. 'I pointed to Giacomo's portrait and said, "May the woman who bore you be blessed!" But she neither moved nor bent her head nor turned towards me; only lifting up her eyes to heaven, she exclaimed: "God forgive him!".'
[2] *Poesie e Prose*, II, pp. 5–6: *Pensieri*, II.

disillusionment and tedium of life, and the numbing of his imagination, would yet not agree to return to childhood, if he had to bear again what he suffered then.[1]

It has not been easy to make a selection from the vast corpus of Leopardi's prose: the 4,526 pages of his great hotch-potch of a day-book, the *Zibaldone*, the 24 *Operette Morali*, the 111 *Pensieri*, the essays and translations of his youth, the fragmentary autobiographical notes or recollections and the unfinished drafts and plans in the *carte napoletane*, and the seven large volumes of his letters. Leopardi was, of course, first and foremost, a poet; but he was also a great classical scholar, a philologist, a speculator, an inquirer, a literary critic; and no one can fully savour his poetry who is not aware of the depth and richness of the soil in which his verse had its roots. The evocative power of his lines, in their deliberate simplicity and restraint, the depth of the chords they awaken, cannot be separated from the rich, complex texture of his culture, through which he reached, by a conscious, disciplined process of elimination, what Sainte-Beuve called 'le grand goût, le goût véritable'. Finally, it is not possible to understand his poetry fully without knowing something about the circumstances of his brief, frustrated life, and in particular about his harsh, intense, imaginative childhood, which no one has described as vividly as himself. In the words of a great Italian poet of our own time, Ungaretti, 'Memory for Leopardi is not so much a process of the intellect, a pure activity of the spirit, as a physical pain, a conscious awareness present not only in the history of individuals, but in that of civilizations and even of the universe. . . . A work of art is convincing when, enriched by our memories, it moves our imagination so completely as to give back to us the gaze of innocence. Memory and innocence are the two inseparable poles of Leopardi's poetry.'[2]

[1] *Zibaldone*, I, p. 255, 1 August 1823.
[2] Ungaretti, Preface to the translation into French of Leopardi's complete works.

This selection has attempted, in so far as is possible in so brief a space, to trace the closeness of the connexion between some of the main threads in Leopardi's life and work, and the recurrence of certain dominant themes, both in his prose and verse: 'the hope that is renewed with every dawn', and always, irrevocably, dies away; the inevitable unhappiness of all human beings, and above all, of any man who has a touch of greatness; the nostalgia for the 'illusions' of our childhood, which he identified with those of the early years, the golden age, of every nation; the search for 'the woman who cannot be found'; the scholar's passion for research, inquiry, definition, and the poet's for what is vague and undefined, leading to infinity; the addiction (as other men are addicted to women, drink, or drugs) to words (*'vagheggiare*,[1] *bellissimo verbo'*, and all that day there is no other entry, as if he had spent the whole day dwelling upon it); the obsession with *noia*, tedium ('which also is a passion, no less than suffering or delight'); the perception, in all the objects before his eyes, of the 'heavenly originals', of which, according to Plato, all earthly objects are but copies.

'To a sensitive and imaginative man,' he wrote, 'who lives as I have lived for a long time, constantly feeling and imagining, the world and its objects are, in a way, double. He sees with his eyes a tower, a landscape; he hears with his ears the sound of a bell; and at the same time his imagination sees another tower, another bell, and hears another sound.'[2]

Readers who are attracted by these translations—which have aimed at reproducing Leopardi's thought and style, rather than giving a literal transcription—will wish (I hope) to read some more of his work in the original, while those who would like a fuller account of his life and a more

[1] *Vagheggiare*—to gaze upon fondly, as a mother does on her child, to cherish. But there are also undertones in the Italian word, connected with *vago* (which means both 'wandering, drifting, vague' and 'charming, pleasing') which are difficult to render. The word, indeed, is a good example of the difficulties one encounters in translating Leopardi.

[2] *Zibaldone*, II, pp. 1230-1, 30 November 1828.

complete critical estimate of his work can also easily find it elsewhere.[1]

As to the translations—Leopardi himself wrote: 'The perfection of a translation consists in this, that the author translated should not seem something Greek rendered into Italian, or something French into German, but should become, in Italian or German, precisely as the writer was, in Greek or French. That is what is difficult, and is not possible in every language.'[2] In other words, I suppose, a translation of Leopardi should read as if Leopardi were an Englishman with a classical education of the early nineteenth century, expressing his thoughts in his native language, English. I know that I have not fully achieved this. I might perhaps find excuses in the general difficulties of translating any Latin language into English, or in the particular cast of Leopardi's mind and style. But the truth is simply this: I have found it, as he himself said, very difficult.

---

[1] See Select Bibliography.
[2] *Zibaldone*, I, p. 1311. Leopardi added, 'In French it is not possible.'

2. The Making of a Poet

'There is no object here which meets my sense
Which does not bring some image back again,
Or raise some sweet remembrance. . . .'

LE RICORDANZE

Among the unpublished papers which Leopardi's friend Ranieri found in Naples after his death, there were some brief, unpolished, often unpunctuated jottings (possibly intended as notes for an autobiographical novel in the manner of Werther) *which were probably mostly set down in 1819, and were eventually published in 1906, under the title* Recollections of Childhood and Adolescence. *These notes are still so fragmentary that an emotion is barely hinted at, a scene faintly etched, sometimes a sentence left unfinished. Leopardi himself, I suspect, would have been much surprised and perhaps annoyed at their having been taken so seriously: they are to his finished work what a scribbled shorthand note is to a finished page of calligraphy. Yet in these rough jottings we do catch an occasional glimpse both of the child and the young man, and of the stuff of which his poetry was made. Some passages, indeed, are the direct source of a few lines in his poems—when, later on, they had been polished, completed, made perfect. But here, in the first faint outline— delicate as the skeleton of a leaf—they have the evocative power, the immediacy, of a scent carried on the breeze or the faint echo of a distant tune. Not poetry yet, but the breath of a wing.*

The passages translated here are set down in their original order, but only about half of the notes are quoted—the ones omitted being either repetitive or too fragmentary, or else quoted in some other chapter of this book.

My face when I was a little boy and even later on had something wistful and serious about it which, being without any affectation of melancholy, gave it charm . . . as I see in a lifelike portrait of me at that time, and which my brother, a year younger than I, remembers very well. This expression, together with manners which were ingenuous and not spoiled or affected by self-consciousness or by a desire to please, but simple and natural, unlike those of boys who are too much spoiled, made me loved at that age by the few ladies who saw that I was so different from my brothers. . . .

Songs after the feast-days. Lambs on the ceiling of my room. The sound of ships. . . .

Fears of the self-flagellations at night of the missionaries. Compassion for all those who, I saw, would never achieve fame. Tears and melancholy at being a man, my mother thinking me a fool and describing me as such. Compassion awakened in Pietruccio [his brother] on my knee. Desire conceived, as I studied geography, to travel.

View after dinner looking out of the window, with the shadow cast by the sheds, the dog on the grass, children, the coachman's door ajar, the shops, etc. Effect of the music I heard in the garden, an air sung from some opera. . . .

First reading of Homer and first sonnet. 'Amore, amore', sung by the children (while I was reading Ariosto) as in Lucian, etc. The Creation of the world (which I should have liked to put to music, since poetry cannot express such things) as I imagined it, while I heard the song of the brick-layers when I was composing. . . .

Description of the view from my house, the mountains, the beach at S. Stefano, and the trees on that side with those little paths, etc. My mournful meditations in the orchard or garden by moonlight, in sight of the deserted monastery, about the fall of Napoleon. . . .

Children on Palm Sunday and the false friendship of one of the bigger ones. Schoolgirls, my cousin, and my comforting speech to them ('My young ladies, you will make me cry too'), producing the good result of a smile, like sunshine in a shower, so that I wrote it down, thinking myself eloquent. . . .

Frequent thoughts of S. Cecilia after dinner, longing, yet

not able, to gaze upon beauty, kisses given to the daughter and sighs about her approaching departure. . . .

Romantic fancies while looking at pictures in the St. Thomas à Kempis and in the little Sacred History and in our books of the Saints. . . . My contempt for men, especially when in love and after reading Alfieri, but, as already appears in a letter of mine to Giordani, my desire to see the world, although I am perfectly aware of its emptiness and have sometimes almost seen and conceived it as a whole. . . .

Accidia and coldness and dryness in January, that is in the Carnival of 1819, when even the sight of women did not move me any more and my delight then in a peaceful domestic life and an inclination to the monastic one. . . .

Discontent in feeling the sensations aroused in me by looking at the landscape, for not being able to penetrate still deeper and enjoy it more fully, since I did not feel that I had reached its depths [*il fondo*]—besides not being able to express them. Singular tenderness of some of my dreams, moving me to tears (which never, never happened to me when awake), and vague fancies, as when I dreamed of Marie Antoinette and of a song to put into her mouth in the tragedy I was thinking about—a poem which, if it were to express the feelings that then came over me, could only have been in music without words. . . .

The effect of reading Virgil; noted the passage about Circe's song as filled with a wonderful childishness and already loved by me as a schoolboy, and also noted his causing Aeneas to return in the Second Book; reading of Xenophon and considerations about his politics, marked the passage about the Persian girls drawing water, comparing it to the hymns to Ceres of Callimachus and Homer. . . .

My considerations on the plurality of worlds and the nothingness of this earth and of ourselves and on the greatness and strength of nature which we measure by the streams, etc., and that I am nothing in this globe, which is nothing in the world—and awakened by a voice calling me to supper.

Whereat our life and time seemed to me nought, and so did time and famous names and the whole of history. . . .

Lying awake at night in the dark with the shutters closed and the cloudy and misty moon and the creaking of the weather-cocks, comforted by the tower-clock, etc. View at night from the top of my house with the moon in a clear sky, as in Homer's image. Fables, and my most vivid fancies in hearing them as on that morning, sunny field, etc. . . .

Songs and airs, how wonderfully sweet is their influence upon my memory! Moschus, etc.

Mad moments of gaiety, especially in times of great anguish, during which, if I did not control myself, I would be capable of throwing chairs into the air and jumping about and perhaps injuring myself, out of sheer gladness. . . .

Fears of an accident and my indifference then; true misfortunes are the enemies of compassion and melancholy, which imagine sham misfortunes, and there is a sweetness in constructing such disasters. . . .

St. Augustine's Day, the blessing on that spring day in the empty courtyard, owing to the suppression [of the monasteries], with the birds singing, having just returned to their nests under the eaves, a clear, cloudless day, sun, the sound of bells close by, and at the first sound my emotion towards my Creator. . . .

Apollo's oxen. What childish virtue in the beginning of the Odyssey, as indeed in the whole poem, to a peculiar degree; did the ancients really continue, owing to their lack of knowledge, to feel the delights that we only feel as children? Oh, we should indeed envy them, and one should see that that is the natural state. . . .

The picture of Noah in the Sacred History, memories of that little window at the top of the ladder from which, from the garden, I could see the moon or the clear sky. . . .

Lying beside a hay-rick at S. Leopardo [one of the Leopardi farms] towards dusk, watching a peasant coming towards me from the horizon. . . .

A peasant saying his *Ave Maria* and *Requiem aeternam*

aloud to himself at the door of his hut, turning towards the moon hanging low over the trees of his field. . . .

The garden near the caretaker's house. I was very melancholy and stood by the window giving on the square. Two young men seated on the deserted, grassy steps of the church, joking under the great lantern, pushing each other about. The first firefly I have seen this year appeared. One of the two got up and went towards it; I begged for mercy to myself for the poor thing, and exhorted it to fly away, but he threw it down and went back to the other. Meanwhile the coachman's daughter, getting up from supper and leaning out of the window to wash a plate, called to those inside, 'Tonight it really will rain: what a night it is! black as your hat', and soon after the light at the window was put out. Meanwhile the firefly had come to life again, and I wished, etc., but he noticed it, blaspheming, and came back, and another blow made it fall, weak as it was, and with his foot he left a shining smear in the dust, until it was wiped out. . . . The laughter increased. I heard the gentle voice of a woman I did not know and could not see, 'Natalino, it's late, we must go.' 'For God's sake, or the dawn will be here,' he replied. I heard a child, who must have been the woman's baby, swaddled in her arms, babbling and stammering, in a laughing, milky voice. . . . The fun increased. 'Isn't there any more wine at Girolamo's?' they asked a passer-by, but there was none and the woman, laughing softly, and commenting 'Oh, what madmen!'(—yet the wine was not for her and her husband would have used the family money for it), and now and again patiently and laughingly asked them to come away, but in vain, etc. At last a voice, 'Ah, here's the rain!' And a light spring rain, and all of them went in, and one heard the sound of doors and locks.

My great desire for glory as a child showing itself in everything. . . . The battles we fought with each other in the garden in imitation of Homer with stones or berries or at S. Leopardo with sticks, calling ourselves by Homeric names or by those of the Civil War, in our Roman history. . . . My

c

Latin oration against Caesar recited to my father and reflecting my hatred for the tyrant and my pleasure and enthusiasm in reading about his death, and other similar performances that we gave, according to what we were reading: note that I chose to be Pompey, although he was vanquished, giving to Carlo the part of Caesar, which he took with reluctance. . . .[1]

At much the same time, that is, early in 1819, Leopardi was setting down some rough 'subjects for idylls'—of which one eventually become The Infinite, *another* The Solitary Thrush, *and yet another,* Fear by Night.

Shade beneath the sheds. Early morning rain in my father's drawing. A rainbow at sunrise. The moon fallen as in my dream, the moon which peasants say turns the skin black; so I overheard a woman laughingly advise her friend to put her arms under her apron, as she sat there in the moonlight. Silkworms, about which two women were talking, and one said, 'I wonder how much you will get out of them', and the other, in a very plaintive voice, 'Be quiet, I have spent such a lot on them, and please God. . . .'

A solitary thrush—the very steep hillside seen from a few steps away, and peasants going down it, almost immediately out of sight—another image of infinity.[2]

These Recollections *are far from being the only descriptions that Leopardi has left us of his early years. Both his voluminous day-book, the* Zibaldone, *and some of his early essays—in particular the* Treatise of an Italian on Romantic Poetry *and the* Essay on the Popular Errors of the Ancients—*hold passages which are plainly autobiographical. Indeed one might almost say that whenever Leopardi was most alive, whenever the poetic spirit stirred in him again, he returned to the source of his early youth, the rich undersoil of his 'fabulous years'. 'If I knew', he wrote, 'how to*

[1] *Poesie e Prose*, I, pp. 673–86: *Ricordi d'Infanzia e di Adolescenza.*
[2] Ibid. p. 377: *Subjects and Drafts for Idylls* (1819).

depict and awaken in others what I saw and felt in my childhood, I would consider myself a divine poet.'

What a fine time that was, when everything came to life according to the human fancy, and behaved in a human manner . . . when we were sure that beautiful Hamadryads and Fauns and Sylvans and Pan lived in the deserted woods, and Naiads in the springs. And, clasping a tree to your breast, you almost felt it tremble in your hand, and believed it to be a human being, like Cypress.[1]

During those years Giacomo lived in an anthropomorphic world, in which trees and flowers and even, he said, 'the letters of the alphabet', took on a human shape:

When thunder and winds, sun and stars, animals and plants, and even the walls of the house, all seemed friends or enemies —none indifferent and none meaningless; when every object that we saw seemed in a certain way to beckon and almost to wish to speak to us; when, never alone, we would speak to images and walls and trees and flowers and clouds, and embraced stones and trees, and caressed or injured, as if they had done us good or harm, objects incapable of either benefiting or harming us: when wonder—so dear to us that we have often wished to believe, in order to be able to wonder— possessed us all the time; when the colours of things and light and the stars and fire and the flight of insects, the song of birds, the transparency of water, all was new and unfamiliar; when no incident seemed commonplace, nor did we know the cause of anything, but made it up for ourselves; when tears were daily events, and all passions still vivid and unruled and never forcibly suppressed. How easily at that time one's imagination took fire, how it enlarged small things and adorned bare ones and lit up darkness; what living images, what happy dreams, what indescribable inventions—what stuff for poetry, what richness, vigour,

[1] *Zibaldone*, I, p. 94.

strength, emotion, and delight! I myself remember hearing in
fancy in my childhood strains sweeter than can be heard in
our real world. I remember looking up at shepherds and
their flocks painted on the ceiling of my room, and imagining
a pastoral life so lovely that were it to come true, this would
not be our earth, but paradise, a home for gods, not men.[1]

*Children, he affirmed, like the poets of classical antiquity,
naturally possess 'an inclination for the infinite', and a capacity to
perceive what he called 'il bello aereo'—an airy, unearthly beauty.*

For then it is our imagination that is at work instead of
our sight, and the fantastic takes the place of the real. The
soul imagines what it cannot see, what is hidden by that
tree, that bush, that tower, and goes off wandering in an
imaginary space. . . . Thence the pleasure that I felt as a
boy, and sometimes do even now, in seeing the sky through
a window or a door or between two houses.[2]

*This theme—the craving for the infinite, which eventually found
expression in the most famous of his Idylls—constantly occurs in
the* Zibaldone, *and is often related to memories of his childhood.*

If, as a child, a view, a landscape, picture, sound, tale,
description, fable, poetic image, or dream please or delight
us, that pleasure and delight is always vague and indefinite;
the idea that it awakens in us is always undefined and unbounded; every comfort, pleasure, expectation, plan, illusion (and almost every idea) at that age is always directed
towards infinity, and they nourish and fill our soul, to an
indescribable degree, even in very little things. . . . Indeed,
we may perhaps remark that the greater part of the vague
images and sensations that come to us, even after childhood
is over, and in the rest of our life, are nothing but a memory

---

[1] *Poesie e Prose*, II, pp. 479–81: *Discorso di un Italiano intorno alla poesia
romantica.*
[2] *Zibaldone*, I, p. 187.

of that time—a recollection, a repetition, an echo, or a reflection of that ancient image.[1]

*It was, however, only a very small part of the boy's life that was
given up to thoughts and dreams as pleasant as these. Later on, when
he wrote about the errors of his education, he said that those which
he most deplored were the quenching of his spontaneous communica-
tiveness, and the deliberate awakening in him of a sense of guilt and
fear. 'Children', he wrote, 'like to talk about the things they have
done, are pleased with themselves'—and he, too, was 'at first inclined to communicate to other people any new impression, whether
inner or outer'. His mother's cold, repressive glance, the 'fierce
veracity' with which she analysed his failings, soon put an end to this.
As a young man he wrote:*

Now I not only dislike and avoid talking about my feelings, but even shun the presence of anyone else while I am
experiencing them. And this is due to nothing but the habit
I have formed of living alone with myself, almost always in
silence. . . . The same thing must happen, I suppose, to true
solitaries: savages, who have no companions or hardly any,
primitive men, who have no language or make very little
use of it, or the dumb, or those who, through some accident,
have been obliged to live for a long time cut off from human
intercourse, such as shipwrecked mariners, pilgrims in lands
in which their language is unknown, prisoners, and monks of
silent orders.[2]

*Fear, too, was awakened very early in this child. When he was
four years old he was taken after dark to watch a penitential procession through the streets of Recanati. The penitents wore the
hoods of their confraternities, with their faces wholly concealed,
but for slits for the eyes; they bore lighted torches, and were followed by monks with dark cowls over their heads. The torches, the
dark, moving shadows, the corpse-like whiteness of the monks' faces
under their black cowls, struck such terror into the boy that many*

[1] *Zibaldone*, I, p. 404.　　[2] Ibid. pp. 1484–5 (11 June 1822).

*years later, as a young man, he still could not bear to see, during the
Carnival, anyone wearing a mask. As he wrote later on:*

No misfortune or fear or danger, however formidable, at
a later age, seems to me strong enough to produce in us
such anguish, frenzy, horror, terror, or in short any torment equal those so-called childish fears. I do not believe
that even the dread of Hell, in a dying man, can be more profoundly terrible.[1]

*The most terrifying of all, however, was the fear of ghosts, 'that
spiritual, supernatural, sacred terror, from another world', which
was deliberately inculcated into the Leopardi children by foolish
nurses, who told them ghost-stories at bedtime, 'so that the impression made upon their spirit by those tales heard in the darkness,
should be indelible'. How these fears were instilled Leopardi fully
described in the* Essay on the Popular Errors of the Ancients,
which he wrote at the age of nineteen.

Hardly can [a child] lisp and make the Sign of the Cross
upon his forehead and breast, to show that he is born within
the true faith, than tales of imps and apparitions have already
found a place in his fearful and wondering mind. . . . He
becomes aghast and afraid; he looks upon the coming of
night as a torment, and on dark places as terrifying caves;
he shakes with anguish in his bed, breaking into a cold sweat,
and draws the sheets over him; he tries to speak and, finding
himself alone, can only shudder from head to foot. The nurse
has fulfilled her intention. . . . She has taken from the child
the chief gift that can render human life as little unhappy as
possible: courage.[2]

*In his essay Leopardi enumerated many of the 'shades, spectres,
ghosts, visions, terrible objects that made the poor ancient peoples
tremble, and, it must be said, still inspire fear in us, too'. They were*

[1] *Zibaldone*, I, pp. 413-14.
[2] *Poesie e Prose*, II, p. 291: *Saggio sugli errori popolari degli antichi.*

the ghosts, or streges, *'from which comes the name of* streghe [*witches*], *which is not yet forgotten', who were accused of sucking children's blood, or eating them alive; the fauns or satyrs, 'particularly insolent by night', 'who would lie in ambush, mocking at everyone who passed . . . or assault them, murder them and barbarously tear their bodies', and the* larvae, *who—according to St. Isidore—'boasted that they were evil men who had turned into demons, and who had the faculty of terrifying children and croaking in dark corners'.[1] For hours, stiff with terror, the child would lie awake, counting the chimes of the tower-clock, which brought the dawn a little nearer.*

> . . . A sound which was my comfort,
> As I remember, in those fearful nights
> Of boyhood, when I lay in my dark room,
> Beset by terrors, longing for the dawn.[2]

Yet the day, when it came, brought its apprehensions, too—chiefly because, like many children whose life has few treats and pleasures, both he and his brothers were acutely, morbidly vulnerable by any small disappointment.

Experience had not yet taught us to have few hopes, and to be prepared to have those hopes destroyed. . . . Thus when we hoped for some good thing, how great were our anxieties, our fears, our tremblings, our anguish, at every little obstacle or apparent difficulty. . . . And if the object of our hopes (however small, according to our present point of view) was not attained, how great was our despair! So that perhaps, in the greatest of life's misfortunes, we have never felt nor ever will feel again such heartfelt grief, as for those little misadventures of our childhood.[3]

His imagination, he wrote, was fixed with great intensity upon a very few ideas ('unlike that of most children, which leaps from

---

[1] *Poesie e Prose*, II, p. 304: *Saggio sugli errori popolari degli antichi.*
[2] *Le Ricordanze.*   [3] *Zibaldone*, I, p. 413.

one thing to another') and this caused him 'to cling most jealously to what was customary and familiar, away from which I could not find peace'. Long before he could formulate his knowledge, he knew that nothing is stable, nothing ours, that the whole of life is a process of losing.

When I saw someone going away, even someone who was quite indifferent to me, I would consider whether it was possible or probable that I should ever see him again. And if I decided that it was not, then I would watch and listen, following our guest with all my eyes and ears, always revolving within my mind, and penetrating more and more deeply into my soul, 'This is the last time, I shall never see him again.'[1]

But this is not, of course, a complete picture. For one thing, Leopardi's childhood was cheered by a close bond of affection with the brother and sister who were nearest to him in age: Paolina— a child as sensitive and melancholy as her brother, though without his genius—and Carlo, a good-looking, normal, high-spirited boy, who always remained Giacomo's closest confidant and friend. Moreover, as Giacomo himself noted, children have a peculiar gift for finding compensations of their own in 'the ease with which they pass in an instant from the deepest grief to joy, from tears to laughter and back again'.

How great must be their inner activity, the multiplicity of their occupations, even when wholly disoccupied, their gift for finding distractions and for lightening or quenching painful thoughts or emotions, the variety as well as the liveliness of their ideas and conceits (each one of which is capable of distracting them completely from what they are doing at the time)—in short, the life of the spirit! and consequently, how great is the happiness of even those children whose outer circumstances are least happy![2]

---

[1] *Zibaldone*, I, p. 472.   [2] Ibid. p. 397.

For Giacomo, the greatest pleasure lay in escaping, with his brother, into an imaginary world. From his earliest childhood he had an insatiable passion for fairy stories; at the age of three or four he would run to everyone in the house in turn, pleading to be told another. These, as he grew older, gave place to long serial sagas, with which he himself would entertain his brothers, describing the imaginary adventures of all the members of their family—tales in which the brave, witty, invulnerable hero was of course always Giacomo himself.

Even the pious teaching of his parents provided him with another fine part.

Seeing some pictures of St. Louis riding through the streets of Rome, with the crowd crying out, 'There goes the Saint!' [the boy] said: 'I, too, when I grow up, will be a Saint, and the people, seeing me pass, will cry, "There goes the Saint!" ' You see what a craving for fame was moving him. But his devout parents took it for devotion, a heroic inclination to sanctity.[1]

But above all, once his early childhood was over, Giacomo found an escape into the world of books. Indeed, from the ages of ten to seventeen, almost the whole of his boyhood was spent indoors in his father's library, in which Conte Monaldo had gathered together a very odd mixture of valuable works and sheer trash: 'grammar and dictionaries and glossaries and commentaries, histories and orations and dissertations, erudite works of Hebrew, Greek, Latin and medieval scholars, subjects sacred and profane, great works and mediocre ones, all mixed together'.[2]

The library may be seen today, as it was when Leopardi worked there: four long narrow rooms, with painted ceilings, lined with books, its windows overlooking a peaceful square. The traveller can still see the table at which the poet wrote, his white china ink-stand, his thin brown rugs, and the manuscripts of some of his

[1] *Poesie e Prose*, I, p. 690: *Alla vita del Poggio*.
[2] De Sanctis, 'La prima canzone di Giacomo Leopardi' in *Nuovi Saggi Critici*.

*childish works. Before he was twelve, he had produced his first
sonnet on the death of Hector, translated the first two books of
Horace's Odes, composed tragedies, parodies, poetic epistles. 'I
would not know anything,' he wrote later on, 'if I had not had the
incentive of making little books.' But at the same time he had no
illusions about the value of such compositions. 'Children, when they
begin to write, consider the value of a work to consist in what lies
farthest from simplicity and do their best to achieve it, that is, to
be mannered, elaborate, etc. Signs of a childish art.'*[1] *And he wrote
elsewhere that 'such simplicity as does lie there* [in children's writ-
ings], *is not simplicity, but childishness'.*[2]

*By the time that he was fourteen, however, his period of ap-
prenticeship was already over. His teachers having told his father
that they had nothing further to teach him, he took his education
into his own hands. Not satisfied with Latin, he began to teach himself Greek, and then Hebrew; he lived surrounded by lexicons and
grammars, only allowing himself an hour of conversation with his
brothers in the evening, while he paced up and down in the dark, to
rest his tired eyes. His genius for philology developed as suddenly and
remarkably as Pascal's for mathematics; he compiled a commentary
on four Greek rhetoricians of the second century; he wrote an* Essay
on the Popular Errors of the Ancients; *he translated into*
Latin *and annotated Porphyry's* Commentary on the Life of
Plotinus, *earning the praise of a celebrated Roman philologist, the
Abate Cancellieri. He even, like Chatterton, perpetrated an
ingenious literary forgery: first a* Hymn to Neptune, *which he
said he had discovered in Greek 'in a torn codex' and had then translated into Latin, and then two Greek odes which he declared to be
by Anacreon, and which completely took in the scholars to whom he
showed them. He translated into Latin verse a part of the* Odyssey,
the Idylls *of Moschus, the* Battle of the Frogs and the Mice, *and
the Second Book of the* Aeneid, *for which he had always had a
special affection. In a prefatory note he wrote:*

When I read the Aeneid, as I constantly did, I eagerly
attempted to find a way of making that divine beauty mine,

[1] *Zibaldone*, I, p. 963.   [2] Ibid. p. 29.

if it was remotely possible, nor could I find peace until I had come to terms with myself and flung myself upon the Second Book of that most sublime poem which had touched me more than the others; so that, when I read it, I found myself inadvertently reciting it aloud, and changing tone at the appropriate moments, and catching fire and perhaps sometimes letting a tear fall.[1]

So Leopardi spent his youth, and it was the only period of his life which, later on, he could say had been happy.

The happiness I felt when I was writing, the most wonderful time I have ever known, and which I would wish to last my whole life long. The days passed without my observing it, and the hours seemed short: and I myself often marvelled at the ease with which they slipped by.

But this happiness was won at a great cost. Those seven years of sedentary life laid the foundations of the ill-health which never left him, and also produced a slight curvature of the spine, throwing the thorax out of place in such a way as to produce a slight double hump on his back and chest, and eventually affecting the functions both of his lungs and his heart. Leopardi, at seventeen, looked one day in the glass, and realized that he was a hunchback.

I have miserably and irremediably ruined myself, for my whole life, with mad and desperate studies, at an age when one's constitution is being formed, making my appearance hideous, and rendering despicable all that great part of a man which is the only one to which most people look.[2]

It was then that he began to feel a bitter resentment against his parents for having permitted him to lead such a life. He was subject to long attacks of black, capricious melancholy, which would either drive him to study even harder than before, or else into

---

[1] *Poesie e Prose*, I, p. 617: Preface to Leopardi's translation of the Second Book of the Aeneid.

[2] *Epistolario*, I, To Giordani, 2 March 1818.

idleness and apathy; sometimes, too, he played with thoughts of suicide, and, leaning over the rim of the deep well in the garden,

> thought of ending there
> Beneath those waters all my grief and pain.[1]

Yet even in such moments common sense and self-knowledge would hold him back.

I stood by the rim of the pool in the garden unutterably weary of life, and, looking at the water and leaning over it with a slight shudder, thought: If I were to throw myself in, I would at once float up again and climb out on to the rim, and—having made the effort to come out, unharmed, with a great fear of losing my life—I would then feel some moments of pleasure at having saved myself, and of affection for this life, which I now so much despise![2]

At one time he believed that he had not, in any case, more than a year or two to live, and he wrote a long visionary poem entitled The Approach of Death. *'Composition of* Cantica,*' he noted in the* Recollections, *'at night, in great grief.'*
Then this apprehension, too, receded.

I have begun to realize and to persuade myself . . . that there is really nothing in me that will necessarily cause me to die soon, and that if I take infinite care of myself, I shall be able to go on living, though clinging on to life by the teeth and doing only half of what other men do. . . . I have not yet seen the world, but when I do see it, and gain some experience of men, I shall certainly have to withdraw bitterly into myself, not on account of the misfortunes that may befall me . . . but because of the things that will wound my heart.[3]

It was with a mind set in this key, that he stumbled into his first romance.

[1] *Le Ricordanze.*   [2] *Zibaldone*, I, p. 40.
[3] *Epist.* I, To Giordani, 2 May 1818.

3. 'The Woman who Cannot be Found'

'Great solace: a dream in exchange for truth.'[1]

The passages quoted in this chapter contain the story of Leopardi's various romantic attachments. It is essentially always the same story, since whoever the protagonist might be, the lady was always, as he himself has said, 'the woman who cannot be found'.

She is one of those images [he wrote in a note to his poem *Alla sua donna*], those phantoms of celestial and indescribable beauty, which we summon up between sleeping and waking, when we are little more than children. . . . The author does not know whether this lady of his—and in calling her so, he shows that he loves no one but her—was ever born, or ever will be; he only knows that she does not live on this earth, and we are not her contemporaries. He searches for her in the ideas of Plato, in the moon, the planets of the solar system, the constellations of the stars.[2]

I

On 11 September 1817 some distant relations arrived in casa Leopardi: Conte Lazzari from Pesaro, his little girl, Vittoria, who was to be placed in a convent-school in Recanati, and his wife Geltrude Cassi, a Junoesque beauty. Her dark, flashing eyes, her voluptuous figure, and her warm, effusive manner, at once captivated the sad, serious boy of nineteen, still dressed in a priest's gown, who was waiting at the door to greet her. Three days later, when she had gone away, Giacomo set down, with a Proustian minuteness and detachment, a detailed account of every hour spent in her company,

[1] *Dialogue between Torquato Tasso and his Familiar Spirit.*
[2] Leopardi's Note to his Ode, *Alla sua donna*, in the edition of his *Canzoni* published in Bologna, 1821, in *Poesie e Prose*, I, p. 152.

and every shade of his emotions. These pages, which have no title in the original, were first published in the Scritti vari inediti dalle carte napolitane (*1906*), *with the title,* Diario d'amore.

For more than a year, since I first began to feel the sway of beauty, I had been wishing to speak and converse, as all other men do, with attractive women, of whom a mere smile, accidentally cast upon me, seemed to me a very strange thing, and marvellously sweet and flattering: and this desire, in my enforced solitude, had remained unfulfilled. But last Thursday evening a distant cousin of ours arrived in our house, a lady from Pesaro—unknown to me, but awaited by me with pleasure, since I believed that she might be able to bring some relief to my old desire.

With a husband of over fifty, heavy, stout, and phlegmatic, she was twenty-six years old, taller and with a finer figure than any woman I had ever seen, but with a face that was not at all coarse, features that were both strong and delicate, a fine complexion, very black eyes, chestnut hair, and manners which were friendly and, to my mind, charming, being quite unaffected, and not at all like the primitive ones of the ladies of the Romagna and especially those of Pesaro, as well as entirely different, in some indescribable fashion, from our ladies of the Marches.

That evening I saw her, and she did not displease me; but I could only say a few words to her. On Friday I said a few cold words to her before dinner; we dined together, I as silent as usual, but keeping my gaze fixed upon her, with a cold and curious delight in looking at a rather beautiful face, considerably greater than if I had been admiring a fine portrait. I had done the same the evening before, at supper. On the Friday evening my brothers played cards with her, but I, envying them very much, had to play chess with someone else. I tried hard to win, so as to obtain the Lady's praise (and only hers, though many others stood around me) since she, though she did not know the game, esteemed it highly. It was a drawn game, but the Lady, thinking of other things, paid no heed; then, leaving her cards, she asked me to teach her the moves; I did so, but together with some other people, and so without much pleasure. But I observed that she learned very easily and did not confuse in her mind the rules explained to her in a hurry (as certainly I would have done). I therefore concluded, what I have heard since from others, that she was a lady of some intelligence. Meanwhile to watch and observe her playing with my brothers had aroused in me a great wish to do so myself, and thus fulfil my wish to speak and converse with an attractive woman; so that I heard with great pleasure that she would stay on until the following evening.

At supper, the same cold observation. On the morrow, during my very empty day, I awaited the game with plea-sure, but without feeling troubled or anxious; either because I expected to find full satisfaction in it, or because it certainly never entered my head that I might be discontented after-wards. The time came, and I played. I came out of it most dis-concerted and uneasy. I had played with great pleasure, but had only stopped against my will, owing to my mother's insistence. The Lady had treated me kindly, and for the first time I had made a handsome woman laugh at my jokes, and had spoken to her and obtained from her many words and smiles. Therefore, wondering why I was dissatisfied, I could not discover the reason. I did not feel the regret that sometimes pierces one's heart after some pleasure, because one has not made the best use of the opportunity. It seemed to me that I had done and obtained as much as was possible or as I could have expected. Yet I very well knew that this pleasure had been clouded and uneasy, that this was not only my fancy, but I could not see where the flaw lay. In any case my heart felt very soft and tender, and at supper, attentive to the Lady's every act and word, I found that they pleased me very much and moved me more and more; and in short, the Lady was very dear to me. And when she went out I realized that on the morrow she would be gone, and that never should I see her again.

I lay in bed, considering the feelings in my heart, which in substance were a vague disquiet, a disconsolate melancholy, some sweetness, much affection, and a desire for I knew not what, nor could I imagine anything that would satisfy it. I fed upon the constant and most vivid memories of that evening and of the preceding days, and so I stayed awake until it was very late, and when sleep came I dreamed, as in a fever, of the game and the play and the Lady; although, while still awake, I had wondered whether I would dream of her and believed I had observed that I had never yet dreamed about anything of which I had expected to dream. But these feelings had become the masters of my whole being and had seized hold of my mind, so that they could in no way leave me, not even in my sleep.

Waking before dawn (and not falling asleep again), the same thoughts returned, as is natural, or rather continued, and I must also say that before falling asleep I had considered that sleep generally weakens and almost deadens the thoughts of the previous day, especially the appearance and behaviour of unfamiliar persons, and I feared that this time, too, the same thing would occur. But on the contrary these thoughts, having gone on during my sleep, dawned again upon my mind with freshness and with almost greater vigour. And since the window of my room looks out upon an open court, which lights the entrance hall of the house, I heard people moving early, and at once became aware that the strangers were preparing to depart, and I waited for a long time with the greatest patience and impatience, first hearing the horses clattering, then the arrival of the carriage and people walking up and down, and hoped every moment that the Lady would come down, that I might hear her voice for the last time; and so I heard it.

That departure did not grieve me, because I had foreseen that if the strangers had stayed, it would have been a very sad day for me. And now I am spending it with the emotions I have already described, with a bitter little pain besides, which comes over me whenever I remember these past days, a recollection more melancholy than I can ever tell, which, as the same hours and circumstances come round again, recalls to me the memory of those days, while I see a great emptiness around me, and bitterness clutches at my heart. For it is very soft, and opens tenderly and suddenly, but only towards one object, since towards any others these feelings have rendered me most reserved and shy both in my thoughts and looks, so that I cannot bear to fix my gaze on any other face, whether beautiful or ugly (I do not know which disturbs me most), nor even on portraits or similar things, for it seems to me that such sights might contaminate the purity of my thoughts and of the breathing and living image I hold in my mind. And thus to hear that person spoken of shakes and torments me, as if someone had touched or handled an ailing part of my body, and even arouses my anger and nausea; as indeed my gorge rises and I feel despair when I hear cheerful talk, and so generally, holding my tongue, I shun as much as possible the sound of any voice, especially during the onslaught of these thoughts. By comparison with them, everything else disgusts me, and I despise many things which I did not before, even study, to which my mind is entirely closed, and almost, though perhaps not entirely, to fame as well. And I have no wish to eat, a thing not customary to me even at the time of the strongest emotions, and therefore a sign of true disquiet.

If this is love, which I do not know, this is the first time I have felt it since reaching the age of reflecting about it: and here I am, at nineteen and a half, in love. And I plainly see that love must be a very bitter thing, and that unfortunately (I speak of tender and sentimental love) I shall always be its slave. Although I feel sure that this present one (which, as I thought last night almost immediately after the game, is probably the fruit of inexperience and of the newness of this delight) will soon be healed by time; and I do not well know whether this pleases or displeases me, except that wisdom bids me to accept it. Yet, wishing somehow to relieve my heart, and not knowing how to do so save by

D

writing, and since today I could not write about anything else, I have set down these lines, in order to examine minutely the course of love, so as to be able to renew at any time the first true entry into my heart of this sovereign passion. (Sunday, 14 December 1817)

Yesterday, having spent the second night in a fitful and delirious sleep, the same emotions continued much more intensely than I had expected, hardly less strong than on the preceding day, and having begun to describe them in verse during the wakeful hours of the night, I went on all yesterday, and finished this morning, as I lay in bed. Yesterday evening and last night, having slept hardly at all, I noticed that her image, which was at first most vivid (especially her face), was gradually fading away, to my very great regret, and I could only call it back with much effort, also because I would have liked to finish the verses, with which I was much pleased, before the heat of my melancholy mood had cooled. Before falling asleep I regretfully foresaw that my night would not be as troubled as the previous ones, and this was so, and now all these emotions have become very weak, partly because the eager composition of these verses has not only reconciled me a little with fame and has drained my heart, but because the industrious and continuous stirring up and evocation of those feelings and images has caused them, as they became less spontaneous, to grow weaker. But their gradual disappearance did not heal the emptiness of my heart, but rather increased it, and I am still inclined to melancholy, fond of silence and meditation, and averse to all pleasures, which seem to me far less precious than what I have lost. In short, I am attempting to foster as carefully as I can those dear and painful emotions which are flying from me, and which seem to me to have broadened my ideas and raised and ennobled my soul, while opening my heart to passion. Not, however, at all to love, save of that one image, since a distaste for every other form of human beauty is, I may say, the strongest and most vivid of the emotions I have

described that still remains with me. And one of the causes of
this (apart from the fact that my heart is too much under the
sway of a single image), as indeed of my whole mood, is—
as I think I can now affirm—the sway that, unless I am mistaken, two things will always hold over my nature. The first
consists in strong features (so long as they are not virile,
but tinged with something delicate and graceful), dark hair
and eyes, a vivacious expression, a tall stature; and indeed
I had observed even before now, but very uncertainly, that
languid, virginal faces, or those which are too refined, with
fair hair and a small stature and insipid manners and so
forth, have little effect upon me, and sometimes, when those
qualities are excessive, none at all, though they sometimes
are very effective with other men. The second consists in
manners which are gracious and kind but not at all affected,
and above all free from any observable distortion or any
airs and graces or grimaces, in short, as I have said above,
the manners of Pesaro, which also have, in their grace and
modest vivacity, something else that I cannot express: and
in this and in their naturalness and unaffectedness (at least
in the Lady of whom I write) they are a hundred times
superior to the ladies of the Marches, who now seem to me
much more affected and less attractive. For these two reasons, the sight or thought of any other figure (for I do not
see any but *marchigiane*, and never have) seem to me to
trouble and soil the beauty of the image in my mind, so that
I avoid them with all my might. (Tuesday, 16 December
1817)

The day before yesterday it seemed to me that my cherished
sorrow was really about to depart, and yesterday morning,
too. My appetite came back, the thought crossed my mind
that I would do well to take up my studies again, I seemed
to have become less averse to laughter and less disinclined
for certain small pleasures, and I began quietly to reason
with myself about this matter, as I usually do about other
ones, so that I regretfully concluded that I would soon again

be the man I was before. Last night my dreams twice brought back the same object to my memory, but only for a short time and peacefully. But yesterday, almost suddenly, and chiefly because I had heard the Lady's name mentioned, the familiar melancholy seized hold of me, with such a violent onslaught that I almost felt I had gone back to the beginning of my disease. The same nausea when I heard cheerful talk, the same grief, the same deep and prolonged meditation, and almost the same frenzy and oppression, both of which I realized I had never truly felt before, except on the evening and night of Saturday, all Sunday and (though much more blunted) during the early part of Monday. And in truth in these last days—since my melancholy, owing to the passage of time, could no longer remain as fiery and intense as at first—it has taken the form of occasional waves, some longer and some shorter, and some more or less strong, but sometimes almost as violent as the first. And in particular the discontent has endured which, on reflection, seems to me to have arisen at the time when I would have liked to go on playing a little longer; not that I precisely felt that I had played too little, or less than I had expected; nor even that, while I was playing, I was content, and only grieved at having to stop so soon; nor finally that even if I had played longer, for a month or a year, I would ever have come away satisfied, for I am well aware that I would never have been anything but most discontented. Yet nevertheless it seems to me that this discontent that takes hold of me is tinged with eagerness, as if it arose from a wish to prolong my enjoyment, and from a blind, unsatisfied greed, which, while I was still playing, caused me a still greater oppression and anguish, almost as if I had been hastening to enjoy a blessing which I knew would soon, too soon, be lost to me.

Already on Monday evening the much desired image of her face had almost completely vanished from my mind, perhaps because I had gazed upon it too eagerly; and since then I must say with great regret that it has never appeared to me again, save as a flash of lightning, seen in passing and very faintly, while the image of her companion, which I was not seeking at all, appears to me with complete freshness and vividness, whenever I recollect it. Every evening, lying in bed awake for a long time, I have tried with all my strength to recall her dear image, which probably flies from me just because I seek it with such ardour, but I can only see its outline, and wear my brain out so completely that I fall asleep, with my head clouded, aching, and on fire. This occurred last night, but this morning, waking very early, in the very moment between sleeping and waking, the desired vision suddenly flashed vividly and truly before my fancy, and at once my thoughts rushed after it, and if I was not fully able to recall it, yet in the freshness of the mind at dawn, I saw and observed enough of her expression and her movements, gestures, features, speech and enunciation that, far from wondering at having been captivated by her, I thought that if these things were still present now in my fancy, I would be even more frenzied and troubled than I am.

Now I am proceeding much as in these last days, and my only pastime is the writing of these lines, with an empty spirit, or rather one filled with tedium (except in the heat of those thoughts), for I can find nothing worthy of occupying my heart or mind, and indeed consider the good I have lost to be the only desirable and worthy one, or at least greater than any other I could obtain. Everything that does not lead to it seems vain; and therefore study (which I yet do sometimes idly return to for a little while) no longer attracts me and cannot fill the emptiness of my soul, since the fruit of this labour, fame, no longer seems to me the great thing it once seemed, or assuredly I can imagine a still greater one, and fame having become an object of secondary value, I do not see why I should spend the whole day pursuing it, thus distracting myself from thoughts of that other good. . . . And therefore I do not see how I shall ever be able to acquire again my old love of study, for it seems to me that even when this infirmity of mind has passed, the knowledge will always remain with me that there is one thing

more delightful than study, and that once I experienced it.
(Friday, 19 December 1817)

[*Entry of Sunday, 21 December, omitted.*]

I will bring to an end this babbling, which I have kept up
to relieve my own heart and to gain a better knowledge of
myself and of my passions; but I will not go on, for, having
nothing more to say, I feel I am wasting my time, which
usually I value, and I had better start to make use of it again,
since passion no longer holds me back. For it is fading
away, so that I am again beginning to enjoy the routine of
my occupations, which in the past days I did not keep to and
found distasteful, and I can bring myself to laugh again, and
to think about other things and to study; except that I am
trying to conciliate my love of study with my passion, since
I vaguely plan to write something in which I could converse
with that Lady or induce her to talk to me, and I imagine
myself some day achieving something great in literature, and
appearing before her in such a way that she would receive
me with pleasure and esteem. And these same thoughts have
nourished me now and again even during these past days.
So I am taking up the usual tenor of my life again, for my
fading passion can no longer fill my days and it is declining
from lack of food, having been strangled at the very moment of its birth by the departure of its object. . . .
   But I am so far from being ashamed of my passion, that
since the moment of its birth I have taken pleasure in it and
still do, congratulating myself on feeling one of the emotions
without which no man can become great, and on being
capable of grieving intensely for things that do not appertain
to the body. Thus I have learned by experience that my
heart is unusually sensitive and tender, and perhaps will
some day move me to do or write something of which the
memory will endure, or which at least I shall enjoy myself. . . .
   I therefore do not deny that I have assisted and cultivated
these feelings of mine with great care, and that part of my

sorrow in seeing them diminish does not only arise from my desire to enjoy and love. But since I have always sincerely detested any taint of false romanticism, I do not think I have had any feeling or impulse that was not spontaneous, and I have not set down anything that I have not truly and spontaneously felt. . . . (Monday and Tuesday, 22 and 23 December)

Not having until now related or shown any sign of my passion to anyone whatever, I told my brother Carlo about it, showing him my verses and these papers on 29 December, while very plain traces of past emotions still remained in my soul, as indeed they still do today, on 2 January 1818, and nothing but opportunity is lacking to bring them to life again.[1]

II

Soon after Contessa Geltrude's departure—'while melancholy was still fresh'—Leopardi composed a Petrarchian idyll in her praise, a stiff and stilted work, much less vivid than his diary, and six years later he wrote in her honour the ode Alla sua donna. *But the real epilogue to this episode is to be found in three passages in the* Zibaldone.

When a man has fallen in love, the whole world fades before his eyes, he sees nothing but the beloved object, and if he finds himself in a crowd at a party, it is as if he were alone. . . . I have always been disgusted by men's folly and by the trivial, vile, and ridiculous things that are said and done by the people I live with. But never have I felt such horrible, tormenting disgust with regard to those things (almost to the point of nausea) as when I felt love within me, or some lingering of love, when it was necessary for me to retire within my shell, having become even more sensitive than usual to any meanness, baseness, or coarseness, whether in deeds or words, whether physical or moral or even philological, that is, in offensive jests, insipid chatter, coarse

[1] *Poesie e Prose*, I, pp. 657–72: *Memorie del primo amore.*

jokes, rough manners, or anything of that sort. I have never been so aware of being alive as when I loved, even though the rest of the world was dead to me.[1]

I remember noting down and awaiting and observing and spending with indescribable emotion, as if they were holy days, the weekly and then the monthly and then the yearly anniversaries of the day on which I first felt the breath of a very dear passion.[2]

In the transports of love, in speaking to the beloved, in the favours she grants you ... you are seeking happiness rather than experiencing it; your uneasy heart always feels something lacking, something, you know not what, that is less than what it hoped for, a longing for something, for a great deal, more. The best moments of love are those of a still and gentle melancholy, in which you weep and know not why, and are almost at rest, resigned to a misfortune you cannot define. ... Your spirit, thus finding rest, is less tormented, indeed almost fulfilled, and can almost savour happiness.[3]

The other two romances of Leopardi's youth were equally remote from reality: indeed the figures he describes are so faint and transient, so much the creatures of his own imagination, that his biographers have had some difficulty in identifying them. Both of them—the 'Silvia' and 'Nerina' of his poems—were, according to his brother, 'distant and imprisoned loves'—girls of whom the two young men had mere glimpses as they passed them in the street, or saw one of them sitting by an open window, singing at her loom.

The first passage referring to one of them appears in Leopardi's fragmentary Recollections of Childhood and Adolescence, *set down in 1819, and first published, after his death, in the* Scritti vari inediti.

My musings about a girl of humble birth, beautiful but very flighty, whom I often saw and then dreamed of with much intensity, who always used to greet me. After the dream I would think about what we might say to each other, but in the daytime I saw her and she did not greet me and I was in a turmoil. ('You fool, she had other things to think about, and she does not even please you, and you have never said nor will say a single word to her.') And yet I should have liked her to greet me.[1]

The next passage describes an evening in May, at sunset.

Children's voices, the house-door ajar, etc., and on one side a thicket of low bushes, and behind it, fleetingly (since the hill sloped sharply), my much-desired glimpse of *la Brini*. . . . She was looking back often at her master, who had just gone by . . . then she ran away in a great hurry, in a red dress with a fine handkerchief on her head and something wrapped up in a white cloth in her hand. For a moment as she turned we could see her face, but she was unstable as a bee, resting here and there, and jumping up to see the game of *pallone*, but all with a sweet seriousness. . . . We followed her until she paused beside a few other women and took off her handkerchief (but not out of coquetry) and passed close to her in a very narrow lane; and she at once followed and went with a man into her master's house, etc. My thoughts that evening, and my turmoil looking out over the fields and the setting sun and the city turned to gold and the valley below with its rows of vines, and my spirit soared and was stirred into a frenzy, and in my thoughts about that day I knew that love could truly make a hero of me and render me capable of great things, even of killing myself.

By pure chance I met her again and she even greeted me sweetly (or so I thought) and her face did indeed seem to me lovely. . . . And without any hope I saw her unexpectedly once more. My dreams that night, and it was true heaven to speak to her and be questioned by her, while she listened with a smile, and then I asked if I might kiss her hand and

---

[1] *Poesie e Prose*, I, p. 677: *Ricordi d'Infanzia e di Adolescenza*.

she, twisting some kind of thread, held it out to me, looking at me with a simple and candid air. And I kissed it, without daring to touch her, and with such delight that only then in my dreams did I realize for the first time what these satisfactions consist in, and this so truly that waking up at once and fully conscious, I saw that the pleasure had indeed been exactly what it would have been in reality, and was astounded. And thus I discovered that it is true that the soul can melt into a kiss, and so lose sight of all the world.[1]

About Silvia we know a little more. She was a coachman's daughter, Teresa Fattorini, and she lived in a small house that gave upon the same square as the Palazzo Leopardi, the one which the poet later on described in Il sabato del villaggio (Saturday Evening in the Village). *From the windows of his library Giacomo could see Teresa at her loom and could hear her singing; but one day he was told that she was ill, dying of consumption, and began to feel for her 'the interest I feel in all who must die young, as I know I shall, too'. Her illness dragged on for many weary months, until even her friends and parents had come to accept her death as inevitable, and almost with indifference.*

As some men enjoy their fame during their life-time, so she, owing to the length of her illness, saw her parents already consoled for her death, forgetful of her and indifferent to her pain. She could not even die peacefully, poor girl, but racked by cruel suffering. . . . The life of man then seemed to me to be like the time when, as a child, I was taken to visit a friend's house, and began to play with the other boys at a table, and then my parents got up and called me and my heart was wrung, but I had to go, leaving my occupations half begun and the chairs upset and the children weeping.[2]

[1] *Poesie e Prose*, I, pp. 684–5: *Ricordi d'Infanzia e di Adolescenza.*
[2] Ibid. p. 680,

III

There were only two other romances, or attempts at romance, in Leopardi's life, and in these, too, he never found fulfilment. At the age of twenty-five he had written in his notebook:

The first feeling that beauty in the other sex arouses in a man is fear . . . and that fear arises from his feeling that it is impossible to go on living without the object of his desire, and at the same time equally impossible to possess it as he would wish; for even physical possession (though at that moment far from his thoughts) would never fully satisfy him nor fulfil his desire. . . . And the violence of his longing fills him with terror.[1]

During his first visit to Rome he would gladly have given all his erudition, all his poetic gifts, for the self-assurance and easy conquests of his handsome brother Carlo.

Whether it be spring or autumn [he wrote to him wistfully], I really do not know what finer occupation there can be than making love—and assuredly it is ten times better to speak to a pretty girl than to wander, as I am doing, round the Belvedere Apollo and the Capitoline Venus.[2]

But such conquests were not for him, nor was he any more successful when, on a more sophisticated plane, he attempted an amitié amoureuse with a lady of Bologna some eleven years older than himself, Contessa Teresa Carniani Malvezzi. The lady was herself a poetess, though not a good one; she had studied philosophy and read the classics; she held a literary salon; and for a short time it seemed to him that in her at least he had found the spiritual companion he had always desired.

I have entered into a relation [he wrote to his brother in the spring of 1826] with a lady of Florentine birth and

[1] *Zibaldone*, II, p. 453, 16 September 1823.
[2] *Epist.* II, 5 April 1823.

married into one of the chief families here, which now forms a great part of my existence. She is not young, but she has a grace and wit which—believe me, who thought this impossible until now—make up for youth, and create a marvellous illusion. In the first days of our acquaintance I lived in a sort of delirium and fever. We have never spoken of love, save in jest, but we live together in a tender and sensitive friendship, with a mutual interest and confidence in each other which is like love without anxiety. She esteems me very highly; when I read her some of my work, she sometimes sheds tears from her heart, without affectation. The praises of other people have no reality for me; hers enter my blood and remain in my soul. She loves and well understands both literature and philosophy; we never lack a subject of conversation. I spend almost every evening with her from sunset until midnight, and it seems to me a moment only. We confide to each other all our secrets, we reprove each other, we point out each other's faults. In short, this acquaintance forms and will form a new epoch in my life, for it has disenchanted me of my disenchantment, and has convinced me that the pleasures I thought impossible really do exist in this world, and that I am still capable of lasting illusions.[1]

The romance lasted all through the summer, but in the autumn Leopardi was obliged to return to Recanati, and though the lady had promised to write to him, five months passed without a word from her. When at last a parcel came addressed in her hand, he opened it eagerly—to find only her translation of 'The Fragments of Cicero's Republic', without a line of her own.

At last a book has reached me from you, which shows me that you have remembered me once, at least, since my departure, and the address in your handwriting assures me that the book is not a posthumous work, and comes to me as a gift, not a legacy. The many letters you meant to write to me, and promised many times, have turned into one

[1] *Epist.* III, To Carlo, 30 May 1826.

address. If you should feel inclined to begin now, that is, after five months, you must know that it is now too late, for I am leaving for Bologna this week, or, at latest, at the beginning of next.

Therefore I will say nothing about your book, in which I admire the sobriety and good sense of the preface, the purity of the language and the style, and the many difficulties you have overcome. Nor will I ask you for your news, for I hope soon to be able to tell you all you wish to know, and ask of you all I wish to hear. Meanwhile love me, as you certainly do, and believe me *your most faithful friend or servant, or both, or what you like.*[1]

He returned to Bologna and went to see the Contessa. What exactly happened we do not know, though one malicious account states that the poet flung himself at his lady's feet—and she summoned a footman to give il signor conte a glass of water. What is certain is that he never called upon her again, and that, before going to Florence in the spring, he sent her the following letter.

My Contessa, on the last occasion I had the pleasure of seeing you, you told me so plainly that my conversation *en tête à tête* was tedious to you, that you left me no excuse for continuing my visits. Do not think that I am offended. If I were to complain of anything, it would be that your words and behaviour, although clear enough, have not been still clearer and more open. Now, after this long interval, I should like to bid you farewell, but dare not do so without your permission. I beg you to grant it, wishing intensely to repeat to you that I am, as you well know, your true and cordial friend.[2]

We do not know what the Contessa replied, but she seems to have chattered about her conquest and her words were repeated to

[1] *Epist.* IV, To Teresa Carniani Malvezzi, Recanati, 18 April 1827. The last words are written in English in the original.
[2] Ibid. undated: Moroncini places it in May 1827.

Leopardi, for in his last reference to her, he flung chivalry to the winds.

How can it come into your head that I should go on see-ing that —— of a Malvezzi? May my nose fall off, if, after hearing her gossip about me, I went back there again, or ever shall. . . . The other day, having met her by chance, I turned my face to the wall, so as not to see her.[1]

Once again, love had turned into contempt.

IV

One more episode—the last—came four years later. In the summer of 1830, when Leopardi was living in Florence, he wrote to his sister Paolina:

Unbelievable news! My blue suit has been turned in the latest fashion, with long lapels; it looks as good as new again, and suits me very well.[2]

Dressed in his blue suit, and with a new self-confidence, Leopardi was going out in Florentine society, and it was then that he met the lady to whom he gave the name of Aspasia: Fanny Targioni Tozzetti—the wife of a celebrated Florentine doctor and botanist, Antonio Targioni—a lively, amorous, pretentious, commonplace coquette. At that time Leopardi was living with his friend Antonio Ranieri, a handsome, vain young man, whom (though his own affections were given to an actress in Rome, Maddalena Pelzet) Fanny greatly preferred to the silent, melancholy poet.

We have, from Ranieri's pen, a description of Leopardi at this time: 'His stature was mediocre, slight, and bent, his complexion pale; his head was large, with a broad, square forehead, languid blue eyes, a sharp nose, and fine-drawn features. His voice was low and very faint, and he had an indescribable, heavenly smile.' The picture

---

[1] *Epist.* VII, p. 83, no. 1062.   [2] Ibid. VI, 21 August [1830].

is not unprepossessing, but it is hardly that of a Don Juan. 'This man', Ranieri also wrote, 'took the flower of his virginity untouched to the grave, and for that very reason loved twice, although without hope, as no man has ever loved before. . . . Almost all his affections were one-sided, and unnoticed by the person he loved. They became all the more intense and ardent.'[1]

Thus with every lost opportunity, every hope denied, Leopardi's adolescent attitude towards love hardened and crystallized. What he feared was not merely a rebuff; perhaps his real dread was rather of success, and of then finding 'the unaccountable void that nothing can fill'. Geltrude Lazzari, Teresa Malvezzi, Fanny Targioni, what were they for him but shadows on a wall, paper silhouettes of his 'heavenly original', 'the woman who cannot be found'?

Fanny, however, at first made use of her little hunchback to collect autographs for her and often allowed him to call, in the hope that he might be a link with his friend. On one spring day he found her on the sofa, surrounded by flowers and with her children playing round her—and discovered, as he wrote in his poem about her, As-pasia, 'a new heaven and new earth, almost a divine light'.

In the evenings, in his solitary room, he would indulge, according to Ranieri, 'in vain and unrestrained soliloquies of love, unworthy of the dignity of so great a man', and it was then that he wrote a poem addressed, not to his lady, but to the obsessive idea of love, Il pensiero dominante (The Dominating Thought).

During the winter Ranieri insisted on carrying him off to Rome (to be near his own mistress) and the only letter that Leopardi sent to Fanny was in a tone of friendship, rather than love.

Dear Fanny, I have not written to you before, so as not to bore you, since I know how busy you are. But I do not want my silence to seem forgetfulness—although perhaps you know that to forget you is no easy matter. You said to me one day that you often do not answer letters from your closest friends, but only those from others, because the former would not be offended, like the latter, by your

---

[1] A. Ranieri, 'Notizie intorno alla vita ed agli scritti di G.L.', printed as an Appendix to his *Sette anni di sodalizio con Giacomo Leopardi*.

silence. Do me the honour of treating me as one of your greatest friends, and if you are very busy or writing tires you, do not reply. I wish for news of you very much, but shall be content to have it from Ranieri or Gozzani.

I do not believe that you expect any news from me. You know that I abhor politics, because I believe, indeed I see, that men are unhappy under any form of government, which is nature's fault for having created men to be unhappy; and I smile at the happiness of the crowd, for my little brain cannot conceive a happy crowd made up of unhappy individuals. Still less can I give you any literary tidings. I must confess that I am in great danger of forgetting the alphabet, from having lost the habit of either reading or writing. My friends are horrified, and they, for their part, are right to pursue fame or the welfare of mankind, but I, who do not presume to improve humanity and do not aspire to fame, am not wrong either to spend my days lying upon a sofa, without moving an eyelid. And I find much common sense in the habits of the Turks and other Orientals, who are content to sit cross-legged all day, vacantly contemplating this ridiculous existence of ours.

But I am wrong to write these things to you, who are beautiful and privileged by nature to shine and to conquer the destiny of mankind. I know that you, too, are inclined to melancholy, as all sweet and talented natures always have been and will be. But in all sincerity and in spite of my genuine philosophy of despair, I believe that melancholy is unsuitable for you, so that, although natural, it is not wholly reasonable. At least that is what I should wish. . . .

Good-bye, dear Fanny; greet the little girls. If you will deign to command me, remember that for me, as for everyone else who knows you, it is a happiness and an honour to serve you. Your Leopardi.[1]

When the spring came, Leopardi returned to Florence, and both he and Ranieri resumed their visits to Fanny's house, but when

[1] *Epist.* VI, 5 December 1831.

summer came, both Ranieri and Fanny left the city, and Leopardi
remained alone, waiting for a letter from his Aspasia. At last it
came, a dull, flat little note which he forwarded to Ranieri, and
when he replied, he only dared to speak about his friend's love, not
his own.

Ranieri is still in Bologna, and still absorbed in that love
of his, which is making him unhappy in more ways than
one. Yet certainly love and death are the most beautiful
things in the world, and the only ones worthy of our desire.
Good-bye, lovely and charming Fanny. I hardly dare ask
for your commands, knowing that I am good for nothing.
But if a wish and desire have some value, as one is told, you
should indeed consider me fit to obey you.[1]

This was Leopardi's second and last letter to Fanny. For some
months more, after returning to Florence, she continued to see both
the poet and his friend, and the three-cornered relationship seems to
have caused some amusement to the provincial society of Florence.

My poor Ranieri! If men laugh at you because of me, I
am comforted by the thought that they are certainly also
laughing at me because of you. . . . The world always mocks
the things which, if it did not mock, it would be obliged to
admire, and, like the fox, criticizes what it envies.[2]

What happened next, we can only surmise. Perhaps Ranieri said
to Leopardi that Fanny had only been amusing herself with him, or
perhaps Fanny herself told the poor poet brutally that it was
Ranieri whom she loved. We only know that the break was final,
and that Leopardi's sense of betrayal, his weariness and loneliness,
found expression in the most concise, poignant, and nakedly self-
revealing of his poems, A sè stesso (To Himself).
After his death, some of her friends persistently asked Fanny
who Aspasia was and she, somewhat disingenuously, asked Ranieri
for an answer. 'For pity's sake, tell me . . . and save me from a

[1] *Epist.* VI, 5 January [1833].   [2] Ibid. 29 January [1833].

E

number of unnecessary and tedious letters.' She received a very clear answer: 'You are Aspasia, and you know it.'[1]

Among Leopardi's papers in Naples, there was a rough draft of an ode, written in Florence at the time of his love for Fanny Targioni, addressed to Arimane, the Persian god of evil, 'whom some call nature, fate or God'.

Why, god of evil, have you given life an occasional semblance of pleasure? of love? Was it to torment us with desire, with self-comparison, with regrets for our youth? . . . If ever a boon was asked of Arimane, grant that I may not live beyond my thirty-fifth year. All my life I have been your chief preacher, the apostle of your religion. Grant me a reward. I do not ask for what the world calls gifts; not for riches nor love, the only thing worth living for. I ask for what is considered the greatest of evils, death. I've had enough, enough of life.[2]

[1] Moroncini, *Purezza di Leopardi* in *Italia Letteraria*, 21 May 1933. The 'carte Ranieri' also contain the rough draft of a letter from Ranieri to Giordani, which shows that Leopardi's friends, too, had asked him to reveal the identity of Aspasia. 'How can I tell you who Aspasia is, without her own permission? Many women have been willing to purchase a journey to posterity with a ticket of . . . ['ill-fame'?—the word is left blank in the draft] when they cannot get a better one, but it is not a thing that one can do without their permission.'
[2] *Poesie e Prose*, I, p. 434.

4. Some Early Letters 1817–19

When, early in 1817, Leopardi completed his translation of the Second Book of the Aeneid, he sent copies of it to the three leading literary men of his time: the poet Vincenzo Monti, whose own translation of the Iliad had recently appeared, the Abate Angelo Mai, and the Abate Pietro Giordani. His letter to Monti was written in a tone of extreme humility.

If it is a fault in a very little man to write of his own accord to a very great man of letters, then I am greatly at fault, for both these superlatives suit both of us. Neither can I proffer anything in my excuse but an incomprehensible craving to make myself known to my prince (for assuredly I am your subject, like every other lover of letters) and the trembling that comes over me as I write, which I would not feel in writing to a king. You will receive on my behalf from Sig. Stella[1] my translation of the Second Book of the Aeneid, a most wretched gift, indeed hardly a gift, but a pretext for a smile, to the man who has been the first translator of the Iliad in Europe and the great emulator of the great Annibale Caro. Pray smile, for your smile will be one of compassion, and your compassion is more welcome and honourable to me than the envy of a thousand others. I do not ask you to read my book, but only not to reject it; and in accepting it, to make clear to me that you are not offended by my daring. . . .[2]

[1] Antonio Fortunato Stella was one of the most liberal and intelligent publishers in Milan, who from the first recognized Leopardi's talents.

[2] *Epistolario*, I, p. 49: Recanati, 21 February 1817. That Leopardi's admiration for Monti soon came to be more critical than this letter implies, is shown in a note in the *Zibaldone* written a few months later. '[Monti's] images have a certain soft, easy, fluent flexibility, but all that belongs to the soul—fire, feeling, or true and deep or sublime emotion—is entirely lacking. He is truly the poet of the ear and the imagination, never of the heart.'

Monti sent only a condescending word of encouragement, but the Abate Pietro Giordani—to whom a similar letter had been sent— wrote, after learning that Leopardi was only nineteen, an answer which changed the whole course of the young man's life. 'I like to think,' Giordani prophesied, 'that in the twentieth century Count Leopardi (whom I already love) will be remembered among the men who have restored to Italy the honour she has lost. . . . You will soon be an honour to Italy, as you are already a miracle in Recanati. . . .'[1]

At the time of writing this letter Giordani, already a man of forty-three, was one of the leading figures in the group of patriots and writers—Vincenzo Monti, Ludovico di Breme, Silvio Pellico— who were making Milan a centre of Italian liberal thought. Both by temperament and personal experience, he was well suited to sympathize with Giacomo and to become his mentor. He, too, had taken refuge in childhood from unsympathetic parents in a preco- cious addiction to study. At the age of twenty-three he had entered a monastery, mainly to get away from home, but after three years he had come out again, having acquired an intense and uncompromising anti-clericalism, which later on—in Conte Monaldo's opinion—was responsible for the destruction of Giacomo's faith. A loquacious, rhetorical, impulsive, generous, and sometimes touchy man, he could be extremely good company, and indeed Byron said that he was the only literary man in Italy whom he ever wished to see twice. But above all he possessed the two qualities of which Giacomo stood most in need: enthusiasm and simple human warmth.

To be praised by such a man, of whom he had heard since his boyhood, was indeed encouraging, and in Giacomo's reply all reserves were thrown aside. His letters to Giordani during the next two years contain the pent-up confidences of his lonely youth.

That I should actually see and read Giordani's writing, that he should write to me, that I may hope to have him as my future master—these are things I hardly dare to believe. Nor would you wonder, if you knew how long and how lovingly I have nourished this thought, for the things one longs for most seem most impossible, when they have come

[1] *Epist.* I, p. 59: Milan, 12 March [1817].

to pass. I should like you to believe without reserve all that I write to you now, or shall write to you in the future, for even the smallest phrases, I promise you, will come straight from the heart. This I demand; everything else I will request.

My first letter was the fruit of respect rather than of affection, for the latter, if welcome and honourable towards one's equals, may be insulting to one's superiors. But now that your two very dear letters permit me to do so, you may be sure that it will be with all my affection that I shall write. . . . Nothing but your writings has ever told me about you, for where I live, there is no soul who can converse about men of letters. But I do not know how one can admire a man's qualities, especially when they are so great and unusual, without feeling affection for him, too. When I read Virgil, I fall in love with him, and I do so even more with the great living writers—of whom you justly say that they are very few, and so much greater must one's affection for them be, being divided between only three or four. I cannot tell you with how great a need, disgusted and discouraged by the mediocrity which besieges and suffocates me after reading the papers and other modern scribblings . . . I turn to the Classics among the dead, and to you and your great friends among the living, finding in them my comfort and my strength, since it is thus that I realize that true literature is still alive. When I write or read over things I think of publishing and see a passage which appeals to me (and here I must remind you of my promise to speak frankly to you) it comes naturally to me to ask myself: 'What would Monti or Giordani say about this? . . .'

I have a very great, perhaps immoderate and insolent, desire for glory; but I cannot endure that any of my work which does not satisfy me shall be praised, nor do I know why those writings have been reprinted, with greater damage to myself than profit to those who circulate them, unknown to me. You will have laughed as you read those things, but your laughter was certainly not malicious, and that gives me pleasure. And so that you may forgive me my madness in ever letting them appear, I will tell you that almost everything of mine that has been published will never be seen again with my consent, and that two other fat (but not great) works which I had already prepared and sent to press, have been condemned to oblivion.

As to the Second Book of the Aeneid, which I have not yet condemned, no one has had a copy of it from me, except the three men of letters you know of. I wrote to them only and from the heart, to satisfy, though with some trembling, an old and intense desire. That my book had many defects I knew before, and would swear to now, because Monti has told me so. . . . But it is of little use to say to a blind man, 'You have taken the wrong turn', unless you also add, 'Go that way.' . . . You say, as a Master, that translating is very useful at my age, which is indisputable, as practice has made very plain to me. For when I first begin reading one of the Classics, my mind is in a turmoil and confusion. Then I begin to translate, as best I can, and its beauties, while I am obliged to examine them and handle them one by one, find a place in my mind, enrich it and bring me peace. Your opinion encourages me and impels me to persevere.

Do not speak to me of Recanati. It is so dear to me that it would furnish me with fine ideas for a treatise on *Hatred of One's Birthplace*, for which, if Codrus was not *afraid to die*, I would be *afraid to live*. My country is Italy, and I burn for love of her, thanking heaven that I was born an Italian, for after all our literature, even if it is little cultivated, is the only legitimate daughter of the two truly great ancient ones. . . . You may be certain that if I do live, it will be for letters, because I neither wish, nor would be able, to live for anything else.[1]

The next letter is even more explicit.

Oh, how often, most dear and desired Signor Giordani, have I implored Heaven to let me find a man who was not

[1] *Epist.* I, pp. 61–64: Recanati, 21 March 1817.

only kind but also outstanding in gifts and erudition, and whom, once found, I might beg to honour me with his friendship! But I did not really believe that this desire would be granted, for I hardly thought it possible that these three things, each one of them so rare to find by itself, could indeed exist together. May God be blessed (I say it with a full heart) for granting me what I asked for and revealing my mistake to me! And therefore, I implore you, let there be complete confidence between us—respectful on my part, as befits a younger man, and very free on yours. You recommend to me some temperance in my studies with so much warmth and as if it were so important to you, that I would like to open my heart to you and to let you see the feelings that have been awakened in me by reading your words— feelings which, unless my heart changes entirely, will never, never perish! And to reply as best I can to so much affection, I will tell you that in truth my health is not only delicate but very delicate, and will not deny that it has been somewhat affected by the labours I have imposed on it for six years. But now I have reduced them very much: I do not study more than six hours a day, and very often less; I scarcely write anything; I regularly read the Classics of all three languages in small volumes, which can easily be carried about, so that I almost always study like the Peripatetics, and—*quod maximum dictu est*—I even endure many, many hours of merely holding my hands in my lap.

But who could ever have thought that Giordani would undertake the defence of Recanati? . . . It is all very well to say that Plutarch loved Chaeronea, and Alfieri, Asti. They loved those towns—they did not live there! So shall I, too, love my birthplace when I have left it. Now I say that I hate it because I am still there, for indeed this poor city is only guilty of never having given me a single good thing, except my family. It is easy to say: 'You are born here, this is where Providence means you to be.' Try saying to a sick man, 'If you try to get well, you are going against Providence.' Say to a poor man, 'If you try to get richer, you are going

against Providence.' Say to a Turk, 'Don't dream of being
baptized, for Providence created you a Turk.' This maxim is
akin to fatalism. 'But here you may be among the first; in a
larger town you would stand fourth or fifth.' This seems to
me a miserable form of pride, unworthy of a noble soul. . . .
'But here you could be more useful than elsewhere.' First
of all, I do not intend to give up my whole life for this
handful of men, renouncing everything else, and to live and
die for their benefit in this cave. I do not believe that it was
for this that nature created me, nor that virtue demands so
dreadful a sacrifice. Secondly, do you indeed believe that
the Marches and the southern part of the Roman States are
like the Romagna and Northern Italy? There the name of
literature is often heard; there, there are papers, academies,
conversazioni, bookshops, in great abundance. Gentlemen
read a little; ignorance belongs to the common herd, which,
if it were not ignorant, would not be common; but very
many try to educate themselves, many believe themselves to
be poets or philosophers. They are far from being so; but
at least they wish to be. Here, my dear Sir, everything is
dead, everything is folly and stupidity. Foreigners marvel at
this silence, this universal sleep. Literature is a word unknown. The names of Parini, Alfieri, Monti, Tasso, Ariosto
and all the others need a commentary. There is no one who
cares to make something of himself, or to whom it seems
strange to be called ignorant. They frankly apply the word
to themselves, knowing that it is true.

Do you believe that a fine mind would be appreciated
here? As a pearl in a dung-heap. You have truly said (and
will remember where) that the rarer studies are, the less they
are appreciated, for their value is not realized. So it is in
Recanati and in these provinces, where intelligence is not
included among nature's gifts. I am certainly not worth
much; but I have some friends in Milan, I order news-
papers, books, I have had something printed; all this no
citizen of Recanati has ever done, since its foundation. . . .
No one cares about my works, and in that they may be right,

but they care even less about anyone else's. Indeed I can tell you without boasting that our library has not its equal in the province, and only two others inferior to it. Over the door an inscription says that it is for the use of our citizens and is open to all. How many people do you think frequent it? Never a one. . . .

If one wishes to read a book one has not got, or even to glance at it, one must order it from somewhere else, without being able to see or choose before buying, with a thousand difficulties on the way. . . . And do you think it amusing to have no man of letters to speak to, to keep all one's thoughts to oneself, never to be able to air or discuss one's own opinions nor to take an innocent pride in one's studies, never to be able to ask for help or advice, and to keep up one's courage during so many hours and days of exhaustion and indifference?

In my early days my head was full of modern maxims, and I disdained and scorned the study of our language: all my early scribblings were translations from the French, I disdained Homer, Dante, all the Classics; I would not read them, I delighted in the works which I now detest. What has made me change my opinion? The grace of God, certainly no man. Who assures me that I am not constantly taking the wrong turn? No one. But let us say that all this is trivial. What is there beautiful in Recanati? What is there that a man can care to see and learn? Nothing. Yet God has made this world of ours so beautiful, man has created such loveliness within it, there are so many kinds of men, whom anyone who is not senseless must long to see and know, the earth is so full of marvels—and must I say, at the age of eighteen: 'In this hole I shall live, and die where I was born?'

Do you think that these desires can be restrained, that they are unfair, immoderate, unfounded, that it is folly not to be content never to see anything, not to content oneself with Recanati? You are misinformed that the air of this town is healthy. It is most changeable, damp, impregnated with salt, trying to the nerves, and, owing to its thinness, not at all suited to some constitutions. Add to this the obstinate, black, barbarous melancholy which consumes and devours me and increases with great strides, both when I study and when I do not. I well know, for I used to feel it, the gentle melancholy which gives birth to beauty, a melancholy sweeter than happiness, like twilight, while this is blackest night, a poison which destroys both body and soul. But how shall I free myself from it, while I do nothing but think? How can you speak of diversions? My only diversion in Recanati is study, my only diversion is what is killing me: all the rest is tedium. . . . I plainly realize that to be able to continue my studies it is necessary now and again to interrupt them and to turn for a while to the things called worldly; but to do this I want a world which attracts me and pleases me, a glittering world (even if the glitter be false), which has the power of making me forget for a few minutes what I care for most; not a world which makes me draw back at the first step. . . .

I see with joy that in your very kind letter of 15 April you condescend to speak to me about my studies. I will answer what you say, telling you sincerely when your opinions have encountered opposing ones in my mind, so that you may see how truly I need you to be my teacher. That a propriety of conception and expression is precisely what distinguishes a classic author from a second-rate one, and that, the richer a language is, the more difficult it is to preserve this propriety, is so evident a truth that I became aware of it as soon as I seriously began to think about literature, and after that I realized that the quickest and safest way of achieving this propriety would be to translate good writers from one language into another. But that—when one's intelligence has reached a sufficient firmness and development to know with some certainty in what direction its nature is calling it— one should necessarily write in prose before one attempts verse, with this I must frankly tell you that I do not agree. Since I am speaking about myself, I may be mistaken, but I will tell you what, in my view, has happened and is happening to me.

Ever since I first began to know what was beautiful, it was only the poets who aroused in me a most ardent desire to translate and render mine what I was reading, and only nature and passion that gave me a great wish to write, but with much strength and sublimity, so that my spirit expanded in every direction and I said to myself, 'This is poetry indeed, and to express what I feel, I need verse and not prose.' And so I began to write verse. Will you not now allow me to read Homer, Virgil, Dante, and the other greatest poets? I do not know whether I could refrain, for in reading them I feel an inexpressible delight, and often, when I have been quiet and alone and thinking of something quite different, it has happened to me suddenly to hear some verse of a classical author recited by a member of my family, and then to catch my breath and find myself obliged to follow those lines. And it has happened to me, too, alone in my study with my mind free and at rest, in an hour most friendly to the Muses, to take up Cicero, and to try, in reading him, to lift up my mind, but to be so tormented by the slowness and heaviness of that prose that I could not go on, and instead took up a Horace. And if you allow me to read these works, how can you expect me to recognize their greatness and examine and analyse every part of their beauty, without trying to fling myself in their pursuit? When I look at nature here, in this truly pleasant landscape (the only good thing my birthplace provides), at this time of year in particular, I feel carried away beyond myself so completely that it would seem to me a mortal sin to pay no heed, and to let this ardour of youth pass, while I attempt to write good prose, after which, firstly, I shall no longer be alive, and secondly, those thoughts will have fled and my spirit will be colder or at least cooler than it is now. Will you grant nothing to the *mens divinior* of Horace? And if you do, how can you demand that it should stay hidden, and that the man who possesses it should not become aware of it in the fervour of his youth, when he looks at nature or when he reads the poets? . . .

How can I crave your forgiveness, my signor Giordani, for having written a volume instead of a letter? I blush and don't know what to say, and yet I do ask you to forgive me. . . . This is the first time that I have opened my heart to you: how could I damn the flood of my thoughts? Another time I will be briefer, much briefer. I would not like you to be angered by my great indiscretion: your anger would be very justified, but I trust in the kindness of your heart.[1]

Soon after this letter, however, Giacomo's ill-health increased—in particular a form of ophthalmia, which, while it lasted, cut him off entirely from his books—and another long, despairing letter went off to Giordani, telling him that it was more than six months since he had been able to do any real work.

. . . What makes me most unhappy is my lack of health. . . . I get up late in the morning—for now, which is the devil, I prefer sleeping to waking. Then at once I start out for a walk, and go on walking, without ever opening my mouth or seeing a book, until dinner time, then walk again until supper. So I live and have lived, but for a few intervals, for six months. My other source of unhappiness is thought. I believe that you know, but trust you have never experienced, how thinking can harass and torture a man whose opinions are unlike other people's, I mean when that man has no other relaxation or diversion but study, and study does him more harm than good. . . . In short, solitude is not made for those men who burn themselves up from within.[2]

More than ten years later, in his Zibaldone, *he was setting down a similar reflection:*

[1] *Epist.* I, pp. 79–88: Recanati, 30 April 1817.
[2] Ibid. pp. 113–14: Recanati, 8 August [1817].

My error lay in attempting to live a wholly and exclusively inner life, with the object and hope of finding peace. But the freer I was from external efforts and occupations or from any external cares, and even from the necessity to ask for what I needed (so that I spent whole days without uttering a word), the less my spirit was at rest. Every slight incident that disturbed my daily habit and routine (and this happened every day, since such small details are inevitable) took my peace away. Constant fears and anxieties, about this and other nonsense of the same kind, and also unceasing torments of the imagination, unpleasant forecasts, disgusting fancies, imaginary evils, panic. . . . People with a certain kind of imagination . . . tend to seek solitude, and they make a great mistake. In order to live peacefully, they have a greater need than other men of escaping from themselves, and therefore of distractions and external occupations, even if they bring troubles or anxieties. For the troubles which, without any real foundation, they would inevitably conjure up with their imagination in their solitude, would be far greater.[1]

But where could any outer distractions be found? Very early in their friendship, Giordani had let slip a promise that he would pay a visit to 'Recanati which you find so tedious, and stay there for a while to interrupt your studies, provide you with an ear and a heart which would gladly be open to your words, and take you for long and frequent walks upon those hills'. Giacomo was of course overjoyed.

I love you so much and so truly that I almost go mad at the thought that next year—if you have not been indulging me with vain hopes—I shall see you and talk to you![2]

The visit did not, in the end, take place until 10 September 1818. It lasted for five days, which were momentous in the history of the Leopardi family. Conte Monaldo had only heard of Giordani as a

[1] *Zibaldone*, II, p. 1092.   [2] *Epist.* I, p. 97: 30 May 1817.

famous writer, without knowing his political or religious views, or he would never have allowed him to enter his house, and later on he complained that, during the single day in which he allowed Giacomo to go alone with Giordani to Macerata, Giordani's diabolical influence corrupted his son's mind and heart, destroyed his religious principles, and cut him off for ever from his father's influence. 'When Giordani left, he took with him the secrets of my children.'

A month later Giacomo—who in the interval had pleaded with his uncle in Rome, Marchese Carlo Antici, to help him to obtain his father's permission to go to Milan or to Rome—wrote to Giordani, complaining that there was very little hope of these plans being carried out: he would for ever remain a figlio di famiglia, *dependent on his father for every penny he needed.*

Since it is impossible for me to find something to live on at once on leaving here, as you affirm, you may be certain that I shall never get out of Recanati, except as a beggar, until after my father's death, which I do not wish to take place before mine. You must consider it to be as certain as the love I feel for you that neither your eloquence, nor that of Pericles and Demosthenes—no, not the Goddess Persuasion herself—could change my father's mind. . . . What I ask, which is not to live like a gentleman, or even comfortably or without hardship, but only away from here, is unimaginably beyond my reach.[1]

But when the following summer came, a return of his ophthalmia, which kept him even from his books, goaded him into action. He planned to leave Recanati secretly and go to Milan, where, with Giordani's help, he hoped to find some work. He took no one into his confidence, but wrote to a Liberal friend in Macerata, Conte Saverio Broglio d'Ajano, asking for his help in getting a passport for Lombardy and the Veneto—implying that the request was made with his father's approval.

While he was waiting for a reply he wrote two letters, one to his brother Carlo, and one, enclosed in it, to his father.

[1] *Epist.* I, p. 26: Recanati, 26 April 1819.

Mio Signor Padre,

Although when you have learned what I have done, you will feel that this letter does not deserve to be read, yet I hope that your kindness will not refuse to hear the first and last words of a son who has always loved and loves you, and who is sincerely sorry to give you pain. You know me, and know what my behaviour has been until now; and perhaps—if you will divest yourself of any local considerations—you will perceive that in the whole of Italy you could not find a young man of my class, even if younger and with intellectual gifts considerably lesser than mine, who has shown half the prudence, abstinence from youthful pleasures, obedience and submission to his parents, that I have shown. Although you may have a poor opinion of those slight talents that Heaven has granted me, you cannot completely disbelieve the writers and eminent men whom I have known, and who have formed the opinion of me which you know, and I shall not repeat. Neither can you fail to know that even among the men who know about me, those who share your general principles think that I might produce something above the common level, were I given the opportunities which, as the world is now, are indispensable for the success of a young man of even moderate promise. . . . Nevertheless you considered me unworthy of a father's sacrifice, nor did you think that what was best for my present and future deserved to bring any alteration to your family plans. . . .

I know your plans for us very well, and that, in the interests of something that I have never known, but you call home and family, you have required from us both the sacrifice, not only of wealth or protection, but of our inclinations, our youth—our whole life. . . . You were also well aware of the wretched life I led, owing to my terrible attacks of melancholy and the other torments caused by my strange imagination, and you could not fail to know what is obvious: that for these troubles and for my health, which was visibly affected by them, and always has been, no remedy can be found but much diversion, and everything that cannot be found in Recanati.

Nevertheless you have permitted a man of my constitution to wear himself out for many years in fatal studies, or else to be swallowed up in the deepest tedium. . . . It did not take me long to realize that your mind was proof against every imaginable argument, and the extraordinary inflexibility of your nature, veiled by a constant dissimulation and apparent flexibility, was such as to leave me no shadow of hope. All this convinced me that, although I lacked everything, I must trust in myself alone. . . . I would rather be unhappy than mediocre, rather suffer from pain than boredom. . . . I find comfort in the thought that this is the last trouble I shall cause you.

My dear *Signor Padre*, if I may still call you so, I implore you on my knees to forgive me, who am unhappy both in my nature and my circumstances. I wish that my unhappiness had been mine alone, without affecting anyone else, and hope that it will be so in future. If fortune is ever kind to me, my first thought will be to pay back to you what necessity now obliges me to use. The last favour I ask of you is that if you should ever call up the memory of the son who always respected and loved you, you will not spurn that memory nor curse him. If fate has not ordained that you should be able to be proud of him, do not deny him the pity that is granted even to evil-doers.[1]

This letter was never delivered, but was put away by Carlo and never published until after Giacomo's death. Meanwhile Conte Broglio had indeed procured a passport for Giacomo, but the Macerata chief of police, recognizing the name, wrote to Marchese Antici to wish his nephew a fortunate journey—and so the secret was out. Monaldo at once demanded that the passport should be sent to him instead, and summoned his eldest son to his presence.

[1] *Epist.* I, pp. 288–92. Undated, but written at the same time as the preceding letter.

I was going to escape from here [Giacomo wrote to
Giordani], but I have been discovered. It did not please
God that they should use force; they used supplication and
grief. I no longer hope for anything.[1]

*To Conte Broglio he sent a long letter in which he tried to justify
his attempt.*

The resolution I had taken was neither immature nor sudden. I had taken it a month ago and had conceived it ever
since I first realized my position and the inflexible principles
of my father, that is many years ago. I have not repented
nor changed my mind. I have given way for the present, not
from compulsion or conviction, but because my feelings
were played upon and taken advantage of. . . . I will not
live in Recanati. If my father will provide the means for me
to go away, as he has promised, I will be grateful and respectful, like any other good son. If not, what was to have
happened, and has not, is only postponed.

What I regret most of all, is the knowledge that certain
literary men whom I have only known for a short time, are
being blamed for this very old decision of mine. If it is
permitted in this case, I swear to you by all that is most holy,
that none of them ever dreamed of giving me such advice. . . .

If my father, in his abhorrence for anything great or even
unusual, now regrets that he allowed me to study, if he is
sorry that Heaven did not make me a mole, if he denies me
what any father anywhere would grant to a son with even a
spark of talent, and resolutely insists on my living and dying
like his ancestors, is it rebellion in a son to refuse submission
to such a rule? . . . I know for certain that he has declared
that none of us shall get away from here, so long as he is
alive. Now I want him to live, but I want to live myself, too,
while I am still young, and not when I am old and of no
more use to myself or anyone else. . . .[2]

[1] *Epist.* I, p. 303: 20 August 1819.   [2] Ibid. 13 August 1819.

F

Meanwhile Conte Monaldo put the passport away in his desk, together with a brief, but not altogether frank, account of the episode. 'And thus,' he complacently added, 'the matter ended.'

What must have rendered the whole episode peculiarly hard to bear, both for father and son, was that a few months before it occurred, Giacomo's position had changed: he was no longer only an unknown figlio di famiglia *with scholarly tastes, but had published his first two patriotic poems,* A l'Italia *and* Sopra il monumento di Dante, *which—while they greatly upset both his father and his uncle—had caused a considerable stir in Milan and among all patriotic Liberals. 'Oh, Giacomino,' wrote Giordani, 'what a great man you are already! . . . Your songs are running through the town like wild-fire; everyone wants them, everyone is overwhelmed by them. . . . Oh, what a fool I was when I advised you to write prose, before you attempted verse—do you remember? Do what you will: you are fit for any high enterprise.'[1]*

These two poems, and the one which soon followed them, Ad Angelo Mai, *are not included in this volume because, of all Leopardi's works, they are the ones which, for all the genuineness of their emotion, now seem most rhetorical and out of date. But it is necessary, in order to understand the effect they produced at that time, to remember the climate in which they were written. Throughout Europe the spirit of liberty was beginning to stir, and the seed of new ideas found a fertile soil in Leopardi's mind. In the year before the one in which the* Canzoni *were written, we find among his papers a rough outline of 'subjects for elegies':*

Oh, my country, my country, what can I do for you? I cannot shed my blood for you, since you no longer exist. In what enterprise, for whom, for what country, shall I bestow my sweat, my pen, my blood?[2]

But already, in the region in which Leopardi lived, events were beginning to move. An insurrection against the Austrians in Macerata in 1817 had recently been followed by a Congress of the

---

[1] *Epist.* I, 5 February [1819].
[2] *Poesie e Prose*, I, p. 381, *Argomenti di elegie.*

Carbonari *in Bologna, and every little city of the Marches and the Romagna was astir. On the one side were the reactionary* Sanfedisti, *men who had sworn 'to show no mercy to any man belonging to the infamous rabble of the Liberals'; on the other were the* Carbonari, *pledged 'to give their strength and their lives to the independence of Italy'. (And often, within the same family, both parties were to be found.) To these patriots Leopardi's poems were a call to arms, the first patriotic poems (except for Monti's* Congresso d'Udine) *to appear since Petrarch, the first in which the name of Italy, as a free and united country, was called upon once again. In his dedication of the two* Canzoni *to Vincenzo Monti, Leopardi wrote:*

I offer [these poems] to you humbly and simply . . . in the fire of my love for our poor Italy, and therefore in a state of most intense affection, gratitude, and reverence for the almost imperceptible number of Italians who still exist.[1]

In 1848 the young men of Naples, still under Bourbon rule, would visit Leopardi's tomb, muttering his stanzas under their breaths, and when, a few months later, the Roman volunteers passed through the Marches on their way to the battles of the Po, they paused at Recanati, 'as on a pilgrimage'. 'Do you remember', wrote the great patriot, Luigi Settembrini, 'the days of our youth, when the Austrian police were at our heels, and we created in our books a world in which we found life and liberty? . . . All that world, that excitement, those unfettered plans, those dreams, was represented by Leopardi in those Canzoni. . . . *Those words were a real flame; we repeated them and they were repeated at their death by those who died for our country.'[2]*

[1] *Poesie e Prose*, I, p. 147. Dedication of the first edition of Leopardi's first two *Canzoni*.

[2] L. Settembrini, *Lezioni di letteratura italiana*, III, p. 354.

5. *The* Zibaldone

*The same year—1819—which saw the publication of Leopardi's
patriotic* Canzoni *and his first open breach with his father, was also
marked by the composition of his first three early idylls,* L'Infinito,
Alla luna, *and* Lo spavento notturno, *while in the following year
he composed* La sera del dì di festa—*poems which, if he had
written nothing else, would assure his place among the greatest
Italian poets. This time was followed, however, from 1820 to 1822,
by a period of numb emptiness, punctuated by feverish letters to
everyone he knew, begging for employment in Rome, Milan, Bologna
—anywhere that was not Recanati. But each fresh faint hope was
followed by renewed disappointment, and a retreat into what he
called resignation, but which seemed more like a dull despair. In his
father's presence he maintained a sullen silence, constantly fiddling
with a small bone paper-knife in his pocket, and it was only very
rarely, even in his letters, that he returned to his old intensity of
feeling.*

I too am longing intensely for the spring [he wrote to
Giordani in March 1820], as my last hope of finding some
healing for my exhausted spirit; and a few evenings ago,
before going to bed, I opened my window and seeing a clear
sky and bright moonlight, with a mild breeze blowing and
some dogs barking from afar, some of the old images awoke
in me and I felt my heart come to life again, so that I began
to cry out like a madman, imploring some mercy from
nature, whose voice I thought I heard, after so long. And
at that moment, looking back at my recent state, to which I
felt certain of returning at once—as indeed occurred—I was
frozen with terror, being unable to understand how life can
be endured without illusions or lively affections, without
imagination or enthusiasm. For a year ago [when he was
writing the Idylls] these things filled all my life, and made me

happy in spite of all my labours. But now I am as parched
and withered as a dry reed, so that no passion can enter this
poor soul, and even the sovereign and eternal power of love
has been destroyed.[1]

*During this period, however, Leopardi was beginning to think
about 'certain little satirical pieces of prose' which were to become
the* Operette Morali, *and in 1820 alone he filled some 1,167 pages
of his encyclopaedic notebook, the* Zibaldone. *Its title means a
hotch-potch or compendium—and indeed it is a hotch-potch, part
notebook and part diary, of every thought that crossed its author's
mind during the fifteen years in which he kept it. It came to consist
of no less than 4,526 pages of minute, fine script, the first entry
being dated July 1817, and the last, December 1832.*
The Zibaldone *throws open the workshop of Leopardi's mind,
and shows us the raw material of everything he ever wrote. A considerable part of the book is given up to philological notes, which cannot easily be quoted in translation, but which reveal, as well as his
scholarly equipment, his passion for his own language and his respect
for both the traditional and the popular sources which contributed
to its formation. There are notes (some of them consisting in a
single line, some in many pages) on philosophy, archaeology, religion,
science, politics, art, and history; there are pages of literary criticism,
comments on articles in contemporary reviews, quotations that struck
him, fragments of popular songs and sayings that caught his ear,
reflections which he subsequently developed or pruned for the*
Operette Morali *or the* Pensieri. *There are odd and unexpected
pieces of information or observation—such as the story (which he
mentions as an example of the faculty of compassion, 'the only
human quality or passion that has no slightest taint of self-love')
about 'a dog in my house, who, from a balcony, used to throw down
a loaf of bread to another dog in the street below'. There is an
account of how, in ancient times, 'when the snake was considered a
protective genius and a symbol of eternity', a drawing of this reptile
would be placed on street-corners or walls, so that they should not
be defiled, whereas in Leopardi's own time men would draw or*

---

[1] *Epist.* I, To Giordani: Recanati, 6 March 1820.

*carve 'long rows of crosses, like hedges', for the same purpose. There
are, embedded in all this, like a fine vein of gold in a rock, occasional
exquisite lines of verse, or a poetic image. There are (under the
title he gave them himself,* Memorie della mia vita) *scattered
autobiographical notes—confessions, descriptions of his personal
habits, recollections of childhood, hopes, dreams, and regrets. And
there is also, to be honest, a good deal that is repetitious and long-
winded, some self-pity, and some unconvincing irony. The* Zibaldone,
*in short, is Leopardi himself—sitting alone in his library at
Recanati, writing and writing until his eyesight failed, with his
lexicons and encyclopaedias beside him—a tribute to scholarship,
taste, and addiction to truth, and also (for no man who could share
his thoughts with his fellows would keep such a diary as this one) a
tragic record of human solitude.*

*After attempting in vain to classify the few passages I have
chosen—chiefly for their autobiographical or literary interest—I have
thought it best to leave them in their chronological order, as perhaps
giving the truest impression of this rich, disconnected, tedious, re-
warding medley.*

SELECTIONS FROM THE *ZIBALDONE*

Various Thoughts about Philosophy and Belles-Lettres

I have just finished reading, in No. 91 of *Lo Spettatore*,
Ludovico di Breme's[1] *Observations* on modern or (if we
prefer to call it so) romantic poetry, and since I have found
in them a series of arguments which might be confusing or
disturbing, and I am myself, by nature, always prone to
doubt, even with regard to things considered indisputable,
but yet have in my mind the answers which can and should
be given to these observations, I will set them down, for
my own peace of mind. The writer (like all the Romantics)
wishes modern poetry to be based on an ideal which he calls

[1] Ludovico Arborio Gattinara di Breme (1780–1820), an ardent follower
of Napoleon in his youth, became well known in Milan as a man of letters
and a Liberal, and one of the leading figures of the Romantic movement.
He was a friend of both Byron and Hobhouse, and also of Stendhal.

poetic and which is more commonly called sentimental, and he rightly makes a distinction between pathos and melancholy, since pathos, he says, is the depth of feeling experienced by sensitive hearts, through the impression made on their senses by any natural thing, for instance—he says—the bell of their native city, or—I would add—the sight of a landscape or a ruined tower, etc. That is, in short, to his mind, the difference between modern and classical poetry, for the ancients did not feel these emotions, or much less than we do; so that, according to him, we are superior *in this* to the ancients, and since, to his mind, it is *in this* that poetry truly consists, therefore we are infinitely more poetic than the ancients. . . . So this pathos, this depth of feeling, must be stirred up in our hearts, and it is in this, naturally, that the poet's most sublime art will consist.

It is here that Breme and all the Romantics and Chateaubriandists etc., etc., are taking a wrong turn. What is it that excites these feelings in men? Nature, pure nature, as it is, as the ancients saw it. Now what did the ancients do? They described nature, and the objects and circumstances which must perforce awaken these feelings, very simply, and they knew how to depict and imitate them in such a manner that we see those very objects in their verses, that is, we feel as if we were seeing them, in so far as possible, as they are in nature. . . .

And behold, thus the ancients achieved the great effect which the Romantics require, and did so in such a way as to transport us and raise us up and plunge us into a gentle world of delight, and every age and century and all the great men and poets who have come after them, can bear witness to this. But are we to believe that when these poets imitated nature like this, and prepared this wealth of sentiment for their readers, they did not feel it themselves, or did not say that they did so; but very simply, like shepherd-boys, described what they saw, and added nothing to it of their own; and that therein lies the great defect of ancient poetry, owing to which it is not poetry any more, and the moderns are a hundred times superior to the ancients, etc.? The Romantics do not realize that, if these feelings are awakened by *naked* nature, it is necessary, in order to re-awaken it, to imitate nature's *nakedness*, and to transpose into poetry those simple and innocent objects which *by their own strength alone*, and *unawares*, produce that effect upon our spirit, just as they are, and neither more nor less; and that, if they are so well and divinely imitated, adding the wonder and attention aroused by each minute part of them, which we did not observe in reality but do see in the imitation, they cannot fail to awaken in us those very sentiments that the Romantics are seeking, and which they are very far from knowing how to awaken in us. For the more a poet speaks in his own person and the more he adds of his own, the less well does he imitate (an observation already made by Aristotle, to whom, whether one wishes to or not, one always inadvertently returns) and sentiment is not produced by sentiment, but by nature, *as it really is*, and it is this nature, *as it is*, that one must imitate, and that the ancients did imitate. That is why a simple simile of Homer's, without convulsions or swoonings, or an ode of Anacreon's, arouses in us a multitude of fancies, and fills our mind and heart incomparably more than a thousand sentimental verses; for there it was nature speaking, and here, a poet. And they [the Romantics] do not realize that it is precisely this great ideal of our time, an intimate knowledge of our own heart, and the analysing, foretelling, and distinguishing of every most minute emotion, in short the art of psychology, that destroys the very illusion without which poetry will be no more.... (I, 21–23)

Were I to express the indefinable effect that Anacreon's odes have upon me, I could find no more fitting image than that of a summer breeze, scented and refreshing, which somehow suddenly gives you new life and opens your lungs and heart to delight, but which—before you have fully savoured that pleasure or analysed its quality, or discerned why it has refreshed you so much—has already fled. Precisely as it does in Anacreon, in whom that indefinable sensation is almost instantaneous, and escapes you if you try to analyse it: you do not hear it any more, you read it over again, but only the bare, dry words are left, while the melody, so to speak, is gone, and you can scarcely remember in your heart the sensations which, a moment before, had been aroused in you by the very words that lie before your eyes.   (I, 46)

Our true Theocritan idylls are not the Eclogues of San-nazzaro, etc., but rustic poems like *La Nencia, Cecco di Varlunga*, etc.—most lovely and similar to Theocritus in their beautiful roughness and admirable truth.   (I, 86)

Everything has been perfected since Homer's time: not poetry.   (I, 87)

The illusion of anniversaries is truly a beautiful one, by means of which, even though that particular day has nothing more to do with the past than any other, we say: 'Such and such a thing happened today, I felt this or that delight, or I was so cast down', and it truly seems to us that those things, which are dead for ever and never can come back, have yet come to life again and are present in the shade.   (I, 90)

La speme che nasce in un col giorno.
[The hope that is renewed with every dawn.]   (I, 108)

It seems absurd, yet is precisely true, that since all reality is nought, illusions are, in this world, the only true and substantial things.   (I, 126)

Melancholy and sentimental poetry is a breath of the soul. An oppression of the heart, whether caused by passion, by discouragement with life, or by a deep sense of the nothing-ness of things, constrains it and gives it no room to breathe.

. . . I believe that Tasso's continual misfortunes are the
reason why, in originality and invention, he remained inferior to the other three greatest Italian poets, while certainly his soul was equal if not superior to theirs in sentiment,
affection, grandeur, tenderness, etc., as is shown by his
letters and his other writings in prose. But although a man
who has not suffered some misfortune knows nothing at all,
it is indisputable that both imagination and a melancholy
sensibility lose some of their power without a certain aura
of well-being, a certain vigour of spirit, which cannot exist
without a gleam, a ray, a glimmer of joy. (24 June 1820)

(I, 156)

Once, when I was feeling very much disgusted with life
and entirely hopeless and so anxious for death that I was in
despair at not being able to die, a letter came from a friend
of mine, who had always encouraged me to hope and implored me to go on living, assuring me (he being a man of
great intelligence and renown) that I would become great
and would make Italy proud of me. In this letter he said
that he now had become so conscious of the extent of my
afflictions that if God should send me death, I should accept
it as a blessing, and that for both my sake and his own, he
hoped it would be soon. Will you believe that this letter, far
from detaching me more completely from life, caused me to
feel some affection again for everything I had already given
up? Thinking of my hopes in the past and of the consola-
tions and forecasts which this same friend had offered me,
and which he now no longer seemed to care to see confirmed,
nor to see my promised greatness realized, and looking
back at my writings and my studies and remembering my
childhood with its thoughts and desires and the fine pros-
pects and occupations of youth, my heart was so oppressed
that I no longer knew how to give up hope, and death
terrified me—not indeed in itself, but as bringing to an end
all those great expectations of the past. . . .

I had taken pleasure in the thought of death, but as

something imaginary. I had thought it certain that my
friends—few in number indeed, but at least those few, and
especially that one—would prefer me to be alive, would not
abandon me to my despair, and that, if I died, they would be
astonished and cast down, saying, 'So it is all over? Oh,
God, so many hopes, such greatness of soul, such gifts, and
all without fruit! No glory, no pleasure, all is passed as if it
had never been.' But to think that they would say instead:
'Praise God, his sufferings are ended, I rejoice for him, for
nothing else was left to him, may he rest in peace', that
seemed to me like sealing down the tomb over my head, and
this sudden and complete acceptance of my death, however
reasonable, stifled me with a sense of my complete annihila-
tion. . . .

From this one may learn how to behave in comforting a
friend in trouble. Do not deny his suffering, if it is real. You
would not convince him, and would cast him down still
deeper, by depriving him of compassion. He knows his
afflictions well, and you, in admitting them, will agree with
him. But remember that in the last recesses of his heart a
drop of illusion still lingers. . . . Beware of drying it up, and
err rather in minimizing his sufferings and showing yourself
too unpitying, than in making him feel certain of those
things as to which his imagination is still contradicting his
reason. If even he exaggerates his calamities to you, be
assured that within his own heart he is doing just the
opposite. I say within, that is, at a level hidden even from
himself. Agree not with his words, but with his heart.

(I, 157–9)

Speech is an art acquired by men, as is proved by the
variety of tongues. Gesture is a natural thing, and taught by
nature. . . . Therefore in great gusts of passion, even as the
force of nature is greater than usual, words do not suffice to
express it, and men are so occupied that the practice of an
art, however familiar, is impossible to them, while gestures
come naturally. . . . Silence is the language of every strong

passion, of love (even in the sweetest moments), of anger, wonder, fear. (27 June 1820)   (I, 160)

In my poetic career my spirit has followed the same course as the human spirit in general. At first my imagination was my strong point, and my verses were full of images, and when I read poetry I always sought what would feed my fancy. I was most sensitive to emotion, too, but did not know how to express it in verse. I had not yet meditated on these things, and had only a glimmering of philosophy, and that a very vague one, with the common illusion that the world and life would always make an exception on my behalf. I have always been unfortunate, but then my misfortunes were vital ones, and only aroused despair in me because I thought (unreasonably, but owing to my strong imagination) that they held me back from happiness, a thing which I believed other men to enjoy. In short my condition was in every way that of the ancients. . . .

This complete change in me, and the passage from the old condition to the new, occurred within about a year, that is in 1819, when—being deprived of the use of my sight and of the constant diversion of reading—my unhappiness seemed much darker, and I began to give up hope, to reflect deeply about such things . . . to become a professional philosopher instead of the poet that I had been before, to feel the world's certain unhappiness, instead of only knowing about it—and this also owing to a certain physical lassitude, which made me less like the ancients and more like the men of our own time. Then my imagination became much less vivid, and although my faculty of invention greatly increased, indeed almost began to exist, it chiefly took the form of prose or sentimental poetry. And if I tried to set my verses down, the images came with the greatest effort. Indeed my imagination was almost dried up (even apart from poetry, that is in contemplating beautiful natural scenes, etc.), as it is now, when I am as cold as a stone.

                                                        (I, 161–3)

Often it has happened to me to fall asleep with some
verses or words on my lips which I had often repeated to
myself during the day, or in the hours before sleep, or else
with the recollection of the air of some melody; and, having
thought or dreamed during my sleep about quite other
things, I would wake up repeating to myself the same verses
or words, or the same air. It would seem that the soul, in
falling asleep, lays down the thoughts and images it holds
as we lay down our clothes, in some place very near at hand,
so as to find them at once again, on waking.   (I, 198)

Illusions, however weakened and unmasked by reason,
yet still remain in this world, and form the chief part of our
life. Even if we have learned to know all and to realize that
they are vain, this is not enough to make us lose them. Nor,
once lost, are they lost in such a way that they do not retain
a very vigorous root; and, in continuing to live, they
flower again, in spite of all the experience and certainty we
had acquired. . . . And to me, too, the same thing has happened a hundred times: to fall into despair because I could
not die, and then to return to my old plans and castles in
the air about my future life, and even to a little passing
cheerfulness.   (I, 221–2)

Reading is, in relation to the art of writing, what experience is to the art of living in the world, and of discovering the nature of men and things.   (I, 227)

Lord Byron, in his notes to *The Corsair*, quotes historical
examples of the effects of the passions and of the characters
he had described. That is bad. The reader should feel
and not learn the relation between your description and
truth and nature . . . otherwise the poetic delight fades away
. . . and the poem is transformed into a treatise and acts
upon the intellect, no longer upon the imagination or the
heart.   (I, 229)

A house suspended in the air, held by ropes to a star.

(I, 251)

What is peculiar to works of genius is that, even when they vividly show the nothingness of things, and plainly represent and convey to us the inevitable unhappiness of life, even when they express the most terrible despair, yet to a man of a noble soul, even if he finds himself in a state of extreme despair, disillusionment, blankness, and discouragement with life, or suffering from the most bitter and deadly misfortunes . . . they always bring consolation, reawaken enthusiasm, and, though they do not describe or represent anything but death, they yet give back to him, at least for a while, the life that he had lost. (I, 252–3)

Generally fame, especially in literature, is sweet when a man nourishes it in the silence of his own study, and uses it as a spur towards other successful enterprises, and as a foundation for new hopes. For then fame still holds the power of an illusion, its only real power. But when it is enjoyed in the world and in society, it usually turns out to be either nothing at all or a very little thing, incapable in short of filling your soul or of satisfying it. So, too, all pleasures seem great from far off, and from near by seem small, arid, void, and null. (I, 260)

An old man who has no present or future is not consequently devoid of life. If he has never been a man, he needs nothing more than the trifles which suffice to distract him, and anything is enough to keep him alive. If he has been a man, he has had a past, and lives in that. . . .

A young man has no past. The little of it that he has, only serves to sadden and oppress his heart. The memories of his childhood and early youth, the pleasures of those years, irreparably lost, the flowery hopes, the radiant ideas, the airy plans for future prosperity, for action, life, glory, pleasure— all have vanished. His desires and passions are most ardent and exacting. A little is not enough: he needs the most. The more intense his inner life has been, the greater the intensity and extent of his need of the outer life that he desires. And if this is lacking, his sense of death, of nothingness, of tedium, is proportionate to his inner life. . . . The young man suffers mortal despair, reflecting that he will only pass through this world once, and that during this one time he will not enjoy life, will not live, and will have lost, without finding any use for it, his only existence: every moment of his youth that passes in this manner will seem to him the irreparable loss of a time that never can return. (16 October 1820)

(I, 264)

His pleasure was in walking, counting the stars. (I, 265)

It is not enough to know that a statement is true, one must also *feel* its truth. There is a feeling of truth, as of passion, emotion, beauty. . . . (I, 307)

Just as among the peoples who do not know or value gold or silver, the richest among us, scattering money, would not be held in esteem . . . so where intelligence or wit are not valued, the most able and wittiest and greatest man, if he has no other gifts, will be despised and given the last place. . . . In every place and every time, one must use the common currency. The man who is not provided with that, is poor. (23 December 1820) (I, 371–2)

On the few occasions on which I have met with some little piece of good fortune, or a reason for joy, instead of showing it outwardly, I have yielded to an external melancholy, though inwardly, I was happy. But I feared to trouble this peaceful and hidden content, to alter, spoil, or lose it by scattering it to the winds. And so I handed over my content into the care of melancholy. (27 December 1820)

(I, 375)

Not only the faculty of the mind or the heart, but even that of the imagination, cannot attain infinity, nor even conceive it, but can only recall or conceive the idea of what is indefinite, unbounded. And this delights it; because the soul, not perceiving any boundaries, receives an impression of a sort of infinity, and confuses the indefinite with the infinite, but does not either comprehend or conceive infinity at all. For indeed it is especially in its most vague and indefinite fancies, which are therefore the most sublime and delightful, that the soul feels a certain constraint, a certain struggle, a certain insufficiency of desire, an impotence which is yet determined to seize to the full its fancy or conception or idea. So that, although these may fill and delight and satisfy it more than any other thing obtainable upon this earth, they yet do not entirely fulfil or satisfy it, and when they fade away, they leave it discontented, for the soul feels and knows (or thinks it does) that it has not conceived or seen these fancies nor delighted in them in their entirety, and persuades itself that it could have done so, and therefore feels a certain remorse, which in truth is wrong, for it was not its fault. (4 January 1821)   (I, 382–3)

It is said as a joke, but not without some truth, that one must satisfy a child's desires, if one does not wish to find him dead behind a door.   (I, 454)

'La solitude est l'infirmerie des âmes.'
[Madame de Lambert, quoted by Leopardi.]   (I, 467)

'Nous ne vivons que pour perdre et pour nous détacher.'
[Ibid.]

That is so. Every day we lose something; one of the illusions, which are our only riches, perishes or diminishes. Experience or truth divests us every day of part of our possessions. We do not live, except in losing.   (I, 467)

I do not usually believe in allegories, or look for them in mythology, or in the inventions of the poets, or in popular beliefs. But the fable of Psyche, that is of the Soul, who was very contented without knowledge and happy just to enjoy, and whose unhappiness came from her desire for knowledge, seems to me so apt and precise and at the same time so profound a symbol of the nature of men and things, and of our true destiny upon this earth . . . that I can hardly believe that this myth is not a fruit of the deepest wisdom and knowledge of the nature of man and of the world. (I, 468)

I praise the Italians for turning away from a blind love and imitation of foreign things, and still more for beginning again to use and to value their own; I praise the men who try to reawaken a national spirit, without which there has never been any greatness in this world—not only national greatness, but even individual greatness; but I cannot find it admirable that our present condition and, in the field of study, our contemporary literature and the greater part of our writers, should be exalted and celebrated every day as if they were almost superior to the greatest men abroad, when they are inferior to the least of them; that they should be offered us as models, and that finally we should be advised to go on following the path which we already tread. If we are to wake up at last and recover a national spirit, our first emotion should be, not pride or satisfaction in things as they are with us now, but shame. And it is this that should spur us on to take a new road altogether, and to renew everything. (I, 579)

England . . . has one of the freest languages in Europe in its nature and in practice the freest of all, and similarly perhaps the most free literature and literary taste in Europe. I am referring to her own literature, both modern and Shakespeare's in the past, not to the second-hand one she has borrowed from France. (I, 703)

When a language, generally speaking (that is, not in one or more sentences, or in this or that particular subtlety, but

G

in general), is not sufficient to render in a translation the refinements of another language, that is a certain proof that the nation into whose language one is translating has a less deep culture than the first.   (I, 731)

Some other reasons for the richness and variety of the Italian language are the following:

(1) That we have never given up any of our riches, however old. . . .

(2) The great liveliness, imagination, fecundity, and variety of the gifts of our writers, qualities which appertain to a nation which has adapted itself to all sorts of circumstances, enterprises, characters, and purposes.

(3) The large extent to which our written language (for it is of this that we are speaking, and comparing with foreign languages) is indebted to the spoken speech of the people. . . .

A nation, especially as lively a one as the Italian, and in particular the Tuscan, and very civilized besides (as the Tuscans and Italians were before any other people in Europe), and constantly in touch with other peoples (as indeed Tuscany has been, both owing to her reputation for culture, her political circumstances, her freedom, and especially her trade), naturally invents or adopts a very large number of words and idioms and many forms of both. These, however, unless the use and form of them is spread by the written word (which varies all over the country), to establish their form and meaning and ensure their permanence, will not spread very far nor become very precise, but will remain uncertain, fluctuating, and arbitrary, and will soon be lost, with new ones taking their place. But Italian literature has done precisely what I have specified. It has adopted with a greater care than any other literature, and with great goodwill and delight, many popular expressions, idioms, and forms, especially the Tuscan, and has itself been formed by them. . . .

The pseudo-philosophers may say what they please. A richness which consists of variety, beauty, expression, efficacy, force, brio, grace, ease, softness, naturalness, will never belong and never has belonged to any language that has not been drawn from the popular tongue, not only originally but constantly, and not by writing as the people speak, but by turning what has been adopted from the people into the universal forms and rules of literature and of the national language.   (I, 838–41)

Rapidity and concision of style are pleasing because they present to the mind a multitude of simultaneous ideas, or of ones which succeed each other so rapidly that they seem simultaneous, and flutter the soul with such an abundance of thoughts, images, and spiritual sensations that it is incapable of embracing all of them, or each one fully, and has no time left in which to remain idle and feelingless. . . .

The beauty and charm of Horace's style, and of other vigorous, swift styles, especially in poetry—since the qualities I am about to describe belong chiefly to poetry, and especially to lyric verse—also derive chiefly from this, that it keeps the mind in constant and lively movement and action, transporting it suddenly, and often abruptly, from one thought, image, idea, or object to another, and often to one very remote and different; so that the mind must work hard to overtake them all, and, as it is flung about here and there, feels invigorated, as one does in walking quickly or in being carried along by swift horses, in taking part in some energetic action or in being in some centre of activity. It is overwhelmed by the multiplicity and variety of things (see my theory of pleasure), etc., etc. And even if those things are neither great, vast, or new, nevertheless this single quality in a style is enough to please the soul, which needs action, because it loves life above all things, and therefore enjoys, both in life and literature, a certain but not excessive effort, which compels it to behave in a lively manner. And this is the case with Horace, who after all is a lyric poet only in his style. That is how style, even considered separately from its subject, can yet be a thing in itself, and an important one: so that a man can be a poet who has nothing poetic about him but his style, and a very true and universal poet, for reasons which are inward, and very deep and elemental qualities, and therefore universal in the human soul.

Horace constantly produces the effects I have described, with a boldness of phrase with which, in a single digression, he transports and flings you about several times, leaping from one idea to another very remote and different one. (As he also does with his very figurative use of words, and with the effort and consequent activity which he produces in his readers.) Courageous metaphors, singular and far-fetched epithets, inversions, placement of words, suppressions, all within the limits of what is not excessive (*it might seem excessive to the Germans, and insufficiently so to Orientals*), all these produce these effects anywhere you please in his poems.

> Pone me pigris ubi nulla campis
> Arbor aestiva recreatur aura,
> Quod latus mundi nebulae malusque
> Juppiter urget.[1]

Here first you have *sluggishness*, then this is applied to the *plains*, and here at once are *the trees* and the *summer breeze* and then *a side of the world*, the *mists*, and then *Jove* instead of the *sky*, and *hostile* instead of *contrary*, *jostling* or *pushing* or *harassing* that part of the world. . . .

It is in the nature of such styles (proper to all great and true poets, more or less, and especially to those who are also distinctive in their style) that many of their images—often contained in a very brief phrase or a single word—etc., should be only suggested, and that there should also be no more than a suggestion of their connexion and relation with their subject and with the other images, ideas, or

---

[1] *Carm.* I, XXII, 17–20. 'Set me in sluggish plains where no tree is restored to life by the summer breeze, the side of the world harassed by mists and hostile Jove.'

maxims which they resemble, or to which they belong or
refer, etc. And this, too, is pleasing, for it compels the mind
to a constant activity, to supply what the poet does not say,
to finish what he has only begun, to colour what he has
outlined, to discover those distant relationships that he has
scarcely pointed out, etc.

> et aridus altis
> Montibus audiri fragor.[1]

What has that *cracking* to do with *dry*? Our thoughts must
realize that it is justified in so far as it is cracking among the
dry branches of a wood. That is how the mind must supply
the connexion of ideas (barely suggested, indeed almost
neglected by the poet), within one very short sentence. And
it must then complete the image that is only suggested by
that *aridus fragor*. (I do not know whether the interpretation
I have given to this passage is true. See the commentators. It
is enough for me that this example explains my thoughts to
myself.) That is how the very suppression of words, phrases,
conceptions, is turned into beauty, because it pleasantly
compels the mind to action and does not leave it idle. Such
qualities in style may sometimes be excessive, as in the
seventeenth century. Then the mind does not delight in
them, at least not in all periods or people, etc. For an excess,
like a defect, in this and in everything else, is relative.

$$(I, 1269-73)$$

People always prefer to call a man who has a physical or
moral defect, or else to hear him called, by nothing but the
name of this defect: the deaf man, the cripple, the hunchback,
the madman. . . . In using such names or in hearing them,
these people feel superior to those others, enjoy the image of
their defect, feel and remind themselves, in a sort of way, of
their own superiority, and their self-love is flattered and
satisfied. It has happened to me to see a common man with

[1] '. . . and a dry cracking [begins] to be heard in the high mountains'
(Virgil, *Georg.* I, 357).

such a defect, talking and playing with some people of his own class, who never called him by any other name than that of his defect, so that I never succeeded in hearing his real name. (13 May 1822)   (I, 1466-7)

So long as a young man keeps some *tenderness* towards himself, this means that he continues to love himself with that most lively, sensitive, and vulnerable love which is natural; and until he has cast himself adrift into the world, and has learned to think of himself almost as he would of anyone else, he will never be able to avoid suffering, nor to enjoy a single moment of comfort and pleasure in the habits and incidents of social life. To enjoy life, a state of despair is necessary. (6 July 1822)[1]   (I, 1524)

Ideas are enclosed and almost bound in words, like jewels in a ring, indeed they become embodied in them, as the soul is in the body, so as to form one entity. Thus ideas are inseparable from words, and if parted from them, are no longer the same; they escape our intellect and our powers of conception, and become unrecognizable, as would happen to our soul, if it were separated from our body. (27 July 1822)   (I, 1536)

The Italians have no customs: they only have habits. And so it is with all civilized peoples that have not become nations. (9 July 1823)   (II, 172)

A Frenchman, an Englishman, or a German, who have cultivated their talents and are capable of thought, have nothing to do but to set them down. Each one of them finds a modern national language which is already formed, established, and perfected, of which he only has to make use, once he has learned it. . . .

[1] In a letter from Rome, written on 19 April 1823, Leopardi gave almost similar advice to his sister Paolina, who was grieving over a disappointment of her own: 'I assure you, my Paolina, that if we do not acquire a little indifference towards ourselves, it is not possible, I do not say to be happy, but even to remain alive.'

It is more than a hundred and fifty years since Italy has either created or cultivated any kind of literature, for she has not produced any original writers during this time in any field, and those whom she has produced, having never done anything but copy their predecessors, do not deserve the title of cultivators of literature, since a man does not cultivate his field who only walks about it carefully observing it, but leaving everything as it was before.[1] Neither has any branch of our literature been advanced or improved by any of these writers, nor any new branch introduced. So that Italian literature has come to a stand-still. . . .

An ancient language cannot serve to say modern things, and to say them as they should be said, in a modern fashion; nor was our language in particular fit to express new kinds of knowledge, and to provide what is needed for so many and such vast novelties. As we gradually heard what was happening in the literatures and disciplines of other countries, the few Italians who were excited by the new sciences and who possessed the necessary mental equipment to add to these something of their own . . . having found that the old Italian language did not suffice them, gave it up altogether, and went to school to foreigners, not only for their new ideas and thoughts, but for their language; and having taken their ideas from those men (sometimes merely repeating and sometimes increasing and improving them), they also took from them their idioms, and their ways and forms of speech and writing; and the true scientists—with regard to whom our country has never at any time been second to any other—since they always cared little for questions of language, followed this barbarous new habit, using the language which was to hand. . . .

Now we have a language of our own; very old indeed, but very rich, beautiful, powerful, in every sort of way; for we have a literature, which is also ancient, but vast, varied,

---

[1] Elsewhere Leopardi said that Alfieri was the only exception, 'for he had a free spirit and rebelled against his time and the notions of the government under which he lived'. (I, 336)

most beautiful, most rich in splendid classical authors and in styles, and which lasted for three centuries or more. . . . So what is necessary, evident, and certain is that in the wish to give a modern literature to modern Italy, we should not change her ancient tongue, nor dissolve it nor renew it, but preserve its fundamental character and attributes and modernize them, in such a way that the fine living Italian language should be a true derivation of the old, indeed a continuation of it. Just as the French language of the second half of the past century and of the present one, is nothing but that of the time of Louis XIV, passed on from hand to hand.

Now this was easy for the French, since their literature has never been interrupted since the time of Louis XIV, so that their language has a natural and effortless continuity, and, having gradually adapted itself to the times, has been modern in each period, but also a single whole, when all its periods are considered as one. But we must force the matter, and almost erase or conceal what has happened to us in the past, that is, we must behave in such a manner that what did happen, should seem not to have occurred, and that our language should seem never to have interrupted its course. . . . How can this be done? It would seem less difficult to create it anew. If Italy only had a very imperfect language, very poor and childish, it would be less difficult for a great mind to perfect, enrich, and broaden it, and lead it to maturity. But Italy has a language as perfect as it is vast, although put aside a long time ago and now unsuited to her needs, for which it has not yet been adapted or used. So it is indispensable that the man of talent whom we are imagining, before beginning to write, should master this vast language of his perfectly, embrace it wholly, turn it into sap and blood. . . . And this language being old, he cannot learn it from his nurse, but only through study . . . with great sweat and deep research into its properties, and a constant practice in reading and writing and a most assiduous and attentive study of its numerous classics. . . . It is certain that a true knowledge and mastery of the Italian language re-

quire, without exaggeration, almost half a lifetime. . . . But
do not a man's learning, knowledge, and study require a
whole lifetime?   (II, 384–90)

All primitive nations and peoples, like savage ones today,
used to regard a man who was unhappy or unfortunate as
an enemy of the gods, either because of some vice or crime
of which he was guilty, or because of envy or some other
caprice which had caused the divinities to hate either him in
particular or his whole family. . . . A man who was often
unsuccessful in his enterprises, was undoubtedly hated by
the gods. An illness, a shipwreck, or other such misfortunes
whose origins were more directly natural, were even more
certain tokens of divine wrath. So the unhappy man was
shunned, like a criminal; he was denied succour and compassion, for men feared thus to become accomplices in his
crime and so to have to share his penalty. . . . Signs still
remain in classical languages of these opinions: κακοδαίμων
ἄθλιος, and similar names referred to a man who was both
unhappy and a scoundrel.   (II, 397)

What is life? The journey of a sick cripple who, with a
heavy burden on his back, climbs over steep mountains and
through desolate, exhausting, and arduous lands, in the
snow, the frost, the rain, the wind, under the blazing sun,
for many days, without ever resting by day or night, in
order to reach a certain precipice or ditch, into which
inevitably he must fall. (17 January 1826)   (II, 990)

It is natural to man—weak, wretched, and exposed to so
many dangers—to suppose, imagine, and even gratuitously
pretend that a wisdom, sagacity, and prudence, a purpose and
discernment, a perspicacity and experience superior to his
own, exist in some other person, whom he watches during
any time of hard trial, finding comfort or fear according to
whether he sees him looking cheerful or sad, alarmed or
courageous, and thus resting on his authority, without any

reason. . . . So children often feel, especially those of tender years, with regard to their parents. And so did I, even at a ripe and stable age, with regard to my father; for in any difficulty or danger it was my habit, before determining the degree of my own trouble or dread, to examine or conjecture his, and also his opinion or judgement, just as if I had been incapable of judging for myself. . . . And this human characteristic is one of the reasons why a belief is so gladly embraced and still held in an all-provident God, that is, in a being superior to us in sense and wisdom, who watches over our fate. . . .   (II, 1057)

Of our great poets, two have met with much misfortune, Dante and Tasso. We possess and visit both their tombs, which are both far away from their own home. But I, who wept by Tasso's tomb, had no feeling of tenderness by Dante's: and I think this is generally so. And yet neither I nor anyone else fails to have the highest esteem and indeed admiration for Dante: perhaps more so (and rightly) than for the other poet. Besides, the misfortunes of the first were undoubtedly real and great, while as to those of the other, we are uncertain whether they were not, at least partly, imaginary. . . . But we see in Dante a man with a strong soul, brave enough to bear ill fortune, and also to fight against it, and against necessity and fate. All the more admirable, assuredly, but also the less lovable and pitiable. In Tasso we see a man defeated by his wretchedness, laid low in the dust, who had given way to adversity, who was constantly suffering and enduring. Even if his calamities were imaginary and untrue, his unhappiness was certainly real. If less unfortunate than Dante, he was assuredly more miserable. (14 March 1827)   (II, 1087)

To eat alone, μονοφαγία, was considered infamous by the Greeks and Latins and considered *inhuman*, and the title of μονοφάγος, the man who eats alone, was given to a man as an insult, like that of τοιχωρύχος, thief. I would have deserved

that insult. But the ancients were right, for they did not
converse with each other at table, but after eating, or during
the actual symposium, that is while drinking together, as
was their custom after the meal; and as is done today by the
English, at most nibbling some little dry piece of food, to
make one wish to drink. That is the time when one can be
most cheerful and good-humoured, and most inclined to
talk and chatter. But during the meal they were silent, or
spoke very little. We have lost the very natural and gay
custom of drinking at table, but talk when we are eating.
Now I cannot get into my head that the only hour of the
day in which our mouth is occupied . . . should be precisely
the one in which one ought to talk.   (II, 1012–13)

Another reason why I like μονοφαγία [eating alone] is in
order to avoid having persons serving my meal and standing
round my table, as I necessarily must if I eat in company—
'*d'importuns laquais, épiant nos discours, critiquant tout bas nos
maintiens . . .*' [Rousseau, *Émile*]. Unfortunately I have never
become accustomed to enjoying myself in the presence of
people who, to my certain knowledge, are condemning or
mocking my enjoyment, or who are bored by it; I have never
been able to understand how others could bear, and indeed
be proud of, such witnesses, whose occupations and thoughts
everyone knows to be precisely those I have described. The
ancients, too, were served at table, but by slaves, that is by
people whom they considered to be less than men, or certainly less fully men than they. . . . But our servants are our
equals. . . .   (II, 1109)

Having often changed my abode and lived in some places
for either months or years, I discovered that I was never
contented, never at home, never naturalized in any place,
however excellent, until I had some memories to attach to
it, to the rooms in which I lived, and to the streets and
houses I visited. These memories did not consist in anything more than being able to say: 'This is where I was so

long ago, this is what I did, saw, heard here, so many months
ago'; a thing which would not otherwise have had any
importance, but the memory of it, the fact that I could
remember it, made it important and sweet. Therefore I was
always sad in any place during the first few months, and as
time went on I became contented and attached to it.
Through remembrance, it almost became my home.
(Florence, 23 July 1827)　　　　　　　　　　　　　(II, 1121)

It has been observed that great grief, like great passion,
has no external language. I must add that it has also not got
an inner one. I mean that in great grief a man is incapable of
circumscribing and defining to himself any idea or emotion
concerning the subject of his passion which he can express
even to himself, thus directing and exercising, so to speak,
his thoughts and his grief. He feels a thousand emotions,
sees a thousand confused ideas, or rather does not see or
feel anything but one very vast emotion or idea, which
absorbs his whole capacity for thinking or feeling, without
being able either to embrace it as a whole or to define its
parts. . . . If he weeps (and I have noticed this in myself) he
weeps as if by chance, without even being able to say to
himself, *for what*.　　　　　　　　　　　　　(II, 1231)

In my solitary walks in the city, very pleasant sensations
and beautiful images are aroused in me by a glimpse of the
interior of the rooms which I see from the street below,
through their open windows. These same rooms would not
awaken any feeling in me if I saw them from within. Is not
this an image of human life? . . . (Recanati, 1 December
1828)　　　　　　　　　　　　　　　　　　　(II, 1233)

After reading a passage of true poetry of our own time,
whether in verse or prose (but the most powerful impres-
sions come from verse), one can say, even in these prosaic
times, what Sterne said about a smile: that it adds a thread to
the short canvas of our life. . . . (1 February 1829)　(II, 1259)

Certain ideas, certain images, of supremely vague, fantastic, fanciful, impossible things, cause us great delight, whether in poetry or in our own fancy, because they call back to us our most remote memories, those of our childhood, in which such ideas and images and beliefs were familiar and usual. And the poets who have the greatest number of ideas of this kind (which are supremely poetical) are dearest to us. If you will analyse your most poetic sensations and fancies, those which raise you up most, and draw you out of yourselves and out of the real world, you will discover that they, and the pleasure they give you (at least after childhood), consist wholly or principally in memories.
(21 May 1829)   (II, 1321)

6. The Visit to Rome 1822–3

'The timid have not got any less self-esteem than
the arrogant, indeed more . . . and therefore are
they afraid.'

LEOPARDI: *Pensieri*

*The following letters are a selection from those which Leopardi wrote
to his family during the winter of 1822–3, when he was at last
permitted, in the company of two uncles and several cousins, to pay
a visit to Rome. It is noticeable that these letters make no mention
of the beauty, not only of Rome itself, but of the long journey by coach,
though it took them through some of the finest country in Italy. Like
Byron, Leopardi would really have preferred to travel through fine
scenery at night: it was always the inner landscape of the mind which
was his chief concern. And it did not take him more than two days
to write to his brother Carlo that the intensity of his expectations
had met with disappointment in Rome.*

My Carlo, If you think it is your brother Giacomo who
is writing to you, you are much mistaken, for that young
man is dead or stunned, and in his place there is a person
who can hardly call to mind his name. You must know, my
dear Carlo, that I am beside myself; not indeed with wonder,
for if I saw the devil himself I would not be surprised, and I
do not take the least pleasure in all the fine things I see,
because, though I know that they are marvellous, I do not
feel it; and I assure you that their multitude and grandeur
have become wearisome to me, from the first day. Therefore
if I tell you that I no longer recognize myself, do not think
it is from wonder or pleasure or hope, or anything agreeable.
You must know, my Carlo, that during the journey I suffered
all that can be suffered, as happens when one travels at someone else's expense, and in the company of a man who requires
every most refined comfort for himself, whether or not it is

compatible with that of others.[1] Nevertheless I enjoyed the journey . . . if only in forming new and very different habits. And I still had that faint shadow of hope of which I am still capable, and which, without exciting or delighting one, is yet enough to make life tolerable. But having arrived here and seen the horrible disorder, confusion, blankness, unbearable meticulousness and indescribable disorder which rule in this house, and finding myself entirely alone and unprotected among my relations (though I lack nothing) I swear to you, that my patience and self-confidence . . . are not only vanquished, but destroyed. . . .

Yesterday I went to see Cancellieri[2] who is a fool, a torrent of words, the most boring and discouraging man in the world; he speaks of absurdly frivolous things with the greatest interest, and of important things with the greatest possible coolness; he suffocates you with flattery and praise, but offers both with such icy coldness and indifference, that, as one listens to him, one has the impression that to be a remarkable man is the most common thing on earth. In short, I am caught up by so great a melancholy, that once again my only pleasure is in sleep, and this melancholy, and the fact of constantly being in public, so unlike my usual habits, depresses me and extinguishes all my faculties, so that I am no longer worth anything, do not hope for anything, would like to speak and don't know what the devil to say, am no longer myself, and have become in every way like a statue. . . .

Love me, by God. I need love, love, love, fire, enthusiasm, life: the world does not seem made for me: I have found the devil much blacker than he is painted.[3]

His next letter, to Paolina, was no more enthusiastic.

---

[1] The companion to whom these remarks refer was his uncle Girolamo.
[2] The Abate Cancellieri, who was then seventy years old, was one of the most distinguished classical scholars and archaeologists in Rome, and later on showed much kindness to the young poet.
[3] *Epist.* II, Rome, 25 November [1822].

All the size of Rome only serves to multiply the distances, and the number of steps you must climb to reach anyone you want to visit. These immense buildings and these consequently interminable streets are just so many spaces thrown between men, instead of being spaces which contain men. . . . I do not mean to say that Rome seems to me uninhabited; but I do say that if men needed to live with as much elbow-room as in these palaces, and to walk as one does in these streets, churches, and squares, the globe would not be large enough to contain the human race.[1]

The truth was that, while in Recanati he had felt that no one fully appreciated him, in Rome he realized that they were unaware of his very existence.

Truly [he wrote in his next letter to Carlo], there can be no greater solitude, to my mind, than too much company. . . . Ask me whether, in the two weeks I have been in Rome, I have enjoyed a single moment of passing pleasure. . . . I will swear to you, that the only drop of pleasure that has fallen on my spirit since I set foot in this city, has been when I have read your letters. . . . You will say that I don't know how to live: that for you and for others like you, things would take a different course. But listen to the facts and my conclusions. In a small city one may be bored, but, after all, men there have some relation to each other and to the things around them, because the sphere of those relations is small and is in proportion to the human scale. In a great city a man lives without any relation at all to what surrounds him, because the sphere is so large, that no individual can fill it or be conscious of it, and thus there is no point of contact between it and him. Therefore you may conjecture how much greater and more terrible tedium is in a great city, than in a small one; for human indifference—that terrible passion, or rather apathy, of man—must necessarily and

[1] *Epist.* II, Rome, 5 December 1822.

inevitably have its seat in great cities, that is, in very large societies. A man's sensitive faculty, in such a place, is limited only to his sight. . . . The only way that one can live in a big city is the one that, sooner or later, everyone is obliged to adopt—to make oneself a little circle of acquaintances, remaining completely indifferent to the rest of society, which is the same as building around oneself a small town, within the great one. . . .

Let me only say this. You know that the ultimate source of pleasure is self-esteem, and that in the last analysis it is satisfied either through one's ambition or one's feelings. As to sentiment, you can imagine whether a crowd, which thinks only of itself, is ever capable of it. And as to ambition, you must convince yourself that in a big town it is impossible to satisfy it. Whatever the qualities may be which you believe yourself to possess—whether beauty, knowledge, nobility, riches, or youth—there is so much of each one of them in a great city, that no one pays any heed to them. Every day I see men who would suffice in themselves alone to fill the whole of Recanati: here no one looks at them. To attract another man's attention in a big town is a desperate enterprise: truly they are only made for monarchs. . . . In Rome, as in all other great cities, you can only find enjoyment as a pure spectator; and a spectacle in which one cannot take part becomes tedious after a moment or two, however beautiful it may be.

But leaving aside all things of the mind and of letters, about which I will write another time (having already met a good many Roman literary men), I will restrict myself to the women, and to the good fortune which you perhaps believe one may more easily meet with them, in a big city. I assure you that the opposite is the truth. Walking up and down, in church, in the street, there isn't a hag who will look at you. I have walked and walked about Rome in the company of handsome and well-dressed young men, and have often passed with them very close to young women: they have not even lifted their eyes: and it was plain that

H

this was not from modesty, but from a complete and habitual
lack of interest and indifference.[1]

*There are many other letters in a similar strain—of which perhaps
the most interesting (since in this his opinions are confirmed by
Stendhal and other travellers) are those dealing with Roman scholars.*

According to them, the summit of human wisdom, indeed
the only real and true science, is antiquarianism. I have yet
to meet a Roman man of letters who by literature means
anything but archaeology. Philosophy, morals, politics,
psychology, rhetoric, poetry, philology, are all foreign to
Rome and seem child's play, compared to discovering
whether a piece of copper or of stone belonged to Mark
Anthony or Mark Agrippa. The beauty of it is that one cannot find a Roman who has a real knowledge of Greek and
Latin; and without a perfect knowledge of those languages,
you can easily imagine what the study of antiquities can be.
They chatter and dispute all day, and make little jokes about
each other in the papers, and form cabals and parties: and
thus does Roman literature progress.[2]

*Leopardi should, perhaps, have omitted philology from his list
of studies that awakened no interest in Rome, and of this he himself
soon became aware, realizing that it was as a philologist that he
stood the best chance of finding some employment.*

I have changed my coat [he told Carlo], or rather I have
put on again the one I wore as a boy. Here in Rome I am
not a man of letters, but a learned man, a Greek scholar.
You cannot believe how useful I find those remains of
philological scholarship which I have pieced together again
in my mind from my youthful occupations. Without these
I should be nothing at all with these foreigners, who now
esteem me, and show me many signs of their approval.[3]

[1] *Epist.* II, 6 December [1822].
[2] Ibid. 9 December 1822.
[3] Ibid. 22 January 1823.

The Prussian Minister [he added a few weeks later] has sent me obliging messages by several people: I have been to his house; he has told me that this is the real way to treat philology, that my road is the right one, that he begged me not to give it up. . . . He has undertaken of his own accord to have printed in German whatever I have discovered or may discover in the Roman libraries. In short he has shown me so much interest that, on hearing that I should soon be obliged to go away, he asked me whether I would not accept some employment. In the end we left it that I would send him a note for the Secretary of State [Cardinal Consalvi], and that he would present it and recommend me with all his power.[1]

The Prussian Minister was the celebrated scholar, Niebuhr, and his word had some weight with the Cardinal, but when the recommendation reached him, the prelate's first question was whether the young man was prepared, if not to enter the priesthood, at least to wear the mantelletta, *or little cape, of the members of the Papal court.*

A prelate's career [wrote Leopardi to Carlo, after telling him this news] does truly offer very great advantages at the present time, especially to a man of noble birth, for there are very few gentlemen who enter that career, and the Secretary of State prefers to give certain posts to them. . . . I felt very much confused, having to decide about the whole course of my life, and all in a few hours. . . . In short, it is almost certain that if I had agreed to become a prelate, you might soon have heard that your brother in his *mantelletta* was off to govern a province. The great expense of putting on the purple robes could have been met by a loan, which could easily have been found here, once one had been offered a post or the assurance of one. I looked around me, and decided I would have nothing to do with it. The reasons which I might tell you are many; I think you agree with me;

[1] *Epist.* II, 10 March 1823.

if you do not, be sure that I did not reach this decision out
of lack of resolution or courage, but because long ago, before
coming here, and still more after my arrival, I reached the
decision that my life must be as independent as possible and
that my happiness could only consist in following my own
bent.[1]

*Only a few more weeks were left to him in Rome, since every other
attempt to find employment proved unsuccessful. But, before leaving,
he did write home a letter in which he described a genuine emotion
aroused in him by at least one of the sights of Rome. This was the
tomb of Tasso, in the church beside the convent of S. Onofrio on the
Gianiculum.*

On Friday, 15 February 1823, I went to see the tomb
of Tasso—and there I wept. This is the first and only
pleasure I have had in Rome. The way there is long, and one
only goes to that place for the purpose of seeing the tomb;
but would one not come all the way from America, to enjoy
for two minutes the pleasure of tears? . . . Many people
feel indignant at seeing Tasso's ashes marked by nothing
but a bare stone, a span-and-a-half in length and breadth,
hidden away in the corner of a poor little church. But I
would on no account have this dust placed under a mausoleum. You can conceive the variety of emotions that arise
from considering the contrast between Tasso's greatness and
the humility of his sepulchre. But you cannot conceive
another contrast, which strikes an eye accustomed to the
infinite magnificence and size of the Roman monuments,
when one compares them with the smallness and nakedness
of this tomb. There is a sad and fearful consolation in reflecting that this poverty suffices to interest and inspire future
generations, while the superb mausoleums which Rome
contains are observed with complete indifference for the
persons to whom they were erected, of whom one does not
even ask the name. . . .

[1] *Epist.* II, 22 March 1823.

Even the street which leads to this place prepares the spirit to be moved. It is flanked by houses used as workshops, and echoes with the creaking of looms and other similar machines, and the song of women and artisans at their work. . . . Even the expression and manners of the people one meets in that street have something, I know not what, that seems simpler and more human, and that expresses the habits and the character of persons whose life is based upon reality and not upon falsehood—that is, who live by work, and not by intrigue, imposture and deceit, like the greater part of this population.[1]

His final comment on his visit was written several years later, in the Zibaldone.

When I arrived in Rome, the necessity of living with other men, of exteriorizing myself, rendered me stupid, inept, and inwardly dead. I became entirely devoid of an inner life and incapable of it, without becoming any more apt for the outer one. This was, perhaps, the most painful and mortifying time I have ever spent in my life, for . . . I lost almost all my self-confidence, as well as any hope of ever being a success in the world.[2]

At the end of April 1823, after a five months' visit, tired and disillusioned, Leopardi returned to Recanati. 'In coming home,' he wrote to his brother, 'I hope to find nothing but friendship and love.'[3]

[1] *Epist.* II, To Carlo, 20 February 1823.
[2] *Zibaldone*, II, p. 1232.
[3] *Epist.* II, 19 April 1823.

7. *The* Operette Morali *1824*

Leopardi's Operette Morali, *of which nine are translated in this book, were mostly written in Recanati in 1824—the year of the publication, in Bologna, of his* Canzoni-Odi—*and were first published in Milan in 1827. The volume included all the* Operette *except* Copernicus *and the* Dialogue between Porphyry and Plotinus *(both written in 1827), and the* Dialogue between a Pedlar of Almanacks and a Wayfarer *and the* Dialogue between Tristan and a Friend, *written in 1832 and published in the Florentine edition of the* Operette, *in 1834.*

According to a letter to his publisher, Leopardi wished these Dialogues to be considered, 'although written with apparent lightness', a complete exposition of his philosophic system. He added that they were 'the true harvest of my life until now . . . dearer to me than my own eyes'. He also said that it was his intention to enrich the Italian language by adding to it a new literary form: some satirical dialogues in the manner of Lucian, containing 'the true Attic salt'. But he came nearer to the truth when, in a letter to his father, he said that he was 'trying to write poetry in prose', or when, in the Dialogue between Tristan and a Friend, *Tristan referred to the whole work as a 'book of poetic dreams, of melancholy inventions and caprices, or an expression of the author's unhappiness'.*

Leopardi, in short, even when he was writing prose, remained essentially a poet. His philosophic themes could be summed up in a very few words: 'a doctrine', as Benedetto Croce wrote, 'of evil, of suffering, of the vanity and nothingness of existence, which intrinsically . . . was nothing but an expression of his own regret and bitterness'. But this philosophy, throughout the book, is constantly being denied by his own poetic vitality and passion. The finest passages in the Operette Morali *are those in which the poet has vanquished the philosopher and, giving free rein to his fancy, allows his spirit to wander in a region between the earth and the sky, in which a Sprite converses with a Gnome, the Earth with the Moon, and Nature with* an Icelander, *in which a philosopher wishes to become a bird, 'to savour their contentment and delight', and Tasso implores his Familiar Spirit to conjure up for him a vision of his Leonora. It is then that Leopardi is back in his own realm.*

For reasons of space it has been impossible to include all the Operette Morali *in this book; those selected have seemed to me to contain some of the best examples of his style and also to give a picture of his inner life, with its constant conflict between the vitality of his poetic feeling and the despairing negativism of his philosophic creed—a conflict equally observable in the Notes in his* Zibaldone, *on which many of the Dialogues are based.*

There is an extremely close connexion between the Operette Morali *and some of Leopardi's poems, as well as with the Notes in the* Zibaldone. *To give only two instances: we find in the* Dialogue between Porphyry and Plotinus, *written in 1827, the deep pre-occupation with suicide and the justification of it as a moral right, which first appears as a personal experience of Leopardi's youth, set down in the early pages of his notebook, and which later on found expression in his* canzone, *written in 1824,* Bruto Minore (The Younger Brutus). *So, too, the main theme of the* Dialogue between Tristan and a Friend *may first be traced in the* Zibaldone *and later on may be found both in the* Palinodia *addressed to Gino Capponi and in the great poem of Leopardi's maturity,* La Ginestra (The Broom).

Except for the effusive praise of one reviewer, the Operette Morali, *when first they appeared, fell rather flat. Leopardi's Florentine friends pronounced them to be 'very inferior to their author', and his most savage critic, Niccoló Tommaseo, described their author as 'both profane and pedantic', and deplored his 'cold and arrogant mediocrity'. But then Tommaseo had seen in the* Canti, *too, nothing more than 'a little Count, singing like a frog of Cephesus and crying, "There is no God, because I am a hunchback. I am a hunchback, because there is no God!"' Leopardi's greatest Italian contemporary, Alessandro Manzoni, held a very different opinion. 'Have you read Leopardi's prose?' he said to a foreign traveller. 'Not enough attention has been paid to that little volume. As to style, perhaps nothing better has been written in Italian prose in our time.'*

Of all the attacks against this work, the one which Leopardi minded most was the suggestion that his philosophic views were a consequence of his own personal unhappiness or ill-health. After reading a review in a German periodical, Hesperus, *he wrote indignantly to his friend Louis De Sinner:*

Whatever my troubles may have been, which it has been thought appropriate to display and perhaps slightly to exaggerate in this journal, I have had enough courage not to try to lighten their burden either by frivolous hopes of an alleged felicity, which is both in the future and uncertain, nor by a cowardly resignation. My feelings towards destiny are and always have been those which I expressed in *Bruto Minore*. . . . Before dying, I must protest against this weak and vulgar suggestion; and request my readers to concentrate on replying to my remarks and my arguments, rather than on accusing my infirmities.

As for Leopardi's family, he begged his brother Carlo to conceal the book, if possible, from his parents, 'as there are certain ideas in it which might perhaps be displeasing to "Babbo"' *; and in Recanati, Paolina, after her brother's death, regretfully placed the* Operette *in the locked bookshelf in their library containing the works proscribed by the Church. 'Now all the world will know', she sadly wrote, 'that my brother has lost his faith! . . . How true it is that too much learning corrupts!' But in the family register at Recanati, when she set down the day of his death, she added: 'Good-bye, dear Giacomo. Shall we not meet again in Paradise?'*

THE STORY OF THE HUMAN RACE

The story is told that all the men who first peopled the earth were created everywhere at the same time, and all as infants, and were nourished by bees, goats, and doves, as the poets describe in their fable about the nurture of Jove. They say, too, that the earth was much smaller than it is now, and all the land was flat, that the sky was starless and there was no sea, and that there was much less variety and magnificence in the world than we see there now. But men, nevertheless, delighted in taking pleasure in regarding and considering the earth and sky with great wonder, thinking them most beautiful, and not only vast but infinite both in size, majesty, and loveliness; and they also nourished very joyous hopes, deriving an incredible delight from all their awareness of this life, and became most contented, so that they almost believed in happiness.

Having thus passed their childhood and early youth most sweetly and having reached a riper age, a change came over them. For their hopes, which they had postponed from day to day until then, had not yet been realized, so that they lost faith in them; and they did not feel that they could still be content with what they were then enjoying, without some promise of an increase of happiness, particularly as the appearance of nature and of every part of their daily life— whether because they had become accustomed to them, or because their spirits were no longer so lively as they once had been—no longer seemed as delightful and pleasing to them as in the beginning. They wandered about the earth visiting very distant regions—for they could do so easily, since the land was flat and not divided by seas or any other impediments—and after many years most of them became aware that the earth, even though it was large, had definite boundaries, instead of ones so vast that one could not define them; and that, but for a few very slight differences, all the places in the earth and all its inhabitants were just alike. And their discontent increased so much on this account that, though their youth was scarcely at an end, they were all overcome by a conscious distaste for their own nature. And in their manhood, and still more as their years declined, their satiety was converted into hatred, so that some of them came to be so despairing that they were no longer able to bear the light and the life which they had at first loved so much, and thus of their own accord—some in one way and some in another—they brought their life to an end.

It seemed terrible to the gods that living creatures should prefer death to life, and that—without the compulsion of necessity—they should become the instruments of their own destruction. Neither can we easily tell how surprised they were that their gifts should have been thought so valueless and abominable that mankind would use all its strength to remove and reject them; for it seemed to them that they had placed in the world so much that was good and pleasant, and so many orders and conditions, that this dwelling-place should have been not only tolerated but deeply loved by every creature and above all by men, whose race had been formed with singular care to marvellous excellence. But at the same time, besides being moved by considerable pity for the great human wretchedness shown by these events, they began to fear that, if these deplorable examples were renewed and multiplied, the human race would soon perish, against the will of fate, and the earth thus be deprived of the perfection which had been attained by our race, and the gods of the honours they received from mankind.

Therefore Jove, having decided—since it seemed to be necessary—to improve the human condition, and to help it to further the pursuit of happiness, reached the conclusion that the chief human complaint was that things were not as beautiful, various, and perfect, as they had believed at first, but instead very restricted, imperfect, and monotonous, and that they complained not only of their old age but also of their maturity and even of their youth, craving for the

sweetness of their early years, and earnestly implored to go
back to childhood, and to remain in that condition their
whole life long. But this Jove could not grant them, since
it is contrary to the universal laws of nature and to the
functions and tasks which men, according to the divine intention and decrees, should exercise and fulfil. Neither could
he transmit his own infinity to mortal beings, nor bestow
infinity on matter, nor render eternal the perfection and
happiness of things and of mankind.

So it seemed to him best to extend the boundaries of the
created world and to bestow on it a greater variety and
magnificence; and, having taken this course, he increased
the earth's circumference and poured into it the sea, so that
—lying between one inhabited place and another—it should
diversify the appearance of things and prevent men from
knowing their boundaries too well, while interrupting their
journeys and also placing before their eyes a vivid image of
immensity. During this time these new waters were occupied
by the land of Atlantis, as well as by innumerable other vast
areas, although of that one a special memory has remained,
handed down over many centuries. He filled up many low
lands, raising mountains and hills, he sprinkled the night
with stars, refined and purified the nature of the air, increased
and gave greater variety than before to the colours of the
landscape and the sky, and caused the generations of men
to overlap, so that the old age of some of them should
coincide with the youth and childhood of others. And having
decided to multiply the appearances of infinity which men
desire more than anything else—since he could not provide
the reality—and wishing to cherish and nourish their imagi-
nations, from which, as he realized, they had drawn the perfect happiness of their childhood, he made use of a device
similar to the creation of the sea and created the Echo, con-
cealing it in caves and valleys, and endowed the forests with
a deep, dull clamour, and made the tree-tops sway like a wide
wave. And so, too, he created all the people of dreams, and
bade them take on many shapes to deceive men's thoughts

with the appearance of an incomprehensible happiness, which he could not give them in reality, and to produce for them those vague and undefined shapes of which he himself—in spite of his own wish and the ardent desire of mankind—could not produce a true and living example.

With all these measures Jove cheered and lifted up the spirit of men, so that each one of them was convinced once more of the pleasantness and kindness of life, as well as feeling delight and wonder at the beauty and immensity of earthly things. And this happy state lasted longer than the first, principally because of the intervals of time at which Jove had caused births to take place, so that the men whose souls had become chilled and wearied by experience, were comforted by seeing the warmth and hopes of those whose years were still green. But in due course all this novelty came to an end and tedium and contempt for life sprang up and gained strength again, and men were brought to such a state of depression that the custom then arose, as we believe, which history still records as being practised by some ancient peoples, namely, that, when a child was born, its friends and relations came together to weep over the event, and when it died, the day was celebrated with feasting and speeches of congratulation to the dead. And at last the whole of mankind turned to impiety—whether because men thought that Jove was not hearkening to them or because it is the nature of wretchedness to harden and corrupt even the best-disposed souls, destroying their love and honesty and justice. For it is a great mistake to believe that man's unhappiness is a result of wickedness and of disobedience to the gods; on the contrary, the sins of men are caused by their misfortunes.

Now, after the arrogance of men had been punished and their insults avenged by the gods, by Deucalion's flood, the only two creatures who escaped the universal destruction of our species, Deucalion and Pyrrha—who told each other that nothing could be better for the human race than its complete destruction—were seated upon the summit of a cliff, calling upon death with intense desire, for they neither feared nor regretted the common lot. But Jove ordered them to remedy the desolation of the earth, and since they could not bear, in view of their disconsolate contempt for life, to face the labour of generation, they took some stones from the mountain, as the gods had taught them, and, throwing them over their shoulders, brought the human race to life again. But Jove had now become aware by past experience of the nature of men, and that it is not enough for them, as for all other creatures, to live without sorrow and bodily pain, but that, on the contrary, they always crave for what is impossible, and torment themselves all the more with this desire, when they are most free from real evils. He therefore decided to use two new devices to preserve this wretched race, of which one was, to pour real afflictions upon it, and the other, to fill it with a thousand occupations and labours, so as to keep men busy and distract them as much as possible from communing with their own souls, or at least with their desire for that unknown, vain felicity. . . .

In order to leave no room for their previous idleness, he induced in the human race the need and appetite for new kinds of food and drink, which they could not obtain without much severe toil, whereas until the flood men had quenched their thirst only with water and fed upon the herbs and fruits that the earth and trees gave to them of their own accord. . . . He ordered Mercury to found the first city, and to divide the human race into different peoples and nations, and to give them different languages, thus arousing discord and rivalry between them, and also to show them the art of song and the other arts which, on account of both their nature and their origin, were and are still called divine.

He himself gave laws, states, and civilized decrees to these new peoples; and finally, wishing to give them an incomparable gift, he sent among them some phantoms of most excellent and superhuman appearance, whom he allowed, for the greater part, to govern and rule over these peoples: and he called them Justice, Virtue, Glory, Patriotism, and other names of the same kind. Among these phantoms there was also one called Love, who came to the earth with the others in those early times; because, before it was the custom to wear clothes, not love, but desire—not dissimilar in the men of those times from that which brute animals have always felt—drew one sex to the other, in the same way that everyone is attracted to food and similar things, for which we do not feel true love, but only appetite.

It was a wonderful thing how much fruit these divine counsels brought to mortal life, and how much more easy and sweet the new human condition became than it had been before the flood, in spite of labours, fears, and griefs which our race had not known before. And this result was mostly brought about by those wonderful phantoms, whom men sometimes considered genii and sometimes gods, and whom they followed and worshipped with an inexpressible ardour and with great and heavy toil for many ages, being spurred on to do so by the great efforts of the noble poets and artisans, so that many mortals did not hesitate to give their blood and their lives for one or another of those phantoms. . . .

Among those phantoms, so much admired by the ancients, there was one whom in their language they called Wisdom, who, being universally honoured by everyone, like all her companions, and particularly pursued by many men, had contributed as much as any of the others to the prosperity of the recent centuries. Often, very often, indeed almost daily, she had promised and vowed to her followers that she would show them Truth, who she said was a very great genius and her own master, but who had never come down upon this earth, but dwelled in heaven with the gods. She promised that she would bring him down from there, through her own authority and grace, and would induce him to live among men for a while, so that the human race, having become familiar with him through long custom, would change its nature and attain such an excellence of knowledge, institutions, and habits, and so happy a life, as would almost be comparable to that of the gods. But how could a mere shadow and empty image keep such a promise and bring Truth down to earth? So that men, after a long time of faith and trust, became aware of the vanity of her promises, and at the same time craved for anything new, especially owing to the idleness in which they were living, and, partly spurred on by an ambition to be equal to the gods, and partly by their desire for the happiness which, after speaking to that phantom, they thought they would attain by conversing with Truth, they turned to Jove, demanding most insistently and presumptuously that he should send this noble spirit to live for a while on earth, and reproved him for having denied to his creatures, out of envy, the infinite benefits that this presence would bring to them, while at the same time they complained about the human lot, and renewed their ancient and odious laments about the meanness and poverty of all their possessions. . . .

Many things had already turned Jove's goodwill away again from men, and among others their great perfidiousness, of which the extent and blackness had been far greater than that which had been avenged by the flood. He was thoroughly disgusted, after so many trials, with the restless, insatiable, immoderate nature of mankind and was now certain that no device, no condition, no place would ever suffice to bring them tranquillity and still less happiness. For, even if he had consented to multiply a thousand times the space and the delights of the earth and the universal knowledge of things, both the one and the other would soon again have seemed narrow, unpleasing, and of little worth to men, who are incapable of the infinite, even while they crave it. But at last their foolish and arrogant demands stirred up the god's wrath so much that he resolved to set aside all pity and punish the human race for ever, condemning it for all time to a much deeper wretchedness than it had ever known before. And to this end he decided not only to send Truth to live among them for a while, as they had asked, but to give him a permanent dwelling-place among them, and—removing the faint phantoms he had sent there before—to make him the permanent ruler and master of the human race.

And since the gods were astounded by this decision, considering that it would make our state too high and would diminish their own superiority, Jove turned them away from this notion, pointing out to them not only that not all genii, even if powerful, are beneficent, but also that the nature of Truth is not such that he can have the same effect upon men as upon the gods. For whereas what Truth showed to the gods was their own beatitude, to men he would disclose their full unhappiness and keep it always before their eyes, and would also show it to be not merely the work of fate, but to be of such a nature that they would never be able, by any chance, accident, or remedy, to endure it, nor, so long as they lived, to cause it to cease. And since most of their ills are of such a nature that they are ills only in so far as they are believed to be so by those who suffer them, and are more or less heavy according to their own estimate, one can judge what a great evil the presence of this genius would be to mankind. For nothing would then seem truer to them than the illusion of all mortal blessings, and nothing more solid than the vanity of everything but their own pain. And for these reasons they would even be deprived of hope, which, from the earliest times until our own, had nourished their life more than any other comfort or delight. And thus, deprived of every hope and seeing no worthy object for any of their enterprises or labours, they would reach so great a neglect and abhorrence of every profitable and also every generous occupation, that the common life of mankind would come to be very similar to that of the dead. Yet in their despair and sluggishness they would still be unable to escape from the desire for an immense felicity which is inseparable from their nature, and which would sting and torment them even more than before, in so far as it would be less encumbered and distracted by the variety of their occupations or the spur of their deeds. . . .

And finally, since the other phantoms would all have been removed from the earth, and since the teachings of Truth would have rendered men fully aware of their own nature, human life would become deprived of all courage and rectitude, both in thought and deed: and not only learning and kindness, but the very names of nations and peoples would everywhere disappear and all men would be gathered together, as they would like to say, in a single nation, as it was in the beginning, professing a universal love towards their whole race, but in reality divided into as many peoples as there would be individuals. So that, since they would have no native country to love most deeply, and no foreign one to hate, every man would hate every other, and would love himself alone. How many and what great inconveniences would arise from this, would be a tale without an end. Neither would any mortals dare to leave this life of their own accord, because of great and hopeless unhappiness, for the rule of this genius would render them no less cowardly than they were wretched, and, in adding to the bitterness of their life, would also deprive them of the courage to renounce it.

On hearing these words of Jove's, it seemed to the gods that our fate would be more cruel and terrible than it is fitting for the divine pity to permit. But Jove went on to say: Yet shall they have some moderate comfort from a phantom whom they will call Love, whom I am prepared to leave with them, though I shall take all the others away. And even Truth, although he will be very powerful, and will be constantly at war with Love, will never wholly succeed in destroying, and only seldom in vanquishing him. . . .

Thus, having withdrawn from the earth those blessed phantoms, save only Love, the least noble of them all, Jove sent Truth among men, and bestowed perpetual residence and power upon him. Whereupon the deplorable effects ensued, which he had foreseen. . . . Yet pity, which is never

I

wholly extinguished in the celestial mind, moved Jove's will
at the sight of so much wretchedness, and especially at that
of a few men remarkable for the nobility of their customs and
the integrity of their conduct, whom he observed to be more
oppressed and afflicted than the others by the power and the
dark domination of Truth. In ancient times, when Justice,
Virtue, and those other phantoms ruled over human affairs,
the gods would sometimes visit their dominions, one or
another of them coming down to earth and manifesting their
presence here in various ways; a thing which had always
been of great benefit either to all mankind or to some particular man. But now that life had once again been corrupted
and overwhelmed by every form of malice, the gods for
some time disdained the society of men. And at last Jove, in
pity for our great wretchedness, asked the immortals if one
of them felt inclined to visit and comfort these children of
theirs in their great troubles, as they used to do, and
especially those among them who had shown themselves
unworthy of the general wretchedness. Whereupon, while
all the others remained silent, Love, the son of the celestial
Venus—similar in name to the phantom called after him,
but most unlike him in nature, virtues, and words—offered
(for his compassion is greater than that of any other god) to
do what Jove had asked, and to come down from heaven,
which he had never left before—since the council of the
immortals, to whom he is indescribably dear, had never
before permitted him to leave their society, even for a short
time, although occasionally a few of the ancients, deceived
by the various transformations and shapes of the phantom
who called himself by the same name, thought they had
perceived indubitable signs of the presence of that great god.
But he did not decide to visit mankind until it had been
placed under the rule of Truth; and even after that, he comes
down very rarely and only for a short time; both because of
the general unworthiness of the human race, and because the
gods are most unwilling to endure his absence.

When he comes upon the earth, he chooses for his abode

the most tender and gentle hearts of the most generous and
magnanimous persons, and there he abides for a little while,
diffusing so rare and wonderful a sweetness, and filling them
with affections so noble, and such virtue and courage, that
they then feel—and this is something entirely new to the
human race—not a semblance of happiness, but happiness
itself. Very rarely does he unite two such hearts, embracing
both of them at the same time and awakening in both a
reciprocal ardour and desire, although he is often insistently
implored to do so by those whose hearts he holds. But Jove
seldom allows him to gratify more than a very few, since the
happiness that is born of that blessing is barely surpassed by
that of the gods themselves.

In any case, to be filled with his spirit is a condition more
fortunate than any that was known to man in even the
happiest times. Wherever he rests, those wonderful phantoms which had been cut off from human society flutter
around him, invisible to everyone else; since this god has
brought them back for that purpose to the earth, with Jove's
permission; and even Truth cannot forbid it, though he is
a great enemy of those phantoms, and his soul is much
offended by their return. But nature does not grant to genii
to go against the gods.

And inasmuch as the fates endowed him with eternal
childhood, so, in harmony with his own nature, he fulfils to
some extent the greatest desire of men, a return to their own
childhood. For in the souls that he chooses to inhabit, he
stirs and reawakens, during all the time that he abides with
them, the infinite hopes and the dear and beloved fancies of
their tender years. Many mortals, who do not recognize or
are incapable of enjoying the delights he brings, jeer and
scoff at him, day after day, whether he is there or not, with
a most unbridled audacity. But he is deaf to them and to
their insults, and even if he did hear them, would not be
tormented by them, so mild and magnanimous is his nature.
Moreover the immortals, satisfied with the vengeance they
have taken on our whole race and with the incurable

wretchedness which afflicts it, do not heed the individual offences of men; and the fraudulent, the unjust, or the blasphemers of the gods are punished only in this, that their own nature excludes them from the divine grace for ever.[1]

[1] This, the first of the *Operette Morali*, was the one which, on account of its 'irreligious sentiments and fantastic tone', prevented Leopardi from being awarded the quinquennial prize of 5,000 *scudi* offered by the Accademia della Crusca—whose members awarded it instead to a voluminous *History of Italy* by Botta. Cf. G. Ferretti, *La fortuna delle Operette Morali e La Crusca*, in *Leopardi, Studi biografici*. 'Your cause', wrote Vieusseux, in imparting the bad news, 'was defended by Capponi and Niccolini, but what could be hoped from the Canons who formed the rest of the assembly?'

DIALOGUE BETWEEN A SPRITE AND
A GNOME

SPRITE. What, are you here, you son of Sabazius? Where are you going?

GNOME. My father has sent me to find out what the devil these scoundrels of men are doing; he is very suspicious about them, for it is a long time now since they gave us any trouble, and he has never seen a single one of them in his kingdom. He wonders whether they are not preparing some great plot against him, and whether the custom has come back of using sheep for barter, instead of gold and silver, or whether civilized people are now content to use little paper notes for money, as they have often done before, or little glass beads, as savages do; or whether the laws of Lycurgus have been revived, which seems the least likely.

SPRITE. 'You wait for them in vain: they all are dead'—so said the last line of a tragedy, in which all the characters had died.

GNOME. What do you mean?

SPRITE. I mean that every single man is dead, and their race has died out.

GNOME. Oh, that's something for the papers! But I have not yet seen that they have mentioned it.

SPRITE. You fool, don't you realize that, if the human race has died out, no more papers are being printed?

GNOME. Yes, that is true. Then how shall we learn the news of the world?

SPRITE. What news? That the sun has risen or set, or that the weather is hot or cold, that it has rained here or there or snowed or been windy? For, without mankind, Fortune is no longer blindfolded, but has put on spectacles and hung her wheel on a hook, and now she sits with folded arms, watching the world go round, without taking a hand in its affairs. There are no more kingdoms or empires now, swelling or bursting like soap-bubbles, because they have all disappeared; there are no more wars, and the years are as much like each other, as an egg is like another egg.

GNOME. Neither shall we know the day of the month, for no more calendars will be printed.

SPRITE. There won't be much harm in that, for it won't cause the moon to lose her way.

GNOME. And the days of the week won't have a name.

SPRITE. Well, even if they have no name to call them by, are you afraid that they won't come round? or do you propose, when they have gone by, to make them come back by calling them?

GNOME. And we shan't be able to keep count of the years.

SPRITE. Well, we can pretend to be young, even when the time for youth has gone by; and since we shall not measure the past, we shall grieve over it less, and even when we are very old, we shall not be expecting death every day.

GNOME. But how did those scoundrels come to die?

SPRITE. Some of them fought with each other, some died at sea, some ate each other up, some killed themselves with their own hand, some rotted away in idleness, some racked their brains over books, some caroused or indulged themselves in a thousand ways. In short, they discovered every possible way of doing violence to their own nature and of getting into trouble.

GNOME. I can't understand how a whole species of animals could come to an end, as you have described.

SPRITE. You who are a learned geologist ought to know that this is nothing new, and that many kinds of animals existed in ancient times which cannot be found today, except as a few petrified bones. And it is certain that those poor creatures did not make use of any of the means by which, as I told you, men used to bring about their own destruction.

GNOME. It may be so. But I should be glad if one or two of that crew came back to life again, just to discover what they would think when they saw that, although the human race has come to an end, everything else is going on just as usual, while they believed that the whole world was made and kept up for their benefit.

SPRITE. And they refused to believe that it only exists for sprites.

GNOME. You are playing the fool indeed, if you are speaking seriously.

SPRITE. Why? I am good at speaking seriously.

GNOME. Get away with you, you little clown. Who does not know that the world was made for gnomes?

SPRITE. For the gnomes, who always live underground? Why, that's the best joke I ever heard! What good are the sun, the moon, the air, the sea, the fields, and the woods to gnomes?

GNOME. And what good are the mines of silver and gold to sprites, and all the depths of the earth, under its outer crust?

SPRITE. Well, well, whether they are any good or not, let's stop this argument, for I feel certain that even the lizards and midges believe that the whole world was made only for the use of their own kind. And so let each one keep his own opinion, for no one could drive it out of his head: and for my part I will only say this to you, that if I were not born a sprite, I should be in despair.

GNOME. And I, if I had not been born a gnome. But I should like to know what men would have to say about their own arrogance, which caused them—among many other tricks they played on this creature and on that—to burrow deep into the earth and rob us of what belonged to us, asserting that it belonged to the human race, and saying that nature had hidden and buried it away in sport, just to see if they would be capable of finding it and excavating it.

SPRITE. That is hardly surprising, since they not only persuaded themselves that everything in this world had no other purpose than to be at their service, but also considered that everything was of no consequence, except the human race. And so they called their own vicissitudes, the world's revolutions, and the history of their own peoples, the history of the world; although, even within the earth itself, it was possible to count as many different species, not simply of living creatures, but merely of animals, as there are individual men: and yet those animals, which had been created especially for the use of men, were quite unconscious of the world's revolutions!

GNOME. Were even mosquitoes and fleas made for the benefit of men?

SPRITE. Yes, so men said, to teach them patience.

GNOME. As if their patience were not tried enough, apart from fleas!

SPRITE. But pigs, according to Chrysippus, were just pieces of meat prepared by nature for men's kitchens and larders and flavoured with souls instead of salt, so that they should not putrefy.

GNOME. To my mind, if Chrysippus had had a little Attic salt inside his brain, instead of a soul, he would not have conceived such an absurdity.

SPRITE. And this too is entertaining: there are a very great many species of animals which were never even seen or heard of by men, their masters: either because they lived in places where men had never set foot, or because they were too small to be perceived. And men also did not become aware of a great many other species, until quite recently. The same may be said about plants, and a thousand other things. And, similarly, by means of their telescopes, men would from time to time perceive some star or planet, which until then, for thousands and thousands of years, had been unknown to them. And at once they would put it down among their possessions; for they imagined that the stars and planets were, so to speak, wicks which had been set up aloft, to give light to their lordships, who were very busy during the night.

GNOME. So that when, in the summer, they saw those little flames that shoot through the air at night, they must certainly have fancied them to be some spirit snuffing out the stars, in the service of mankind.

SPRITE. Yet now that they are all gone, the earth does not feel their loss. The streams have not ceased to flow, and the sea, although no longer used for shipping and trade, is not running dry.

GNOME. And the sun has not plastered its face with rust, as it did, according to Virgil, when Caesar died, but about whom I think it concerned itself as little as did the statue of Pompey.

DIALOGUE BETWEEN TORQUATO
TASSO AND HIS FAMILIAR SPIRIT

SPIRIT. How are you, Torquato?

TASSO. As a man may be in prison, and in trouble up to his neck.

SPIRIT. Never mind. After supper is no time to complain. Take heart, and let's laugh about it together.

TASSO. I'm not very good at that, but your presence and your conversation always comfort me. Come and sit down beside me.

SPIRIT. Sit down! That's not so easy for a spirit. But so be it: pretend that I am seated.

TASSO. Oh, if only I could see my Leonora again! Every time I think of her, I feel a shudder of delight from the crown of my head to the soles of my feet, and there is no vein or nerve in me that is not stirred. Sometimes, when I think of her, certain fancies and emotions come to life in me again, so that for a short time I still believe myself to be the same Torquato that I was, before I came to know misfortune and mankind, and for whom I now sometimes mourn, as for the dead. Truly, I would say that knowledge of the world and endurance of suffering are likely to bury and deaden within each one of us the man he used to be. From time to time that person wakes up in us again for a little while, but more and more seldom as the years pass; he withdraws farther and farther into himself, falling into a deeper sleep, until at last, even though life still goes on, he dies. Finally, I am amazed that the mere thought of a woman should have so much power to give new life, so to speak, to my spirit, and to make me forget so many calamities. And were it not that I have given up all hope of ever seeing her again, I should believe that I have not yet lost the faculty of being happy.

SPIRIT. Which do you consider sweeter: to see the beloved woman, or to think of her?

TASSO. I do not know. Certainly while she was near me, she seemed to me a woman: far away, she seemed and seems a goddess.

SPIRIT. These goddesses are so kind that when someone draws nigh to them, they suddenly lay aside their divinity and, casting off their haloes, hide them away, so as not to dazzle the mortal who is approaching.

TASSO. Alas, what you say is true. But does it not seem to you a great fault in women, that, put to the test, they prove to be so different from what we had imagined?

SPIRIT. I cannot see what fault it is of theirs, that they are made of flesh and blood, instead of nectar and ambrosia. What is there in this world that holds even a shadow or a thousandth part of the perfection that you attribute to women? And it also seems strange to me that, while you do not wonder at men being men—that is, unworthy and unlovable creatures—you should yet not be able to comprehend that women are not really angels.

TASSO. In spite of all this, I am dying with desire to see her and to speak with her again.

SPIRIT. Well, this very night I will bring her to you in your dreams: beautiful as in her youth and so courteous, that you will take heart and converse with her far more frankly and freely than you ever could in the past, until at the end you will take her hand, and she, gazing at you steadily, will fill your heart with such sweetness that it will overcome you. And tomorrow, during the whole day, whenever you recall this dream, your heart will leap with tenderness.

TASSO. Poor solace: a dream in exchange for the truth.

SPIRIT. What is truth?

TASSO. Pilate did not know, and neither do I.

SPIRIT. Well, I will answer for you. Know that between truth and a dream the only difference is that the latter can sometimes be very much fairer and sweeter than the former can ever be.

TASSO. So a delight only dreamed of may be as precious as a real one?

SPIRIT. I think so. Indeed I have heard about a man who, when the woman he loved appeared before him in a pleasant dream, avoided seeing her again or being with her all the next day, knowing that she would never be able to equal the image left in him during his sleep, and that reality, in wiping out that fictitious image, would deprive him of the extraordinary delight he drew from it. So we must not find fault with the ancients—who were much more swift, skilful, and diligent than we are, with regard to all the pleasures that a man can obtain—for seeking in various ways to enjoy the sweetness and delight of dreams. Nor should Pythagoras be blamed for having forbidden men to eat beans, because he believed them to destroy the peace of such dreams, by clouding them; and we must excuse the superstitious men who, before going to bed, would pray and make libations to Mercury, the bearer of dreams, so that he might bring them happy ones, and indeed would keep a carved image of that god at the foot of their bedsteads. Thus, since they could never find happiness in their waking hours, they sought it in their sleep; and I believe that in some way they partially succeeded, and that Mercury, more than the other gods, granted them their prayers.

TASSO. So that, since men are born and die solely to obtain pleasure, whether of the body or the mind, we had better make up our minds, if it consists solely or chiefly in dreams, to live only for the sake of dreaming, a conclusion to which, in truth, I can hardly bring myself.

SPIRIT. You have already accepted it, since you live and consent to live. But what is pleasure?

TASSO. I have not known it enough to say.

SPIRIT. No one knows it by experience, but only in theory: for pleasure is a conception, not a fact; a desire, not a reality; a sentiment which man conceives in his thoughts but does not realize—or rather an idea, not a sentiment at all. Do you not perceive that even in the very moment in which you enjoy a pleasure which you have desired intensely and pursued with indescribable toil and trouble, you are unable to find satisfaction in your enjoyment of those moments, but are always looking forward to a still greater and truer delight? It is in this expectation, indeed, that your pleasure consists, and you are almost constantly dwelling on the mirage of this same delight. And this always fades away at the instant at which you think you have attained it, leaving you with nothing but a blind hope of a greater and truer enjoyment in some future time, and the comfort of pretending, telling both yourself and your friends that you have enjoyed it—not only out of vanity, but in order to deceive yourself more completely. Therefore, whoever consents to live, does not really do so for any other purpose nor for any other use than to dream again: that is, to believe in a past or future happiness: both false and fanciful beliefs.

TASSO. But can a man never believe that he is happy now?

SPIRIT. If he could believe it, he would be so indeed. Tell me, do you remember a single moment in your life in which you could say to yourself, with complete sincerity and conviction: 'I am happy'? But every day you have said and do say sincerely, 'I will be happy' and sometimes, though less sincerely, 'I have been so'. So that pleasure is always a thing of the past or the future; never of the present.

TASSO. Which is as much as to say that it does not exist.

SPIRIT. So it seems.

TASSO. Even in dreams.

SPIRIT. Properly speaking.

TASSO. And yet pleasure is the whole object and purpose of our life, and by pleasure I mean happiness, which must in effect be pleasurable, from whatever origin it springs.

SPIRIT. Assuredly.

TASSO. So our life, since it never attains its object, must always be imperfect, and therefore living is, by its very nature, a tormented state.

SPIRIT. Perhaps.

TASSO. I see no 'perhaps' in it. But then, why do we live?
I mean, why do we consent to live?

SPIRIT. How should I know? You should know better, being
men.

TASSO. For my part, I swear I do not know.

SPIRIT. Ask a wiser man, and perhaps you will find someone
who will resolve your doubts.

TASSO. I will do so. But certainly the life I lead is nothing
but torment, for, apart from grief, tedium is also destroying me.

SPIRIT. What is tedium?

TASSO. I do not lack experience, to enable me to answer that
question. It seems to me that tedium is of the nature of air,
which fills up all the spaces between material things and
all the voids in each one of them; and whenever a body
changes its place and is not at once replaced by another,
tedium at once comes in. So all the intervals in human life
between pleasure and pain, are occupied by tedium. And
as, in the material world, according to the Peripatetics,
there is no vacuum, so there is also none in our life, except
when for some reason the mind has ceased to think. At
all other times the soul, even if considered as a separate
entity from the body, always contains one passion or another; just as a man, when free from pleasure or pain,
finds it necessary to be filled with tedium; which also is a
passion, no less than sorrow and delight.

SPIRIT. And as all your delights are of the same stuff as
cobwebs, most fragile, wide-meshed, and transparent—
so tedium enters into them, even as air penetrates a cob-
web, from every side and fills them. Truly I believe that
tedium means nothing more than a craving for pure
happiness, unsatisfied by pleasure and not perceptibly
wounded by wretchedness. And this craving, as we said
before, can never be gratified; so that true pleasure can
never be found. Thus the stuff of which human life is
made is partly sorrow and partly tedium; and we only
escape from one of them by falling into the other. And this

is not your peculiar destiny, but is common to all mankind.

TASSO. What remedies are there against this tedium?

SPIRIT. Sleep, opium, suffering. And this last is the strongest
of all: for while a man suffers, he is not bored at all.

TASSO. Rather than have recourse to such remedies, I am
content to endure tedium all my life. Yet a variety of
actions, occupations, and sensations, though they do not
deliver us from tedium, since they do not bring us true
delight, yet do lift and lighten it. But in this prison,
deprived of any human society, not even allowed to write,
reduced to finding a pastime in the ticking of a clock, or
in counting the planks, cracks, and worm-holes in the
beams of the ceiling, in observing the pattern of the brick-
work, in playing with the butterflies and gnats that fly
about the room, and passing almost all my time like this,
I have nothing which can in any way relieve me from the
burden of tedium.

SPIRIT. Tell me: how long have you been obliged to lead this
sort of life?

TASSO. Many weeks, as you know.

SPIRIT. Have you not observed, between the first day and the
present one, some variation in your distress?

TASSO. Certainly I felt it much more at first. For gradually
my mind, not occupied with anything else and with nothing to distract it, has grown accustomed to converse with
itself more freely and with greater pleasure than at first,
and has acquired the habit and power of talking to itself,
indeed of chatting, so that often it almost seems to me
that I have a whole company of people in my head conversing with me, and any trifling subject that comes into
my mind suffices for me to hold a fine conversation with
myself.

SPIRIT. You will see that this habit will grow upon you from
day to day until, when you are once more allowed to talk
to other men, you will feel more disoccupied in their
company, than in your solitude. And do not believe that

the habit of such a manner of life is formed only in men like you, who are already accustomed to meditation; for it happens, to a lesser or greater degree, to everyone. Besides, to be cut off from other men and, so to speak, from life itself, serves this purpose: that a man, even if sated by the world and enlightened and disillusioned about its nature, through his own experience, yet gradually accustoms himself to look at it again from a distance, whence it appears to him far more beautiful and valuable than from near by. And thus he forgets its vanity and misery, and begins to make again and almost to create a new world of his own, and to value, love, and desire life once more. And these hopes—unless he has lost any faint expectations of ever returning to human society—nourish and delight him as they did in his youth. So that solitude almost plays the role of youth, and certainly rejuvenates the mind, gives a new value and incentive to the imagination, and renews in a man of experience the joys of early innocence which you regret.

But now I will leave you, for I see that sleep is coming over you, and I must prepare the fine dream that I have promised you. So, between dreaming and weaving fancies, your life shall pass, with no other fruit that this world can give you and no other object to put before yourself each day on waking. Long have you held on to life, as it were, by your teeth, and the day will be a blessed one in which you can end it yourself, or are released from it. But in effect the hours will pass no more wearily for you in this prison than for your oppressor in his halls and gardens. Farewell.

TASSO. Farewell. But listen. Your conversation always comforts me. Not that it wholly dissipates my sadness, which is most often like a very black night, without moon or stars; while when you are with me, it is more like the shades of twilight, rather friendly than oppressive. But in order that I may summon you or find you again when I want you, tell me where you usually live?

SPIRIT. Don't you know that yet? In any strong wine.

NOTE BY LEOPARDI TO THE DIALOGUE BETWEEN
TORQUATO TASSO AND HIS FAMILIAR SPIRIT

(Composed in June 1824; first appeared, with two other
dialogues in the *Antologia* of Florence, LXI, in January
1826, and then in the Milanese edition of the *Operette
Morali* in 1827.)

'Torquato Tasso, during the time when his mind was
infirm, held an opinion similar to the famous one of
Socrates: that is, he believed that he saw, from time to
time, a kind and friendly spirit, and that he held many
long conversations with him. So we read in the life of
Tasso described by Manso, who was present at one of
these conversations or soliloquies, whichever we choose
to call them.'

K

DIALOGUE BETWEEN NATURE AND
AN ICELANDER

An Icelander who had travelled over the great part of the world and had lived in many different lands, was wandering in the heart of Africa. As he was crossing the Equator, in a place no man had ever visited before, something befell him which resembled what happened to Vasco da Gama, as he was sailing round the Cape of Good Hope, when he saw that very Cape, the keeper of the Southern Seas, coming towards him in the form of a giant, to dissuade him from entering those unknown waters. The Icelander saw in the distance a very large bust, which at first he believed to be of stone, like the colossal figures he had seen many years before on Easter Island. But as he came closer, he discovered that it was a great figure of a woman, sitting erect on the ground, with her back and elbow resting against a mountain. It was no statue, but a living woman, with a countenance both beautiful and terrible, and very black eyes and hair. She gazed at him intently, in silence, for some time, and at last she said:

NATURE. Who are you? and what do you seek in these lands where your race is unknown?

ICELANDER. I am a poor Icelander, who is attempting to run away from Nature; and having fled from her for almost all my life, in a hundred different regions of the earth, I am now attempting to escape from her here.

NATURE. So does the squirrel fly from the rattlesnake, until it falls into its jaws of its own accord. I am she from whom you are trying to escape.

ICELANDER. Nature?

NATURE. None other.

ICELANDER. This grieves me to the heart; I am certain that no greater misfortune than this could overtake me.

NATURE. You might have considered that I was likely to

dwell in these parts, where you must know that my power is more felt than elsewhere. But what was it that made you run away from me?

ICELANDER. You must know that in my early youth, a very short experience of life sufficed to persuade me of its vanity and of the folly of men, who are constantly at war with each other for the sake of pleasures which bring no delight and possessions which give no profit, and who endure and inflict upon each other innumerable anxieties and evils, which both distress and injure them. And the further they are from happiness, the more they seek it. For these reasons, having renounced all other desires, I decided to live an obscure and peaceful life, without causing any trouble to anyone; or attempting in any way to better my condition, or contending with other men for any earthly good; and having given up all hope of pleasure, a thing denied to our race, I had no other aim than the avoidance of suffering. I do not mean that I intended to abstain from every occupation or from physical toil; for you well know that fatigue is as unlike discomfort, as tranquillity is unlike idleness. But hardly had I begun to put this resolve into practice, than I at once discovered by experience how vain it is, if one lives among one's fellows, to believe it possible that, by causing no suffering to others, one can avoid being injured oneself; or that, even if one always gives way to other men, and is content with the least of everything, even that small respite or amount will not be denied to one. But I easily freed myself from the nuisance of other people, by leaving their company and taking refuge in solitude: a thing which can easily be obtained in my native island.

Having taken this step, and leading a life which lacked even a mirage of pleasure, I yet found that I could not avoid suffering; for the length of the winter, with its intense cold, and the extreme heat of the summer, which are characteristic of that region, were constantly tormenting me; and the fire, close to which I was obliged to spend most of my time, parched my flesh, while its smoke hurt my eyes, so that I could not preserve myself from continual discomfort either indoors or out. Nor could I preserve the tranquillity towards which all my wishes were directed, since fearful storms, both from land and sea, the rumblings and threatenings of Mount Hecla, and the dread of fires—very common in wooden houses like ours—never ceased to trouble me. Such discomforts as these, in a monotonous life which had no other desire or hope and hardly any other preoccupation than to achieve tranquillity, acquire a considerable importance, and seem much more weighty than they would be if the greater part of one's mind were occupied with the cares of civilized life or the troubles caused by other men.

Having thus observed that the more I withdrew and almost shrank within myself, so that my existence should neither cause trouble nor injury to anything in the world, the less could I prevent other things from disquieting and troubling me, I decided to try a change of country and of climate, and see if there was any part of the world where, if I gave no offence, I would not be offended, and where, if I could not find enjoyment, I would avoid suffering. And I also reached this decision owing to an idea that perhaps you had allotted to the human race only a single climate and certain regions of the earth (as you have done for all other kinds of animals and plants) and that, beyond this region, men could not prosper or even live, save with a difficulty and wretchedness which should not be imputed to you, but only to themselves, for having disregarded and gone beyond the boundaries which your laws have laid down for human habitation.

I searched through almost the whole world and became acquainted with almost every country, always keeping to my resolve of not causing any injury, or as little as possible, to any other creature, and only seeking a peaceful life. But I have been scorched with heat in the tropics, benumbed with cold at the poles, afflicted in temperate climates by the changeableness of the weather, and shaken everywhere by the violence of the elements. I have seen many places in which no day passes without a storm, which is the same as to say that every day you assault and attack the men who live there, who have never done you any harm. In other places the habitual serenity of the sky is balanced by the frequency of earthquakes, and the number and violence of volcanoes, or of subterranean commotions; while winds and furious hurricanes prevail in regions free from other forms of violence. Sometimes I have felt my roof giving way over my head beneath a great weight of snow; sometimes, owing to an excess of rain, I have been obliged to run away at full speed from streams pursuing me, as if I had done them some injury. Many wild beasts, to whom I had not given the least provocation, have tried to devour me, many snakes to poison me; and in several places flying insects came close to stripping my very bones. I will not enumerate the daily perils by which a man is threatened every day; so that an ancient philosopher could find no better prescription against fear, than the observation that everything should equally be feared. Disease, too, has not spared me, even though I always have been and still am, not only temperate but continent with regard to physical pleasures.

I often greatly wonder that you should have instilled into us such a strong and insatiable craving for pleasure, without which our life, being deprived of its most natural desire, is an imperfect thing; and that, on the other hand, you should have ordained that the enjoyment of such pleasures should be the most harmful of all things human to our physical health and strength, the most calamitous in its general effects, and the most pernicious to the length of life itself. But even though I have almost always and completely abstained from every pleasure, I have not been able to avoid many and various diseases, some of which have threatened my life and others the loss of a limb, or have offered the prospect of perpetually living a life even more wretched than before; and all of them have oppressed me, body and soul, with a thousand hardships and sufferings. Certainly, though each one of us discovers, in times of illness, new and unfamiliar evils and an even greater unhappiness than usual (as if human life were not already sufficiently wretched), you have not granted to us, in compensation, periods of great and exceptional good health, to provide us with some extraordinary delights both in their nature and intensity. In regions which mostly lie beneath the snow, I have nearly been blinded, as often happens to the Laplanders in their own country. Sun and air—elements which are vital and necessary to our life and therefore cannot be shunned—constantly injure us, the one by its heat and even its light, the other by its dampness or cold; so that a man can never be exposed to the one or the other without some major or minor inconvenience.[1]

In short, I do not recollect having spent a single day of my life without some form of suffering, while I cannot even count those which have gone by without a trace of enjoyment. Therefore I perceive that suffering is as unavoidable and necessary for us as the lack of pleasure, and that a peaceful life, of any kind, is as impossible as an unquiet one without wretchedness. And thus I have reached the conclusion that you are the avowed enemy of mankind and of all other animals and even of your own works: for now you ensnare us, now threaten us, now attack us, now sting us, now smite us, now tear us to pieces, and always both injure and pursue us. By habit and by destiny

[1] We should perhaps remember that, during his winters in Recanati, Leopardi often spent several months without setting foot out of doors; that he drove all the way from Florence to Naples in a tightly sealed carriage; that in Bologna he attempted to find some warmth in winter by placing himself in a sack lined with feathers, from which he would emerge looking like Papageno; and that in Florence, during a long attack of ophthalmia, he was so much afraid of any ray of light that for several months he spent his days not only in a darkened room but in bed, with bed-curtains drawn, often not getting up till dusk, and going to bed before the dawn.

you are the destroyer of your own family, your children, your own flesh and blood. Therefore I have ceased to hope, having realized that while men may cease to persecute those who fly or hide from them owing to a real wish for escape or obscurity, you, for no reason whatever, will never cease to pursue us until we are completely laid low. And I already see the approach of the sad and bitter years of old age: a true and evident evil, or rather, an accumulation of all the most burdensome evils and troubles—and these, too, are not accidental, but are planned and ordered by you to be the fate of all living creatures. All this each one of us foresees, from the time of his childhood, and begins to prepare himself for from his twenty-fifth year, as he observes the gradual process, through no fault of his own, of decay and loss; so that barely one third of the life of man is given up to an early flowering, a few moments only to maturity and perfection, and all the rest to decline and the evils that it brings.

NATURE. But did you think that the world was made for your sake? You must have known that in my works, my laws, and my operations, with a very few exceptions, I have always been ruled, as I am now, by considerations which have little to do with the happiness or unhappiness of mankind. When I injure you in any way or by any means, I very seldom am aware of it, as I also usually do not know when I am giving you some delight or benefit; and I do not do certain things or perform certain actions, as you believe, for either your pleasure or your profit. And finally, if I should happen to destroy you, I would do so unawares.

ICELANDER. Let us suppose that a man invited me of his own accord and very pressingly to his country house; and that I accepted, to please him, and were given a crumbling and ruined cell to dwell in, where I was in perpetual danger of being crushed, and which was damp, stinking, open to wind and rain. Imagine that he took no trouble to entertain me or to make me comfortable, but scarcely furnished me with enough food to keep me alive, and that in addition he permitted his sons and household to insult, mock, threaten, and beat me. If I complained to him of this ill-treatment, he answered: 'Did I build this house for you? Do I keep my children and household for your service? I have other things to think about than your amusements and your comfort.' To this I might reply: 'My friend, just as you did not build your house for my use, so it was in your power not to invite me to dwell there. But since it was you who wished me to come, was it not your part to arrange, in so far as you could, for me to live there without suffering and danger?' So I say now. I well know that you have not created the world for the service of men; I am more inclined to believe that you created and ordered it for the express purpose of treating them ill. But now I ask you: Did I request you to bring me into the world? Or did I intrude into it violently, against your will? If you yourself put me there with your own hands, by your own desire and without my knowledge, and in such a manner that I could neither refuse nor resist, is it not your duty, if not to keep me happy and contented within this kingdom of yours, at least to forbid that I should be tormented and molested, and to see that my dwelling there should do me no harm? And I say this, not only for myself, but on behalf of the whole human race, and of all other animals and living creatures.

NATURE. You plainly show that you have not realized that the life of the universe is a perpetual circle of production and destruction, both linked to each other in such a way that each one of them constantly serves the other, and is necessary to conserve the existence of the world; which, if either of them should fail, would swiftly be dissolved. Thus, if anything within the world were free from suffering, the world itself would be harmed.

ICELANDER. All philosophers, I am told, reason like this. But since that which is destroyed suffers, and that which destroys derives no pleasure, and is in turn destroyed itself, tell me what no philosopher will say: for whose pleasure or use is this most unhappy life of the universe preserved, at the expense of the suffering and death of all the things composing it?

While they were engaged in these discussions and others of the same kind, it is said that two lions appeared. They were so thin and so worn out by hunger that they hardly had the strength to devour the Icelander; but so they did; and, having recovered a little, kept themselves alive for another day.

But there are some people who deny this tale, and say instead that a very violent wind, which rose up while the Icelander was speaking, cast him to the ground, and piled above him a splendid mausoleum of sand, beneath which he was completely dried up and turned into a fine mummy. He was then discovered by some travellers, and placed in the museum of a European city, I know not which.

DIALOGUE BETWEEN FREDERICK RUYSCH AND HIS MUMMIES

Chorus of the Dead

Alone eternal in the world, to whom
Every created thing
Devolves, in you, O Death,
Our naked being finds rest;
Joyless, indeed, but safe
From the ancient pain of thought; profoundest night
From the bewildered brain
Blots out that grievous load;
The dry ghost feeling never impulse more
To hope or to desire
Is likewise free from all distress and fear,
And with no tedium consumes the slow
And vacant centuries.
We lived: and as a terror of the night
And an oppressive dream
Is troubled recollection in the mind
Of child as yet unweaned,
The memory remains
Of our lifetime; but far removed from fear
Is it in the recalling. What were we?—
That bitter point of time
Which bore the name of life?
A dark and awful thing
Is life to our conceiving, as appears
To thought of them that live
This undiscovered Death. And as from Death
The living start appalled, just so with us
Our naked being recoils
Back, from the flame of life;
Joyless, indeed, but safe;
Because the Fates deny
To mortals happiness, and to the Dead.

RUYSCH [*outside his studio, looking through the cracks in the door*]. What the deuce! Who has taught these dead men music, so that they crow like cocks at midnight? Truly I am in a cold sweat, and feel almost more dead than they are. I little thought, when I preserved them from decay, that I would see them come to life again.* But so it is: for all my philosophy, I am trembling from head to foot. A plague upon the devil who tempted me to bring such creatures into my house. I don't know what to do. If I shut them up in here, how can I be sure that they won't open the door or pass through the keyhole, and visit me in my bed? It isn't fit for me to call for help, from fear of the dead. Come on, let's gather up our courage, and try to frighten them instead.

[*Entering.*] Children, what are you playing at? Don't you remember that you are dead? What does this uproar mean? Perhaps you are so puffed up by the Czar's visit† that you consider you have ceased to be subject to the old laws? I presume you are doing this for fun, not in earnest. If you have truly risen up again, I congratulate you; but I can't afford to keep the living, as I did the dead: so get out of my house. If what they tell of vampires is true, and you belong to their species, seek other blood to drink, for I am not inclined to give you mine, though I was liberal of the artificial one I put into your veins. In short, if you will continue to be quiet and silent, as you have been hitherto, we shall get on very well together, and you shall lack for nothing in my house; if not, beware, for I will take up the door's bar and kill you all.

MUMMY. Don't be angry: I promise you we will all stay as dead as we are, without your killing us.

RUYSCH. What has come over you, then, to make you sing?

MUMMY. A little while ago, exactly at midnight, the great mathematical year, about which the ancients have written so much, was completed; and this is also the first time that the dead can speak. And not only we, but all the dead—in every churchyard, every tomb, in the depths of

the sea, beneath the snow and sand, under the open sky,
or wherever they may be—have sung at midnight, like us,
the song that you have heard.

RUYSCH. And for how long will they go on singing or speaking?

MUMMY. They have finished singing already. They may go on
speaking for another quarter of an hour. Then they will fall
back into silence again, until the completion of another year.

RUYSCH. If this is true, I don't think you will disturb my
sleep again. So pray speak to each other freely, for I will
gladly stand aside here and listen, out of curiosity, without disturbing you.

MUMMY. We can only speak in answer to a living man. Any
one of us who has nothing to reply to the living, must
fall into silence again as soon as his song is over.

RUYSCH. I am truly sorry, for I fancy it would be very entertaining to hear what you would say to each other, if you
could speak.

MUMMY. Even if we could, you would hear nothing; for we
should have nothing to say to each other.

RUYSCH. A thousand questions come into my mind which I
should like to put to you. But as our time is short and
leaves no room for choice, tell me briefly what you felt in
your body and soul at the point of death.

MUMMY. I was not aware of the exact moment of death.

THE OTHER MUMMIES. Nor were we.

RUYSCH. How was that?

MUMMY. Just as you do not perceive the moment when you
fall asleep, however hard you try.

RUYSCH. But falling asleep is a natural thing.

MUMMY. And don't you think that death is natural? Show me
a man, beast, or plant, that does not die.

RUYSCH. I no longer wonder that you go about singing and
talking, if you were not aware of your death.

> 'So he, incautious of the fatal blow,
>   Continued fighting, though a dead man now.'

So wrote an Italian poet.[1] I expected people of your kind
to know a little more about death than the living. But, to
return to the point, did not you feel any pain at the instant
of your death?

MUMMY. What sort of pain could there be, if one is not aware
of it when it comes?

RUYSCH. At any rate, everyone is convinced that the sensation of dying is most painful.

MUMMY. Almost as if death were a sensation, and not rather
the contrary.

RUYSCH. And both those men who hold the views of the
Epicureans, with regard to the nature of the soul, and
those who follow the common doctrine, mostly agree
with what I am saying: they believe that dying is, by its
very nature, an intense and incomparable pain.

MUMMY. Well then, pray inquire of both the one and the
other: if a man is unaware of the point at which his vital
functions are suspended, to a greater or lesser degree, by
sleep or lethargy or a stroke, or any other cause, how can
he be conscious of the moment in which these same
faculties cease completely—and not for a short space of
time, but for ever? And besides, how can it be that a
vivid emotion should be felt at the time of death, and still
more, that death itself should be a vivid sensation? When
the capacity to feel has not only become weaker and more
restricted, but has been reduced to such infinitesimal terms
that it is failing and ceasing to exist, do you believe that
anyone is capable of a strong sensation? Could this very
extinction of the faculty of feeling be in itself a very strong
sensation? Yet you must observe that even those who die
of acute and painful diseases, find peace and rest for a
while before they draw their last breath, so that plainly
their life has dwindled to so very little, that it is no longer

[1] The reference is to some lines by Francesco Berni in his *Orlando Inna-
morato*:

> 'Così colui, del colpo non accorto,
> Andava combattendo, ed era morto,'

strong enough for pain, and so their strength comes to an end before their life. That is what you should say from us to whoever believes that, on the point of death, he will die of pain.

RUYSCH. This reasoning will perhaps satisfy the Epicureans, but not those who hold a different opinion about the nature of the soul; as I have done in the past, and shall do still more in the future, now that I have heard the dead speak and sing. For, believing death to consist in a separation of the soul from the body, they cannot understand how these two substances, which had been joined and fused together so as to form one single person, can be parted without very great violence and anguish.

MUMMY. Tell me: is the spirit fastened to the body by some nerve, muscle, or membrane, which must necessarily be severed when the spirit departs? Or is it a member of the body, which must be torn or cut away violently? Don't you see that the soul only leaves the body when it is prevented from dwelling there and when there is no place left for it, not because of any violence that tears it out by the roots? Tell me, too: when the soul entered, did it feel itself strongly pressed or fastened in or, as you say, fused with the body? Why therefore should it feel torn to pieces on going out, or feel any violent sensation? Be assured, that the coming-in and going-out of the soul are equally quiet, easy, and gentle.

RUYSCH. Then what is death, if it is not pain?

MUMMY. Pleasure rather than otherwise. You must know that dying, like falling asleep, does not take place in a single instant, but by degrees. It is true that these degrees vary, according to the different causes and kinds of death. In the last of these moments, death, like sleep, brings neither pain nor pleasure. In the earlier moments it cannot cause pain, for pain is a vital thing; and by that time, that is, when death is approaching, a man's senses are themselves dying, that is they are much weakened. Death may well be a cause of pleasure; for pleasure is not always a vital thing; indeed, perhaps the greater part of human enjoyment consists in a kind of languor. Thus it is that men's senses are capable of giving them pleasure even when they are near to extinction, since very often languor is in itself a pleasure, especially when it brings freedom from pain; for you well know that the cessation of any pain or discomfort is in itself a pleasure. So that the languor of death ought to be all the more welcome, in proportion to the extent of the pain from which it frees a man. For my part, although in the hour of death I did not pay much heed to what I was feeling, because the doctors forbade me to exert my brain, I remember that the sensation I had was not unlike the pleasure that a man feels when the languor of sleep comes over him.

THE OTHER MUMMIES. We too remember something like that.

RUYSCH. It may be as you say; although all those with whom I have had occasion to speak about this, hold a very different opinion; but, so far as I remember, they could not speak from their own experience. Now tell me: in the hour of death, when you felt that sweetness, did you believe that you were dying and that this delight was a courtesy of death? Or did you have some other fancy?

MUMMY. Until I was actually dead, I never believed that I would not recover; and up to the last moment in which I had power to think, I hoped that at least an hour or two more was still left to me; and this I believe happens to many men, when they are dying.

THE OTHER MUMMIES. It was the same with us.

RUYSCH. Cicero says that no one is so worn out that he does not promise himself at least one more year of life. But how did you perceive, at last, that your spirit had left the body? Tell me, how did you know that you were dead? They do not answer. Children, don't you hear me? The quarter of an hour must have gone by. Let's touch them gently. Yes, they are quite dead again; there's no danger of their frightening me any more. Let's go back to bed.

NOTES BY LEOPARDI ON THE DIALOGUE BETWEEN FREDERICK RUYSCH AND HIS MUMMIES

(Composed in 1824, first published in 1827.)

* See Fontenelle, *Eloge de mons. Ruysch.* The means used by Ruysch to preserve his corpses consisted in injections of a certain fluid which he himself prepared, which had a miraculous effect.

† Ruysch's study was twice visited by Czar Peter I.

IN PRAISE OF BIRDS

Aemilius, a solitary philosopher, as he sat one spring morning with his books in the shade of his country house, reading, was struck by the birds singing in the fields, and gradually ceased to read, giving himself up to listening and musing. At last he took up his pen, and, still sitting in the same place, wrote the following words:

Birds are by nature the gayest creatures in the world. I do not say this because when you see or hear them they always give you pleasure, but rather because I mean that in themselves they are more light-hearted and joyful than any other living creature. Other creatures mostly seem serious and grave, and a few even appear melancholy; they seldom give any token of joy, or only rarely and briefly; in most of their enjoyments and pleasures they do not show delight or any symptom of merriment; and if indeed they rejoice in green fields, in wide and charming views, in bright sunshine, in sweet, clear breezes, they give no outer sign of it; except that it is said, according to Xenophon, that hares, at night, when the moon is up, leap and play with each other, taking pleasure in the moonlight.

Birds are mostly very gay both in their movements and their aspect; and their power to delight us springs precisely from this, that their whole appearance and behaviour is universally such as to show a special disposition for joy and happiness—an appearance which need not be considered a vain illusion. Every delight and pleasure of theirs causes them to sing: and the greater the delight or pleasure, the greater is their diligence and care in singing. And as they sing for most of the time, we must conclude that they are usually contented and glad. And although it has been observed that when they are mating they sing still better and more often and at greater length than at any other time, yet we must not think that they are not also moved by other delights and pleasures than those of love. For it is noticeable that they

L

sing more on a clear and serene day than on a dark and stormy one; and they fall silent during storms, or during any other fear that may overcome them, and when it is over, they come out again, singing and making merry together. So, too, we perceive that they are wont to sing in the early morning, at waking, being moved to do so partly by their joy in a new day and partly by the pleasure that every creature feels at being restored and refreshed by sleep. They also take great pleasure in the gaiety of green fields, in fertile little valleys, in pure and shining streams, in a beautiful landscape. And in this it is noticeable that what seems agreeable and delightful to us, also seems so to them. . . .

Certainly it was a wise provision of nature to assign both song and flight to the same creatures, so that those whose task it is to delight other living beings with their voice, should usually be in a high place, from which it can extend over a wider space and reach a larger number of listeners, and also so that the air, which is the element given up to sound, should be peopled by vocal and musical creatures. Truly much comfort and delight is brought by bird-song, and not, to my mind, any less to other creatures than to men. And I believe that this does not merely arise from the sweetness of the sound, however great it may be, nor from its variety, nor from their mutual exchange, but rather from the sense of gladness inherent in the nature of song in general, and in particular, in bird-song—which is, one may say, like the bird's laughter, which it utters when it is glad and satisfied with its lot.

From this we might almost conclude that birds share the human gift of laughter, which other creatures do not possess; and this is why some people have thought that, just as man is defined as an intellectual and rational animal, he should also equally be defined as a laughing animal; for it would appear that laughter is as much a peculiarly human attribute as reason. Certainly it is a wonderful thing that man, the most tormented and wretched of all creatures, should possess the faculty of laughter, which is denied to every other animal. And the use that is made of this faculty is remarkable, too: for one can see that many men in some terrible trouble or spiritual affliction, or others who have lost all love of life and are convinced of the vanity of every human good, or are incapable of joy and deprived of any hope, can yet still laugh. Indeed, the more they become aware of the vanity of the pleasures we have spoken of, and of life's wretchedness, and the less they hope for gladness or are inclined to enjoy it, the more are such men inclined to laughter. For the nature of laughter, and its deepest origins and forms, can hardly be defined or explained, in so far as they belong to our spirit, except by saying that laughter is a sort of temporary madness, or else raving or delirium—since men, who are never fully satisfied or delighted by anything whatever, can have no reasonable and just cause for laughter. Moreover it would be curious to learn where and on what occasion men first came to discover and use this faculty of theirs. For there is no doubt that in a primitive state men are mostly serious, like other creatures, and indeed seem melancholy. So I am of the opinion that laughter not only appeared in the world later than tears, which can hardly be denied, but also that some time elapsed before it was first experienced and known. And during all that time, as Virgil says, a mother did not smile at her baby, nor did he recognize her with a smile. For if now, at least wherever people live civilized lives, men begin to laugh soon after their birth, they do so chiefly from imitation, having seen other people laugh. And I am inclined to believe that the first occasion and cause of human laughter was probably drunkenness, a state peculiar to the human race. . . .

That birds should both be and appear to be happier than other creatures, is very natural. For truly, as I suggested at first, their disposition is more fit for enjoyment and happiness. First, they do not seem to be subject to tedium. They are constantly changing place; they pass from one country to another, however far away, and from the loftiest to the lowest region of the air, swiftly and with marvellous ease.

They see and experience most numerous and varied things; they constantly exercise their body; and they are especially rich in their external life. All other creatures, provided their needs are satisfied, like to be quiet and idle; none of them, except for fish and some of the flying insects, go wandering about for long periods, just as a pastime. So, too, a man of the woods, except to provide for his daily needs, which only require little time or trouble, or unless he is driven away by a storm or pursued by some wild beast, hardly ever moves a step, but usually prefers idleness and inactivity; he will spend whole days sitting lazily in silence in his rough hut, or out of doors, or in the clefts and caves of cliffs or rocks.

Birds, on the other hand, stay a very short time in the same place; they come and go continually for no reason whatever; they make use of their flight as an amusement, and, having flown for pleasure for hundreds of miles from their habitual home, they fly back again the same evening. Even during the short time that they stay in one place, they are seldom motionless: they are always turning this way and that, wheeling, bending, stretching, shaking themselves, and fluttering, with an indescribable liveliness, swiftness, and agility of motion. In short, from the moment that a bird emerges from its egg until its death, except for short intervals for sleep, it does not rest a moment. In view of all these observations, it seems to me that we may affirm that the natural state of other animals, including men, is rest; that of birds, motion.

These external qualities and characteristics of theirs correspond to those of their spirit, which render them more fit for happiness than other creatures. Their hearing being very sharp and their sight very clear and accurate, to a degree which we can hardly imagine, they can enjoy wide and varied views every day and can discover from aloft, all at once, as great an expanse of the earth and as many regions as a man can hardly embrace simultaneously in his mind. One infers that they must have very great strength and vitality, and a great deal of imagination. Not the deep, fervid, and tempestuous imagination of Dante or Tasso, which is a most fatal endowment, and the source of very serious and constant anxiety and anguish; but the rich, changing, light, unstable imagination of children, which is a very rich source of pleasant and happy thoughts, of sweet errors, of manifold comforts and delights, and the greatest and most fruitful gift that nature has courteously granted to living creatures. So that birds possess a generous portion of the good and useful aspects of this faculty, without partaking of its harmful and painful side. And just as they have a great deal of external life, so, too, they are rich in what lies within, but in such a manner that this abundance produces boons and pleasures for them, as for children; not harm and great wretchedness, as for most men. For even as a bird has an obvious resemblance to a child in its vivacity and mobility, so we may reasonably believe that it is like one in its inner qualities. And if the blessings of childhood were enjoyed in later years, and the evils of age were no greater than those of childhood, man could perhaps reasonably endure his life with patience. . . .

In short, as Anacreon wished he could transform himself into a mirror, to be constantly gazed upon by the lady he loved, or into a tunic to cover her, or into an ointment to anoint her, or into water to cleanse her, or into a girdle to encircle her waist, or into a pearl at her neck, or into a shoe, that at least she might press him with her foot, so I should like for a while to be changed into a bird, to savour their contentment and delight.

8. Milan, Bologna, Florence, Pisa 1823–8

'Qu'est-ce donc que le bonheur? Et si le bonheur n'est pas, qu'est-ce donc que la vie?'[1]

I

After his return from Rome, Leopardi spent two years in Recanati which were almost entirely lacking in any external incident. Soon after his return, he wrote a revealing and intimate letter, in French, to a young Belgian writer whom he had met in Rome.

Assuredly, my dear friend, either one should not go on living, or one should always continue to feel, to love, to hope. Sensibility would be the most precious of gifts, if only one knew how to make use of it, or if there were anything in the world to which to apply it. I have told you that the art of avoiding suffering is now the only one that I attempt to learn. That is because I have given up the hope of living. If from the time of my first attempts I had not already been convinced that this hope was a vain and frivolous one for me, I would never have followed or even discovered any path but that of enthusiasm. For some time I felt the emptiness of life like a real burden, weighing heavily upon my soul. All that existed for me was the nothingness of things. It always loomed before me like a terrible phantom; I saw nothing but the desert around me, I could not conceive how it was possible to subject oneself to the daily cares that life demands, being very certain that they would never lead to anything. This thought obsessed me so much that I feared it would cause me to lose my reason.

In truth, my friend, the world does not know where its

[1] Leopardi to Jacopssen, 23 June 1823.

true interests lie. I am prepared to admit, if you wish, that virtue, like everything else that is beautiful and great, is only an illusion. But if this illusion were a common one, if all men believed in it and wished to be virtuous, if they were compassionate, kind, generous, magnanimous, enthusiastic, in a word, if everyone had sensibility (for I make no distinction between sensibility and what is called virtue), should we not be happier? Would not each man find a thousand resources in society, and—since human happiness cannot consist in reality—should not society attempt, in so far as possible, to make these illusions come true?

It is true that a habit of reflection, which always belongs to sensitive natures, often destroys a capacity for action and even for enjoyment. An excess of the inner life will always incline a man towards the outer, but at the same time renders him incapable of dealing with it. He embraces everything, he would like to be perpetually fulfilled; yet everything escapes him, precisely because it is smaller than his capacity. He even exacts of his own slightest actions, words, gestures, movements, more grace and perfection than it is possible for any man to attain. And so, since he can never be satisfied with himself nor cease from self-examination, and always mistrusts his own strength, he cannot even achieve what everyone else can manage.

What then is happiness, my dear friend? And if there is no happiness, what is life?[1]

During 1824 most of Leopardi's energies were devoted to the composition of the Operette Morali, *and his letters were comparatively few. One of them, however, addressed to his cousin, Giuseppe Melchiorri, who had asked him for some occasional verses, must be quoted here, as it describes very clearly how his poems were written.*

Dear Peppino, you were not wrong to make that promise for me, for you must have thought that I was like everyone

[1] *Epistolario*, III, To A. Jacopssen: Recanati, 23 June 1823.

else who writes verse. But you must know that in this, as in everything else, I am different from everyone else, and very inferior. And as to the verses, an understanding of my nature may be of service to you for some similar future occasion.

I have only written a very few and brief poems in my life. In writing them I have never followed anything but a brief inspiration (or frenzy) during which, in the course of a couple of minutes, I conceived the plan and arrangement of the whole composition. This done, I usually wait until another moment returns, and when it comes—which is usually not until some months later—I then begin to compose, but so slowly that I cannot finish a poem, however short, in less than two or three weeks. This is my method, and if inspiration does not come of its own accord, water would spring out of a log more easily than a single verse from my brain. Others can write poetry at will, but I do not possess this faculty at all, and however much you implored me, it would be in vain—not because I don't wish to please you, but because I can't.[1]

There is only one occasion on which Leopardi, in this respect, overcame his natural tendencies and wrote a poem to order. It was in Bologna in the following winter, and the poem was not written at the request of any great man of letters or fine lady, but of Angelina, who had been a maid in casa Leopardi, *and who, having married an excellent cook, often asked the poet to dinner. 'I shall eat very well', he wrote to his sister, and in return he sent Angelina a sonnet (which has unfortunately disappeared), written at her request 'for a young priest on saying his first Mass'. Thus what had been refused to many others was not denied to kind Angelina and her* tagliatelle.

In the spring of 1825 the Operette Morali *were completed, and Leopardi, still marooned in Recanati, felt once again to the full the empty dreariness of his daily life. After a silence of many months, he sent a description of it to Giordani:*

[1] *Epist.* III, Recanati, 5 March 1824.

I study day and night for as long as my health allows. When it can stand no more, I spend a few months in walking round my room; then I go back to my studies, and that is how I live. As to the kind of studies I pursue, they are changed, even as I am changed from what I was. Everything that is sentimental or eloquent bores me, and seems to me to have a foolish or ridiculously childish flavour. I seek nothing now but the truth, which I used to hate and detest so much. . . . And now I clearly perceive that when passion is extinguished, no source or foundation of pleasure is left to one's studies but a vain curiosity, the satisfaction of which yet has much power to please. . . .

I am here without any hope of getting away. I would gladly try to entrust myself to change, attempting to earn a little bread by my pen in some big city, but I see no way of getting enough to keep me from dying of hunger the day after I left. . . . Farewell, my soul, I love you with all the strength of my frozen heart.[1]

A few weeks later, however, a most unexpected opportunity did arise: his publisher in Milan, Antonio Stella, wrote asking him to go to Milan to prepare for him a complete edition of Cicero's works, with an Italian translation, while staying with him in his own house. He gratefully accepted and on his way spent ten days in Bologna, which are remarkable as being one of the few periods of his life of which he had nothing but good to say.

I sigh for Bologna [he wrote to Carlo after reaching Milan], where I made more friendships in nine days than during five months in Rome, where no one thinks of anything but living gaily, without being diplomatic, where strangers can hardly rest from the numerous kindnesses that are bestowed on them, where men of talent are invited out to dinner nine days a week, where Giordani assures me that I could live better than in any Italian city except Florence. . . . In Bologna men are wasps without a sting, and believe

[1] *Epist.* III, Recanati, 6 May 1825.

me, I have come to agree with Giordani and Brighenti that kindness of heart really does exist there, and indeed is very frequent, and that the human race there is different from what you and I believed.[1]

He persuaded Stella that he might supervise the progress of his work from Bologna instead of Milan, and moved there, with the intention of settling down for some time, at the end of September. Here, after a long winter of ill-health, he enjoyed, for the first time, the sweets of literary success, surrounded by a group of assiduous and apparently very patient friends, who sat with him in the dark, to rest his eyes, satisfied his perpetual craving for ices and sweets, put up with his frequent complaints about the cold, the heat, the light, the noise, and shared with him their Christmas dinner and their Paschal lamb. One of his new friends was Count Carlo Pepoli, an elegant young man of his own age, to whom he dedicated a poem in the manner of Parini, and Pepoli, who was the Vice-President of the Accademia dei Felsinei—one of the provincial academies that were to be found all over Italy, on the model of the famous Roman academy, L'Arcadia—invited him to recite these verses at one of their Academy meetings.

This was a form of entertainment about which Leopardi himself had always been very scornful. To read one's own works aloud, he wrote, was 'a plague, a public calamity'.

Italians, Frenchmen, Englishmen, Germans, white-haired men, very wise in all other matters, full of wit and valour; men who are familiar with social life, who have finished manners, who are quick to note other men's follies and to smile at them, all, when there is an opportunity of reciting their own work, become like cruel children.[2]

But these opinions did not, on this occasion, hold him back.

On Easter Monday evening I gave a recitation in the Casino of the Accademia dei Felsinei, in the presence of the

[1] *Epist.* III, Milan, 31 July 1825.
[2] *Poesie e Prose*, II, p. 17: *Pensieri*, XX.

Legate and the flower of the aristocracy of Bologna, both men and women. . . . I am told that my verses had a great effect, and that everyone, of both sexes, is anxious to read them.[1]

He felt, he told his father, that he had now entered 'the great world'. 'How fortunate you are!' exclaimed Paolina in her reply, and Carlo's warm congratulations, too, had a wistful note: 'Success is a thing that greatly resembles happiness.'[2]

II

After some fifteen months in Milan and Bologna, during which time he supported himself entirely, Leopardi returned to Recanati, and this time—perhaps owing to his break with Contessa Malvezzi, described in an earlier chapter—not entirely unwillingly. A few days after his return he was noting in the Zibaldone:

Jerocles' observation in his book *On Brotherly Love* is very fine, that since human life resembles an unceasing war . . . our brothers, parents, and relations are given to us as our allies. And I myself remember that, while I was away from my family, even though I was surrounded by well-disposed persons and had no enemies, I lived in a constant state of apprehension and timidity . . . and on the contrary, returning home, I felt a lively sense of security, courage, and peace of mind.[3]

But this state of contentment did not last long. By December he was writing:

I spend my mornings in working, my evenings in shivering and swearing. . . . My body is perhaps a little less cold than in Bologna, but my spirit feels a deadly chill, and every hour seems to me a thousand, until I can get away again.[4]

[1] *Epist.* IV, Bologna 4 April 1826.   [2] Ibid. 7 April 1826.
[3] *Zibaldone*, II, pp. 1054–5 (Recanati, 16 November 1826).
[4] *Epist.* IV, 15 December 1826.

At last, however, the spring came, and he was able to set forth to the city he had always most wished to visit—Florence—which was at this time the centre of a most active intellectual life. Two remarkable men had brought this about: a Tuscan aristocrat, Marchese Gino Capponi, and a merchant of Swiss origin, Gian Pietro Vieusseux, who had founded in Florence a library and reading-room, the Gabinetto Scientifico Letterario Vieusseux, which was also a centre of Liberal opinion and of literary conversation. 'How delightful it is,' said one of the guests, 'on a winter's night, to stay in a warm room in the company of so many able men, all conversing gently about letters and the arts!'

Vieusseux warmly welcomed the poet on his arrival in Florence, found him lodgings, offered him work, and introduced him at one of his literary parties. 'His expression', noted a fellow guest, 'is mild, his manners gentle and courteous, but his body has a defect, the height of his shoulders. He speaks very little, is pale and seems to be melancholy.' Everyone was most cordial to him, but he was not well enough to enjoy it; he had toothache, his eyes were troubling him, he sometimes had not enough money to buy his supper—and worst of all, in the midst of so many cultivated men, he found that he was still alone. For the Florentine Liberals had passionately embraced a number of convictions that Conte Monaldo's son could never share: they believed in the amelioration of the human lot by education and legislative reform; they demanded the abolition of slavery and of capital punishment; they valued literature chiefly as an instrument of social and political progress. In a society which held such convictions as these, Leopardi could not feel at home.

When the winter came he decided—since he would not return to Recanati—to try the milder climate of Pisa, and settled down in lodgings there. He had a room with light, linen, and service; dinner in his room at any time he pleased, a fire in the scaldino *all day and his bed warmed at night, and in a letter to Vieusseux he made use of an expression we have seldom heard from his lips: 'I am content.'*

The appearance of Pisa [he wrote to Paolina] gives me far more pleasure than that of Florence; the *lung'Arno* is so beautiful a sight, so wide and magnificent, so gay and smiling, that one falls in love with it. I have seen nothing like it in Florence, Milan, or Rome, and really I doubt whether in the whole of Europe many such sights could be found. It is a pleasure to stroll there in the winter, because the air is almost spring-like; and at certain hours of the day that part of the town is full of people, on foot or in carriages. One hears ten or twenty languages spoken, while brilliant sunshine lights up the gilding of the cafés, the shops full of frivolities, and the windows of the palaces and houses, all of fine architecture. . . . As for the rest, Pisa is a blending of a big town and a little one, of town and country—a romantic combination, such as I have never seen elsewhere. To every other charm, its beautiful language must be added—and I will add, too, that I am well, am eating with appetite, and have a room looking out westwards over a great orchard— with so wide a view that one can see far towards the horizon.[1]

The fields and lanes of Pisa reminded him—now that he had got away—of those of Recanati.

There is here a delightful path which I call 'the path of memories', and I walk there when I want to dream with my eyes open.

In the foreground of his dreams there was, once again, a young girl: Teresa Lucignani, the sister-in-law of his landlord, a child of not yet sixteen, with blue eyes and large fair curls. What he felt about her—or was it his memories of Nerina and Silvia?—he set down soon after in the Zibaldone.

She has in her face, her movements, her voice, something —I know not what—almost divine that nothing can equal. Whatever her character and taste may be; be she gay or melancholy, capricious or serious, lively or modest, this pure, untouched, fresh flower of youth, this untouched

[1] *Epist.* V, Pisa, 12 November 1827.

hope that you see in her face and gestures, or imagine, as you watch her, to exist in her and for her; this air of innocence, of complete ignorance of evil, misfortune, or suffering —in a word this flower, this very first flower of life—all these things, without making you fall in love or even really awakening your interest, yet make so lovely, so deep, so indescribable an impression, that you never tire of looking at that face.[1]

In six April days during that spring he wrote Il Risorgimento, *the story of his heart's re-awakening, and soon after, in Florence, the most perfect and serene of his shorter lyrics,* A Silvia.

III

During the summer of 1828 Leopardi remained in Florence but, once again, his health broke down: he was unable to go on with the work he had undertaken for Stella—an anthology of Italian poetry and a volume to be entitled An Encyclopaedia of Useless Knowledge—*so that he felt he should no longer accept the publisher's monthly allowance. In November he returned to Recanati, for the last sixteen months that he was to spend there.*

These were peculiarly lonely months, since he had lost even the companionship of his brother Carlo, who had married against his father's wishes and left the house. Yet it was during this unhappy period that the poet's imagination began to stir again and that—in the summer of 1829—he composed his exquisite later Idylls: The Solitary Thrush, Memories, The Calm after the Storm, *and* Saturday Evening in the Village, *and these were followed in the course of the next winter by the* Night Song of a Nomadic Shepherd in Asia.

In this period, too, he was setting down enough literary plans—as yet only vaguely outlined—to fill many years of work. Only a few of them are quoted here.

Parallel between the Civilization of the Ancients (that is the Greeks and Romans) *and that of the Moderns.* If we consider

[1] *Zibaldone*, II, pp. 1143-5, 30 June 1828.

its origins and nature, modern civilization is a renaissance; and a large part of what we think we have acquired, we have only recovered. . . . In any case, it cannot fail to be important, both in theory and practice, to investigate accurately the civilization which is the mother of our own, and to compare it with that of her daughter. The result of this comparison would be, that we have still got a great deal to recover from the ancient civilization.

Of the Nature of Men and Things. This would contain my whole metaphysical system, or transcendental philosophy; but should be intelligible to all. It would be the chief work of my life.

A Treatise on Men's Passions and Sentiments. The science of the intellect and of ideas has been much cultivated in the last two centuries, and fruitfully, and is now full-grown; but that of the sentiments, which is at least equally important, has made no progress at all, as a science, since the days of Aristotle. So it is still in its infancy, if not still uncreated.

A Manual of Practical Philosophy: that is, an Epictetus in my own manner.

A Treatise on Moral Manners: that is, on the respect one must observe in civilized conversation and life, so as not to offend certain of men's passions which are, in general, little regarded.

The Macchiavelli of Social Life.

Moral Discourses: that is, Sermons and Panegyrics, without the Bible and without theology.

The Art of being Unhappy. The one of being happy, is already decaying: taught by thousands, known by all, practised by very few, and by no one successfully.

An Encyclopaedia of Useless Knowledge, and of the things that are not known, or a Supplement to all Encyclopaedias.[1]

These are hardly the plans of a man who thinks he has only a short time left to live. When a second long winter, however, had dragged on at Recanati, he decided that, whatever might come of it,

[1] *Poesie e Prose*, I, pp. 703–7: *Disegni letterari.*

he would take the small sum he had earned by his previous writings and set forth to any place where he could earn the bare necessities of life.

I am resolved [he wrote to Vieusseux], with the little money that is left me from the time when I could work, to set forth to look for health or die, but never, never to return to Recanati. I have no preference as to a profession; any that is reconcilable with my poor health will suit me; I fear no humiliations. . . . I have nothing left to lose. . . . Tell me in all sincerity whether you think that I could earn enough to live by giving lessons or literary entertainments at home [in Florence]. . . . I mean literary lessons of any kind, even the humblest, in language, grammar, and the like.[1]

This letter, however, crossed with one from Florence, written by General Colletta, the Neapolitan historian, and containing what is surely one of the most generous proposals ever made to a man of letters, an offer of a monthly subsidy of 18 francesconi *to enable the poet to live in Florence, among his friends. 'I shall hand over to you, every month, the above-mentioned sum in advance, but I shall have no office or duty besides that of handing over the money. Nothing will come out of my purse. Those who give do not know to whom their gift is destined—and you, who are receiving it, do not know from whom it comes. . . . No obligation is imposed on you. May it be the good fortune of Italy that, as you recover your health, you will be able to write works worthy of your genius! But this hope of mine confers no obligation upon you.'[2]*

So generous a letter could receive only one reply.

I can only tell you that your letter—after sixteen months of horrible darkness, after a life from which God deliver my worst enemies—has now reached me like a ray of light,

---

[1] *Epist.* V, 21 March 1830.
[2] Ibid. 23 March 1830.

more blessed than the first dawn of twilight in the polar regions.[1]

On 29 April, taking leave of his mother and Paolina, but not even seeing his father—who wrote later on that he 'had not had the heart to embrace him or to come downstairs to bid him farewell'—Giacomo Leopardi left Recanati for ever.

[1] *Epist.* V, 2 April 1830.

M

9. *Later* Operette Morali 1829–32

COPERNICUS

A Dialogue

Scene One: The First Hour and the Sun

FIRST HOUR. Good morning, Your Excellency.

SUN. Yes: or rather, good night.

FIRST HOUR. The horses are ready.

SUN. Good.

FIRST HOUR. The morning star has been up for some time now.

SUN. Very well: let her rise and set as she pleases.

FIRST HOUR. What does Your Excellency mean?

SUN. I mean that I want you to leave me alone.

FIRST HOUR. But Excellency, the night has already lasted so long that it cannot go on any longer; and if we delay, take care, Your Excellency, that some confusion does not arise.

SUN. Whatever may come of it, I am not going to stir.

FIRST HOUR. Oh, Your Excellency, what is this? are you not feeling well?

SUN. No, no, I don't feel anything wrong with me, except that I will not move; and so you had better go about your business.

FIRST HOUR. But how can I do so unless you come too, since I am the first hour of the day? and how can the day have being, if Your Excellency does not condescend to rise as usual?

SUN. If you are not of the day, you will be of the night; or else the hours of the night can do double duty, and you and your sisters remain idle. Do you know what has happened? I have become weary of this constant peram- bulation, to give light to a handful of little animals, which live on a handful of clay so small that I, although my eyesight is good, can hardly see it. And so I have resolved tonight not to take any more pains about this matter, and that if men want light, they may keep their own fires burning, or make shift in some other way.

FIRST HOUR. But what other way, Excellency, can those poor creatures find? To keep their lamps fed, or to provide enough candles to burn all day long, will be a very great expense. If they had already discovered that air which one can use for burning, and for lighting up streets, rooms, shops, cellars, and everything else, and all very cheaply, I should agree that the matter was not so serious. But the fact is that about three hundred years must still go by . . . before mankind discovers that remedy, and meanwhile their oil, wax, pitch, and tallow will run short, and they will have nothing left to burn.

SUN. Let them hunt fireflies, and little glow-worms.

FIRST HOUR. And what will they do about the cold? For without the help they used to receive from Your Excellency, the wood of all their forests will not suffice to keep them warm. Besides, they will die of hunger, for the earth will no longer bring forth her fruits. And so, after a few years, the seed of those poor animals must die out, for when they have wandered here and there, groping across the Earth, looking for food and warmth, and when at last they have used up everything that they can swallow, and the last spark of fire has died out, they must all die in the dark, frozen like pieces of rock-crystal.

SUN. What does that matter to me? Am I the wet-nurse of the human race? or am I its cook, to season and prepare its food? Why should I care if a few invisible little creatures, millions of miles away from me, cannot see and cannot bear the cold, without my light? And besides, if indeed I am to serve as a stove or a hearth for the human family, it is reasonable that if this family wants to keep warm, it should move towards the hearth, and not that the fire should move round the house. So if the Earth needs my presence, let her get up and take some trouble to obtain it; since, for my part, I do not need anything from the Earth, to make me go and look for her.

FIRST HOUR. Your Excellency means, if I have understood you rightly, that what you have done yourself in the past, should now be done by the Earth herself.

SUN. Yes; now, and for ever.

FIRST HOUR. Certainly Your Excellency is quite right in this, apart from the fact that you may do as you please with yourself. But for all that, Your Excellency, deign to consider how many beautiful things will have to be destroyed, to establish this new system. The Dawn will no longer have her beautiful golden chariot with its fine horses, that bathe on the sea-shore, and, apart from many other things, we poor Hours will no longer have a place in the sky, and will have to turn into earthly, instead of celestial maidens; unless indeed, as I expect, we dissolve into thin smoke. But let that be as it may: the real trouble will lie in persuading the Earth to go round, which will be very difficult, as she is not used to it; and she will find it strange to be obliged to run and tire herself so much, never having stirred from her own place until now. And if Your Excellency, as it appears, is now inclined towards indolence, I hear that the Earth, too, is not any more disposed to bestir herself than she used to be.

SUN. Necessity, in this case, will goad her, and make her rise up and run as much as is needed. But in any case, the quickest and surest way is to find a poet or a philosopher who will persuade the Earth to move, or, if there is no other way of persuading her, make her go by force. For in the last resort the greatest share of this matter is in the hands of the philosophers and the poets: indeed, it is almost entirely in their power. It was the poets who in the past (for I was young then and paid heed to them), with their fine songs, led me to undertake, as if it were a sport or an honourable exercise, this absurd task of racing about like a madman, in spite of my great size, around a little grain of sand. But now that I am of ripe years and have turned to philosophy, I do not look for beauty, but for use, and the sentiments of the poets, if they do not turn my stomach, make me laugh. I must have a good and substantial reason for doing anything and I see no reason at all to prefer an active life to an idle and easy one, since activity does not pay you for your pains or even for your worry (for there is no fruit in the world worth two pence). Therefore I have decided to leave all this trouble and discomfort to others, and, for my part, to live quietly at home, idle and indolent.

This change in me, as I have told you, has been brought about, in addition to the effects of my age, by the philosophers; people who are rising in power in these times, and will rise still higher. So, if you do indeed wish the Earth to go round instead of me, a poet would really in one way be better than a philosopher: for the poets—with one fable or another—do make people believe that the things of this world are of real value and importance, and also very pleasant and beautiful, and by inspiring a thousand joyous hopes, often persuade other men to toil, while the philosophers dissuade them. But since the philosophers' rule has begun, I fear that a poet would not be listened to by the Earth, any more than by me, or that, if he were, he would not seem impressive. So we had better turn to a philosopher; for although philosophers are not usually fit, and still less inclined, to incite others to work, yet it may be that, in so extreme a case as this, they will go against their usual habit. Unless indeed the Earth considers it better for her to destroy herself, instead of taking so much trouble—and I would not say that she was wrong.

Enough, let us see what happens. But there is one thing you can do: go down to the Earth, or send one of your sisters, whichever you please; and if she can find one of those philosophers who spend their evenings out of doors in the cold, watching the heavens and the stars—and this should be easy, owing to the novelty of this very long night—let her pick him up without more ado, throw him over her shoulders and bring him back to me here; and I will see to it that he agrees to do what is needful. Do you quite understand?

FIRST HOUR. Yes, Excellency. You shall be obeyed.

Scene Two

COPERNICUS [*on the terrace of his house, scanning the eastern sky through a roll of paper, for telescopes had not yet been invented*].

This is a wonderful thing. Either all the clocks have gone wrong, or the sun should have risen more than an hour ago; and yet one cannot even see a glimmer in the east, although the sky is as clear and polished as a mirror. All the stars are shining as if it were midnight. I must consult my Almagest or Sacrobosco,[1] and see what explanation they give for such an event. I have often heard about the night that Jove spent with Amphitryon's wife; and I remember reading in a modern book by a Spaniard about the Peruvians' tale that once, long ago, their country had a night so long that it seemed without an end, and that at last the sun rose out of a certain lake, which they call Titicaca. But until today I believed these tales to be merely idle talk, indeed I felt sure of it, like all rational men. But now that I perceive that reason and science are not worth a pin, I am prepared to believe that these and other similar things may indeed be true; indeed I feel inclined to visit every lake and swamp I can find, to see if I can succeed in fishing up the sun. But what is this sound I hear, like the wings of a great bird?

[1] Almagest: celebrated treatise on astronomy of the second century A.D. by Claudius Ptolemy of the school of Alexandria. It was well known in the Middle Ages in a Latin translation by Gherardo di Cremona.

Sacrobosco: Giovanni di Sacrobosco (John Holywood, from his birthplace in Yorkshire) was an astronomer of the thirteenth century, and author of a treatise entitled *De Sphaera Mundi*.

Scene Three: The Last Hour and Copernicus

LAST HOUR. Copernicus, I am the Last Hour.

COPERNICUS. The last hour? Well, one must resign oneself. Only, if possible, give me time to make my Will and put my affairs in order, before I die.

LAST HOUR. Who said anything about dying? I am not the last hour of your life.

COPERNICUS. Well, what are you then? The last hour of the office of the breviary?

LAST HOUR. I can well believe it to be the one you prefer, when you are in the choir-stalls.

COPERNICUS. But how do you know I am a Canon? And how do you know me? for you called me by my name.

LAST HOUR. I have made inquiries about you from some men who were down there in the road. In short, I am the last hour of the day.

COPERNICUS. Ah, I see: the first hour is ill, and that is why the day has not yet dawned.

LAST HOUR. Let me speak. The day will not dawn again, neither today nor tomorrow nor ever again, unless you see to it.

COPERNICUS. A likely thing indeed, that I should be the one to make the day!

LAST HOUR. I will tell you how. But the first step is for you to come with me at once to the house of the Sun, my master. You shall hear the rest on the way, or from His Excellency, when we arrive.

COPERNICUS. That is all very well. But the journey, unless I am mistaken, must be a very long one. And how can I take enough provisions not to die of hunger, some years before I arrive? Besides, I do not believe that His Excellency's lands will provide me with even a single meal.

LAST HOUR. Lay aside those doubts. You will not have to stay long in the Sun's house, and the journey will be made in a moment. For I am a spirit, though you do not know it.

COPERNICUS. But I am a body.

LAST HOUR. Well, well, you need not trouble yourself with such talk, for you are not a metaphysician. Come here: mount upon my shoulders, and leave the rest to me.

COPERNICUS. Very well: that's done. Let us see where this venture leads us.

Scene Four: Copernicus and the Sun

COPERNICUS. Most noble Lord.

SUN. Forgive me, Copernicus, for not asking you to be seated, since we do not have chairs here. But we shall soon be done. You have already heard my business from my handmaiden. For my part, from what she tells me about your qualities, I think you very well suited to my purpose.

COPERNICUS. Sir, I see many difficulties in this business.

SUN. The difficulties should not alarm a man of your sort. Indeed it is said that, in a brave man, they increase his courage. But briefly, what are they?

COPERNICUS. First, that, great as the power of philosophy may be, I doubt whether it is great enough to persuade the Earth to start running, instead of remaining comfortably seated; and to begin to toil, instead of living in idleness—especially in these times, which are certainly not the heroic ones of old.

SUN. If you cannot persuade, you must compel her.

COPERNICUS. Gladly, Your Excellency, were I a Hercules or even an Orlando, and not a mere Canon of Varmia.

SUN. What has that to do with it? Is there not a tale about one of your ancient mathematicians, who said that if he were given a standing-place outside the world, he would undertake to move both heaven and earth? Now you are not required to move the sky; and here you are already in a place outside the Earth. So, if you are not a lesser man than that ancient, you should be able to move the Earth, whether she will or not.

COPERNICUS. My lord, this might be done, but it would require a lever of such dimensions that not only I, but

even Your Excellency, rich as you are, could not pay for
half its material and its manufacture. And another still
graver difficulty is one which I will tell you now; indeed
it is a tangle of difficulties. Until now the Earth has held
the first place in the world, that is, the centre; being (as
you know) motionless, and having nothing to do but look
about her, while all the other spheres of the universe,
whether great or small, shining or dark, gyrated above
and below and around her all the time: with a swiftness
and busyness and vehemence of which the mere thought is
overwhelming. And thus, since everything seemed to be
occupied in her service, the universe seemed like a court
in which the Earth sat on a throne, with the other globes
around her, like courtiers, guards, or servants, each one
attending to some office. So that, indeed, the Earth has
always believed herself to be the Empress of the universe;
and truly, matters being as they have been till now, one
cannot say that she was wrong; indeed I shall not deny
that these ideas had a sound foundation. But what shall I
say about men? For believing ourselves to be (as we
always shall believe) the first and most important of all
terrestrial creatures, each one of us, even if dressed in rags
and with nothing but a dry crust of bread to gnaw, has yet
esteemed himself an emperor—not only of Constantinople
or Germany, or of half the Earth, as the Roman emperors
were, but an Emperor of the Universe, ruling the sun, the
planets, and all the visible and invisible stars; and the final
cause of the stars, the planets, and of your illustrious
Excellency, and everything else. But now, if we depose the
Earth from her central position and make her run and
whirl round and round and toil unremittingly, and do
everything that has been done until now by all the other
globes—in short, if she becomes just one of the planets—
this will mean that her terrestrial Majesty, and their human
Majesties too, will have to renounce their thrones and their
power; they will be left with only their rags and troubles,
which are not few.

SUN. In short, what does my Don Nicola conclude from these remarks? Perhaps his conscience is uneasy, fearing that this deed would be treasonable?

COPERNICUS. No, Your Excellency, for neither the Codices nor the Digest, nor the books dealing with public or natural law, or with the law of the Empire or the *jus gentium*, make any mention of this form of treason, to the best of my knowledge. What I really mean is that this action of ours will not only alter the order of nature as it may appear at first sight, but will have effects in the realm of physics, changing the hierarchy of everything and the ends for which living creatures are created, and thus will bring about a great revolution even in metaphysics, and indeed in everything concerning the speculative part of knowledge. And the result will be that men, if indeed they are still able or willing to talk sanely about it, will discover that they themselves are something quite different from what they had been until now, or imagined themselves to be.

SUN. My son, these things do not alarm me at all: for I feel just as much respect for metaphysics as for physics, or for alchemy or necromancy if you like. And men must learn to be content to be as they are; and if they do not like it, they can start arguing upside down and in despite of the evidence of things, which will come very easy to them; and so they will go on considering themselves whatever they wish to be, barons or dukes or emperors, or whatever else they please, for this will bring comfort to them and will not cause the slightest annoyance to me.

COPERNICUS. Well, let us leave men and the Earth. But consider, Your Excellency, what may reasonably be expected to happen to the other planets. For when they see the Earth doing precisely what they do, just like one of themselves, and become one of them, they will be dissatisfied with their own bare simplicity and lack of adornment, and the mournful desolation they have known until now, while the Earth alone is so richly adorned. They too will want their rivers, seas, mountains, plants, and also animals and men, for they will see no reason why they should be at all inferior to the Earth. And so there will be another great revolution in the universe: and an infinite number of new races and peoples will spring up in a moment on every side, like mushrooms.

SUN. Well, let them come, and let them be whatever they can be; for my light and heat will suffice for them all, without any extra expense; and the world will be able to feed, clothe, lodge them and provide for them generously, without running into debt.

COPERNICUS. But let Your Excellency consider a little further, and he will see yet another cause for confusion. For the stars, when they see that you have seated yourself, and not only on a stool, but on a throne, and that you are surrounded by this fine court and population of planets, will not only wish to seat themselves too and take their rest, but will also want to reign; and in order to reign one must have subjects, so they too will wish to have their planets, as you have, each one of them his own. And these new planets will have to be inhabited and adorned like the Earth. And it is unnecessary to mention the poor human race, which has already become wholly insignificant with regard to this system alone. What will become of it, when so many thousand new worlds appear, so that even the smallest star in the Milky Way does not lack its own? But considering only your own interests, I must say that until now you have been, if not the first, certainly the second in the universe—that is, after the Earth—and have had no equal, since the stars did not presume to compare themselves with you. But in this new state you will have as many equals as there are stars, each with its own system. So beware lest the change we wish to bring about, may not lower your own dignity.

SUN. Don't you remember what your Caesar said when, crossing the Alps, he happened to pass through the small village of certain poor Barbarians: that he would rather be the first man in that village, than the second in Rome? And I, too, would rather be the first in this world of ours, than second in the universe. But it is not ambition that moves me to desire a change in the present state of things: it is only a love of peace, or more properly, of indolence. So that I little care whether I have any equals or not, or whether I am in the first place or the last; for, unlike Cicero, I have more regard for ease than for dignity!

COPERNICUS. For my part, Your Excellency, I will do the best I can to obtain this ease for you. But even if our purpose is achieved, I doubt whether it will last very long. For in the first place, I am almost certain that not many years will go by before you are obliged to go winding round like the pulleys of a well or like a millstone, though without ever changing your place. And then I have some suspicion that in the end, whether sooner or later, you will even have to begin running again: I don't mean around the Earth, but what good will this do to you? And perhaps the very rotation which you will perform will serve for an argument to make you run. Enough, be this as it may: in spite of every inconvenience and all other considerations, I will try to help you, if you persist in your intention; so that, if I do not succeed, you will know that it was not that I lacked courage or inclination, but simply power.

SUN. Very well, my Copernicus; pray do your best.

COPERNICUS. There is only one other difficulty.

SUN. Well, what is it?

COPERNICUS. That I would rather not be roasted alive, on this account, like the Phoenix; for should this happen, I feel certain that I should not rise from my ashes like that bird, but should never, from that moment, see Your Lordship's face again.

SUN. Listen, Copernicus: you know that at one time, when you philosophers were scarcely yet born—I mean in the days when poetry held the field—I was a prophet. Let me prophesy now, for the last time, and pay heed to me, in remembrance of my ancient power. So let me tell you that

some men who come after you and who approve of what
you have done, may perhaps get a scalding or something
like that; but that, so far as I can see, you yourself shall not
suffer anything at all on account of this enterprise. And if
you wish to make your safety certain, adopt this plan:
dedicate the book which you write on this subject, to the
Pope. For thus I promise you that you will not even lose
your canonry.[1]

[1] Written in 1827, this dialogue was not included in the Florentine edition
of the *Operette Morali* (1834) but appeared for the first time only in 1845.
Copernicus did in fact dedicate his treatise to Pope Paul III.

DIALOGUE BETWEEN A PEDLAR OF ALMANACKS AND A WAYFARER

PEDLAR. Almanacks, new almanacks, new calendars. Do you need almanacks, sir?

WAYFARER. Almanacks for the New Year?

PEDLAR. Yes, sir.

WAYFARER. Do you believe that this new year will be a happy one?

PEDLAR. Oh yes, your lordship, certainly.

WAYFARER. As the past year?

PEDLAR. Much, much more so.

WAYFARER. As the previous one?

PEDLAR. Much, much happier, your lordship.

WAYFARER. But as what other year? Shouldn't you like the New Year to resemble one of these recent years?

PEDLAR. That I should not.

WAYFARER. How many new years have gone by, since you started selling almanacks?

PEDLAR. About twenty years, your lordship.

WAYFARER. And which of those years would you like the New Year to resemble?

PEDLAR. I? I couldn't say.

WAYFARER. Don't you remember any particular year, that you considered happy?

PEDLAR. None, in truth, your lordship.

WAYFARER. And yet life is a fine thing, isn't it?

PEDLAR. So they say.

WAYFARER. Wouldn't you go back to live those twenty years over again, and all the rest of the past, too, from the day of your birth?

PEDLAR. Oh, dear sir, would to God that one could!

WAYFARER. But if you had to live precisely the same life over again, with all the joys and sorrows you have known?

PEDLAR. That I shouldn't like.

WAYFARER. But what other life would you wish to live

again? The life I have led, or the king's, or someone else's? Or don't you believe that I and the king, and anyone else, would answer just like you: and that, if any man were bound to lead precisely the same life as before, no one would wish to turn back?

PEDLAR. I do think so.

WAYFARER. And you, too, would not go back on those terms, if no others were possible?

PEDLAR. Oh, no, sir, truly I would not go back.

WAYFARER. But what life, then, would you wish for?

PEDLAR. I would like just such a life as God might send me, without any conditions.

WAYFARER. Just any life, about which you knew nothing beforehand, as we know nothing about the New Year?

PEDLAR. Just so.

WAYFARER. That is what I would like, too, if I could live again, and so would any man. But this proves that, up to this year, fate has treated us all badly. And it is plain that everyone believes the evil that has come to him to have been greater or heavier than the good; since no one, if asked whether he would wish to have his former life, with all its good and evil, would wish to be born again. The life that is a fine thing is not the life one knows, but the life one does not know; not past life, but the life to come. With the New Year, Fate will begin to treat us well— you and me and everyone else, and a happy life will begin for us. Isn't that so?

PEDLAR. Let us hope so.

WAYFARER. Then show me the finest almanack you have.

PEDLAR. Here it is, your lordship. It costs thirty pence.

WAYFARER. And here are thirty pence.

PEDLAR. Thank you, your lordship; may we meet again. Almanacks, new almanacks! new calendars!

DIALOGUE BETWEEN TRISTAN AND A FRIEND

FRIEND. I have read your book. Melancholy, as usual.

TRISTAN. Yes, as is my custom.

FRIEND. Melancholy, disconsolate, despairing; it is plain that this life seems a very poor thing to you.

TRISTAN. What can I say to you? I had this mad notion in my head that human life is unhappy.

FRIEND. Unhappy, perhaps. Yet after all . . .

TRISTAN. No, no, it is really very happy. I have changed my mind. But when I wrote that book, I had that mad notion in my head, as I said. And I was so convinced of its truth that I would have expected anything rather than to hear my observations doubted, for it seemed to me that the conscience of every reader must bear a ready witness to each one of them. I only imagined that there might be some dispute as to the usefulness or danger of such observations, but not as to their truth: on the contrary, I believed that my sad voice, describing the common lot, would find an echo in the heart of every man who heard it. And when I heard the denial, not of any particular proposition, but of the whole, and the assertion that human life is not unhappy, and that if it seemed so to me, it must be the effect of some peculiar infirmity or sorrow of my own, I was at first stupefied, astounded, and turned to stone, and felt for a few days as if I had been carried off into another world. But then, coming back to my senses, I felt rather indignant, and finally I laughed and said: Men in general are like husbands. A married man who wishes to live in peace, must perforce believe in his own wife's faithfulness; and so he does; even though half the world knows that the truth is very different. If anyone desires or is compelled to live in a country, he makes up his mind to regard it as one of the best in the world: and that is what he does believe. It is best for all men everywhere, if they wish to go on living, to consider life delightful and valuable; and that is what they do think, and are angry with those who hold a different opinion. For in reality the human race believes, not what is true, but what is, or seems to be, most to its advantage. The human race, which has believed and will believe so many absurdities, will never believe that it knows nothing, or that it is nothing, or that it has nothing to hope for. No philosopher who should teach one of those three doctrines would make a fortune or found a sect, particularly among the common herd; since all three are unsuited to anyone who wishes to live, and moreover the first two offend a man's pride, and the third (as well as the other two) demand courage and fortitude from the man who believes them. And men are cowardly and weak, with ignoble and narrow minds, always ready to be hopeful, because always prepared to change their opinion of what is good, according to what their life requires. They are always ready, as Petrarch said, to surrender their arms to fortune, most prompt and determined to console themselves for any mischance, to accept any compensation for what has been denied to them or what they have lost, to adapt themselves on any terms to the most iniquitous and barbarous lot, and, when they have been deprived of everything desirable, to accept beliefs which are false, but are held by them as strongly and firmly as if they were the truest and best-founded in the world.

For my own part, just as southern Europeans laugh at husbands who are in love with unfaithful wives, so I cannot refrain from laughing at the human race, which is in love with life; and I consider it very unmanly to wish to be deceived and deluded like fools, and, in addition to the evils one is obliged to endure, to become the butt of nature and destiny. I am speaking about the illusions of the intellect, not those of the imagination. Whether these sentiments of mine are caused by disease or not, I do not know. I know that, ill or well, I tread human cowardice

N

underfoot, reject every consolation and childish illusion, and dare to endure the privation of every hope and to look steadily upon the desert of life, not conceal- ing from myself any aspect of human unhappiness, and accepting all the consequences of a philosophy that is painful, but true. This, if it has no other use, can give a strong man the proud satisfaction of seeing every veil cast off from the hidden and mysterious cruelty of human destiny.

I was saying these things to myself, almost as if I myself had invented this painful philosophy; for I saw it re- jected by everyone else, as one rejects ideas which are new or unheard of. But then, as I thought the matter over, I remembered that it was as new as Solomon or Homer, or the most ancient poets and philosophers, who are all rich in figures, fables, and aphorisms showing the extreme unhappiness of humanity. One of them says that man is the most wretched of all creatures; another, that it is best not to be born at all, or else to die in one's cradle; others, that those whom the gods love, die young, and a thousand other things in the same strain. And I also remembered that from those times until yesterday or the day before yesterday, all poets and philosophers and writers, great and small, had echoed or confirmed, to a lesser or greater degree, these same doctrines. So that I began to wonder afresh; and passed a long time between wonder and con- tempt and laughter, until, studying the subject more profoundly, I became aware that man's unhappiness was one of the inveterate errors of the intellect, and that the refutation of this opinion, and the happiness of life, was one of the great discoveries of the nineteenth century. Then I grew calm, and now I confess that I was mistaken in thinking as I did.

FRIEND. So you have changed your opinion?

TRISTAN. Certainly. Would you wish me to oppose the truths discovered by the nineteenth century?

FRIEND. And you believe all that this century believes?

TRISTAN. Certainly. What cause is there for surprise?

FRIEND. You believe in the unlimited perfectibility of man?

TRISTAN. Undoubtedly.

FRIEND. You also believe that the human race is improving every day?

TRISTAN. Yes, certainly. It is true that sometimes I think that one of the ancients, in bodily powers, was worth four of us. And the body is the man: for (apart from all the rest) magnanimity, courage, passion, the power to act and to enjoy, everything that makes life noble and alive, depend on the body's vigour, and cannot exist without it. A man who is weak in body is not a man, but a child; indeed worse, for his fate is to remain an onlooker while others live, and the best he can do is to talk, but life is not for him. That is why, in ancient times, bodily weakness was considered ignominious, even in the most civilized periods. But among us, it is a long time since education has deigned to consider the body, a thing too low and abject, and has cared only for the spirit; and precisely in order to cultivate the spirit, it has ruined the body, without realizing that by its destruction, the spirit, too, is destroyed. And even if it were possible to correct this doctrine, it would never be possible to change the whole state of modern society, and to find a remedy for every other aspect of private and public life, which, in their respective ways, always used to unite in perfecting and strengthening the body, and now are conspiring to deprave it. The result is that, in comparison with the ancients, we are little more than children, and that they, in comparison with us, may more than ever be said to have been men. I am talking about individuals compared with other individuals, as well as of the masses (to use this most elegant modern term) compared with the masses. And I will add that the ancients were incomparably more virile than we, even in their moral and metaphysical systems. But all the same, I do not allow myself to be affected by such trifling objections, but steadfastly believe that the human race is always progressing.

FRIEND. You also believe, I presume, that knowledge—or, as they say, enlightenment—is on the increase?

TRISTAN. Most certainly. Although I observe that, as a wish for knowledge increases, there is a proportionate reluctance to study. And it is surprising to count the number of learned men, true scholars, who were living a century and a half ago, and even more recently, and to see how disproportionately larger it was than their number today. And do not tell me that the learned are few today because knowledge is generally not concentrated in a few individuals, but scattered among many; and that the number of the latter makes up for the scarcity of the former. Knowledge is not like riches, which can be divided and put together again, and always come to the same sum. Where everyone knows a little, little is known; for knowledge follows knowledge, and will not be spread out. A superficial education cannot be divided among many, but is merely common to many who are not learned. What is left in the way of knowledge belongs only to the learned, and a large part of it only to the very learned. And, with a few accidental exceptions, it is only a very learned man who possesses a vast store of knowledge, who is capable of increasing and solidly forwarding human knowledge. Now, except perhaps in Germany, where scholarship has not yet been uprooted, don't you think that the existence of very learned men becomes less possible every day?

I am making these reflections just for the sake of argument, and to philosophize a little, and perhaps to make use of sophistry, not because I am not convinced by what you have said. For even if I were to see a world made up of ignorant impostors on the one hand, and presumptuous fools on the other, I should still believe, as I do, that knowledge and enlightenment are constantly on the increase.

FRIEND. Therefore, you believe this century to be superior to all those of the past?

TRISTAN. Certainly. So each age has believed, even the most

barbarous; and my century thinks so, too, and I agree with it. But if you asked me in what respect it is superior to other centuries, whether in the things that appertain to the body or to the mind, I would remind you of what I have just said.

FRIEND. In short, to sum it all up in two words, your opinion about nature and the destiny of man and matter (since we are not now talking about literature or politics) is precisely the one held by the papers?

TRISTAN. Precisely. I believe and embrace the profound philosophy of the daily press, which, while it destroys every other literature and study, as too heavy and distasteful, is the teacher and the light of the present day. Isn't that true?

FRIEND. Very true. If what you are saying is spoken seriously and not in jest, you have become one of us.

TRISTAN. Yes, certainly, one of you.

FRIEND. Well, then, what shall you do with your book? Do you want to go down to posterity with sentiments so contrary to the opinions you now hold?

TRISTAN. To posterity? I am laughing, because you are joking; and if you conceivably were not, I would laugh still more. I will not speak with regard to myself, but in so far as all individuals and individual things of the nineteenth century are concerned, be sure that there is nothing to fear from posterity, who will know no more than our ancestors did. *Individuals have been swallowed up by the masses*, as modern thinkers elegantly word it. Which means that it is unnecessary for the individual to take any trouble, since, whatever his merits may be, he cannot hope, either waking or in his dreams, for even the wretched prize called glory. Leave everything to the masses: though what they can do without the individuals, being made up of individuals, I should like to have explained to me by the experts in individuals and masses who are now enlightening the world. But to return to my book and posterity, you will see that books—which are now mostly written in less time than it takes to read them—only cost what they are worth, and endure in proportion to what they cost. As for me, I believe that the twentieth century will make a clean sweep of the immense bibliography of the nineteenth, or will say: we have entire libraries of books which have cost twenty or thirty years of hard work, and some less, but all of which required great toil. Let us read those first, for it is probable that we shall find more substance in them, and when there are no more of them left to read, then let us open the books that are mere improvisations.

My friend, this is a childish age, and the very few men left in it must hide themselves for shame, like the man who walked upright in a land of cripples. And these dear children want to do, in every field, what was done by grown men in other times, and to do it just as children do —on the spur of the moment, without taking any trouble to prepare themselves. Indeed, they desire that the level which civilization has reached, and the character of the present and future eras, should absolve them and their successors for ever from any need for hard work and the long toil of preparation. A friend of mine, a successful man of business, was saying to me a few days ago, that even mediocrity has become very rare; scarcely anyone is efficient, scarcely anyone is fit for the offices or tasks to which necessity or fortune or choice has appointed him. This seems to me to form the true distinction between this age and those which came before. In all other times, as in this one, greatness has been very rare. But in other times mediocrity held the field, and in ours, nullity. Therefore we have such noise and confusion—since everyone tries to do everything—that little attention is paid even to the few great men whom I do believe to exist, but who, in this vast crowd of competitors, can no longer open a way for themselves. And so, while all the meanest consider themselves illustrious, obscurity and nullity become the common fate, both for the lowest and the highest. But long live statistics! Long live the sciences—economic,

moral, and political—the pocket encyclopaedias, the
manuals, and all the fine creations of our age! And may
the nineteenth century live for ever!—perhaps poor in
results, but very rich and generous in words: which has
always been a good sign, as you know. And let us comfort ourselves, since for another sixty-six years this century will be the only one to speak and express its opinions.

FRIEND. You seem to speak with some irony. But you should
at least bear in mind that this is an age of transition.

TRISTAN. And what conclusions do you draw from that? All
centuries, more or less, have been and always will be
times of transition, since human society does not stand
still, nor will a time ever come in which it has a condition
that will endure. So this fine phrase either offers no excuse
for the nineteenth century, or only one which is common
to all other centuries. What remains to be seen, in view of
the way that society is going, is the result—that is, whether
the transition now in progress is from good to better, or
from bad to worse. Perhaps you would like to tell me that
the present age is pre-eminently one of transition, that is,
a very swift passing from one state of civilization to
another, which will be entirely unlike its predecessor. If
so, I must ask your permission to laugh at your rapid passage and reply that all transitions should take place
slowly; for if made in a rush, one must turn back again
very soon, to make them step by step. So it has always
been. The reason is, that nature does not advance by
leaps, and that if we force nature, we do not produce
lasting results. Or rather, to express myself better, such
hurried transitions are apparent, but not real.

FRIEND. Pray, do not speak like this to many people, or you
will make many enemies.

TRISTAN. No matter. Neither friends nor enemies can do me
much harm now.

FRIEND. Or more likely you will be despised, as incapable of
appreciating modern philosophy, and caring little for the
progress of civilization and enlightenment.

TRISTAN. I am very sorry, but what is to be done? If they despise me, I shall try to console myself.

FRIEND. But in short, have you changed your mind or not? And what is to be done with this book?

TRISTAN. Best burn it. Or if you do not wish to do so, keep it as a book of poetic dreams, of melancholy inventions and caprices, or as an expression of the author's unhappiness. For in confidence, my dear friend, I believe you and everyone else to be happy; but as for me, by your leave and that of this age, I am most unhappy and know it; and all the journals of two worlds cannot persuade me to the contrary.

FRIEND. I do not know the causes of the unhappiness you are talking about. But a man is the best judge of his own happiness or unhappiness, and his opinion cannot be wrong.

TRISTAN. Very true. And what is more, I tell you frankly that I do not submit to my unhappiness, nor bow my head to destiny, nor come to terms with it, as other men do; and I dare to desire death above all things, with such ardour and sincerity as, I believe, few men have ever felt in desiring it. I would not be speaking to you like this, were I not certain that, when the time comes, the facts will not belie my words; for though I do not yet see any way out of my life, yet I have an inner feeling which almost makes me feel sure that the time of which I speak is not far off. I am too ripe for death, it seems too absurd and incredible—being spiritually dead as I am, with the fable of my life already told—that I should linger on for the forty or fifty years more with which nature threatens me. I shudder at the thought. But, like all evils which transcend, so to speak, the powers of our imagination, this one seems to me a dream and an illusion, which cannot come true. Indeed, if anyone speaks to me about a distant future as about something which concerns me, I cannot help smiling to myself: so confident do I feel that the road left to me to tread is not a long one. This, I can affirm, is the only thought which sustains me. Books and studies, which I often wonder I ever loved so dearly, plans of great deeds, hopes of glory and immortality—all these are things at which it is too late even to smile. I do not laugh at the projects and hopes of this age. I wish them every possible success, with all my heart, and sincerely praise, admire, and honour their good intentions: but I do not envy posterity, nor those who still have a long time to live. In the past I have envied fools, and people with a great conceit of themselves, and I would willingly have changed places with any one of them. Now I no longer envy either the foolish or the wise, the great or the small, the weak or the powerful. I envy only the dead, and with them only would exchange. Every pleasant fancy, every thought of the future that comes to me in my solitude, and with which I pass away the time, is concerned with death, and can see no other way out. Nor is this desire troubled, as once it used to be, by the memory of my youthful dreams or by the thought that I have lived in vain. If I can obtain death, I will die as quietly and contentedly as if nothing else on earth had ever been my hope or my desire. That is the only boon that can reconcile me with fate. If on the one hand I were offered the fortune and the fame of Caesar or Alexander, unsullied, and on the other, death today, I would say, death today, and would need no time to make my choice.

10. Selected Reflections

Leopardi's 111 Pensieri, *of which over 70 are based on notes in the* Zibaldone, *were described by him in a letter to De Sinner, on 2 March 1827, as 'Reflections on the Character and Behaviour of Men in Society'. Some of them were written as early as 1820–3, but they were selected and polished only during his time in Naples, and were not published until after his death, in the edition of his works edited in 1845 by Ranieri.*

1. For a long time I refused to believe the things which I am about to say because, apart from the fact that I have myself a nature which is very alien to them, and that one always tends to judge others by oneself, my inclination has always been not to hate other men, but to love them. But in the end experience has convinced me, almost by force, and I am sure that those of my readers who have had many and varied dealings with other men will admit that my observations are true, while all the others will consider them exaggerated, until experience—if the opportunity is afforded them of a real experience of human society—places the truth before their eyes.

I say that the world is a league of scoundrels against honest men, and of the base against the generous. When two scoundrels meet for the first time, they easily recognize each other, as by a secret sign, for what they are; and at once they reach an agreement; or, if their interests do not permit this, they at least feel a great liking for each other, and hold each other in much esteem. If a scoundrel has business dealings with another scoundrel, he very often behaves honestly and does not defraud him; but if with men of honour, he will be sure to break faith with them, and, if it suits his convenience, will try to ruin them, even if they are courageous men, capable of revenging themselves. For he hopes, as almost always does occur, to defeat their courage with his deceit. I have often seen very timid men, who, finding themselves placed between a scoundrel more cowardly than themselves, and an honest man full of courage, have yet taken the scoundrel's part; indeed, this always happens when ordinary people find themselves in this situation, for the ways of an honest and brave man are familiar and simple, while those of a scoundrel are hidden and infinitely varied. Now, as every-one knows, the unknown is more alarming than the familiar, and it is easy to guard against the vengeance of the magnani-mous, from which you are partly saved by your own coward-ice and fear; but no fear and no cowardice will suffice to save you from the secret persecutions, the intrigues, or even the open blows which come to you from mean enemies. Usually in daily life true courage is seldom feared; partly because, not being supported by any make-believe, it has not got the outer appearance which makes it alarming, and therefore no one believes in it; while scoundrels are feared as if they were also brave, because, owing to their craftiness, other men believe them to be so.

Scoundrels are seldom poor, because, apart from anything else, if an honest man falls into poverty, no one comes to his assistance and many rejoice; but if a scoundrel becomes poor, the whole town bestirs itself to help him. The reason is easily understood. It is that we are naturally moved by the misfortunes of our fellows and associates, for we think that similar threats hang over ourselves; and we are willing to help them, if possible, because not to do so almost seems to be equivalent to an inner admission that we ought to be treated in the same way ourselves. Now the scoundrels, who are the more numerous, and also the richer in talent, con-sider other scoundrels, even if they do not know them by sight, their natural comrades and associates, and in times of need feel bound to succour them by the sort of alliance that exists between them, as I have said. . . .

On the contrary, the good and the magnanimous, being unlike most other men, are considered by them as creatures of another species and consequently not only are not treated either as allies or comrades, but are not thought deserving of human rights, and are persecuted more or less severely, according to the degree of baseness or perfidiousness of the people or the period in which they chance to live. For as, in the bodies of animals, nature tends to get rid of those humours and elements which do not agree with those which properly compose their bodies, so in human communities nature herself decrees that any man who is very different from most other men, especially if this difference takes the form of opposition, should by every effort be destroyed or chased away.

The good and magnanimous are also much hated because they are usually sincere and call things by their true names; and this is a fault never forgiven by the human race, which does not even hate an evil-doer or evil itself as much as the man who calls them by their right name. So that very often, while evil-doers become rich, honoured, and powerful, the man who calls attention to them goes to the gallows. For men are ready to bear anything whatever from each other or from heaven, as long as they are safe from hard words.

vi. Death is not an evil; for it frees man from all evils and, in taking away joy, also removes desire. Old age is the greatest of evils, for it deprives man of every pleasure, while leaving every appetite, and brings with it all sorrows. Yet men fear death, and desire old age.

x. Most of the persons to whom we entrust the education of our children have not, to our certain knowledge, been educated themselves. And we do not suspect that they cannot possibly impart that which they have not themselves received, and which cannot be acquired in any other way.

xviii. I saw a man in Florence who, as he was dragging along a heavily-laden cart, like a beast of burden, as is the custom there, went about with great arrogance, shouting, and ordering everyone to give way to him; and it seemed to me a symbol of many men who go about puffed up with pride and insulting others for reasons not unlike his, that is, that they are dragging a cart behind them.

xxv. No one is so completely disenchanted with the world, nor knows it so intimately, nor feels so much anger against it, that he does not become reconciled to it, at least in part, if he suddenly receives from it a kindly glance; and equally we consider no man so perfidious that, if he greets us courteously, he will not appear to us less perfidious than before. . . .

xxvii. There is no more certain sign that one does not possess much philosophy or much wisdom, than to expect that everything in life should be wise and philosophical.

xxviii. The human race, and every small portion of it, is divided into two kinds: the bullies and the bullied. No law or power, no progress of philosophy or civilization, can prevent a man, in the future as in the past, from belonging to the one or the other; but it is open to those who are capable of choosing, to make a choice between them. Yet it is true that the choice is not open for everyone, nor at all times.

xxxi. In every country the universal vices and evils of mankind and of human society are considered to be peculiar to that one place. I have never been anywhere where I have not heard people say: 'Here the women are vain and inconstant, they do not care for reading and are ill-educated; here the people are inquisitive about other men's business, they are gossipy and malicious; here money, favouritism, and baseness are all-powerful; here envy reigns, and friendship is insincere', and so forth; as if things were different anywhere else. It is through necessity that men are wretched, but they are determined to believe that they are so by accident.

xxxiv. Young men often believe that an affectation of melancholy renders them more lovable. And perhaps indeed melancholy, when feigned, can be pleasing for a short time, especially to women. But when it is genuine, it is avoided by the whole human race, and in the long run nothing but cheerfulness pleases in society, or brings good fortune with it. For in the end—whatever young men may think—the world wishes rather to laugh than to weep, and is not wrong.

xxxv. In places which are half-way between savagery and civilization—such as Naples, for instance—a thing that is more or less universally true, is more noticeable than elsewhere. It is this, that a man who is thought to be penniless is scarcely looked upon as a man at all; while a man believed to be rich is in danger of his life. In consequence it is necessary in such places, and indeed is generally the custom, to strive to keep your financial state a secret, so that the public should not know whether to despise or to get rid of you, and so as to be treated like most other men: partly despised and partly respected, sometimes injured and sometimes left in peace.

xxxvii. No human quality is more intolerable in everyday life, nor indeed is less tolerated, than intolerance.

lviii. The timid have no less self-esteem than the arrogant, indeed more or perhaps a more sensitive one; and therefore are they afraid. . . .

lxi. When a man loses his youth, he is also deprived of the capacity of communicating, and almost of making his presence felt; and thus, having lost the sort of influence which a young man exercises on the people around him—which draws them to him and makes them feel a sort of inclination for him—he realizes, with a new kind of pain, that in company he is cut off from everyone and surrounded by sensitive creatures who yet are hardly less indifferent to him than if they were totally insensitive.

LXXVI. Nothing in the world is rarer than a person whom one can put up with all the time.

LXXXIV. Jesus Christ was the first who clearly pointed out to men who is the apologist and teacher of all feigned virtues, and the detractor and persecutor of all true ones; the adversary of every sort of greatness that is intrinsic and truly proper to man; the derider of every high sentiment, unless he believes it to be false, and of every sweet affection, if he believes it to be private; the slave of the strong, the tyrant of the weak, the enemy of the unfortunate, to which Jesus Christ Himself gave a name which it has kept in all civilized languages up to the present day: the World. I do not believe that this general idea, which is so true and which afterwards came into current usage and will always remain so, had struck anyone else before, nor do I remember that it is to be found, I mean as a single term and in a precise form, in any pagan philosopher. Perhaps because until then baseness and deceit were not full-grown, and civilization had not yet reached the point at which a great part of its essence is indistinguishable from corruption. . . .

LXXXVI. The most certain way of hiding the limits of our knowledge, is never to overpass them.

XC. I once knew a child who, whenever his mother refused him anything, would say, 'Oh, I see, I see, Mama's naughty.' Most men speak with as much logic about their neighbours, although they do not express themselves so simply.

XCVI. An honest man, as his age increases, easily becomes indifferent to praise and honours, but never, I believe, to blame or contempt. Indeed the praise and esteem of many distinguished men will not make up to him for the pain given to him by a jeer or a sign of indifference, even from someone who is quite insignificant. Perhaps the reverse occurs with scoundrels, who are so accustomed to blame and unaccustomed to praise, that they care nothing for the former and greatly enjoy the latter, if a taste of it happens to come their way.

XCIX. People are never ridiculous, except when they try to seem or to be what they are not. The poor, the ignorant, the rustic, the sick, the old, are never ridiculous so long as they are content to appear just as they are, and to keep within the limits required by their own character, but only become so when the old try to seem young, the sick strong, or the poor rich; when the illiterate try to seem learned or the rustic polished townsmen. Even physical defects, however serious they may be, would not arouse more than a passing smile, if a man did not attempt to conceal them, that is, if he did not wish to appear as if he had not got them, and different from what he really is. . . .

Those men who, to become more lovable, pretend that they have a different character from their natural one, make a great mistake. The effort, which cannot be kept up after a short time and soon becomes evident, and the contrast between the assumed character and the real one, which is frequently perceptible, render that person much more unamiable and unattractive that he would be if he frankly and steadily showed his true nature. Every character, even the most unfortunate, has something in it which is not ugly, and which, being real, will please a great deal more, if shown at the right moment, than the finest simulated qualities.

Generally speaking, the endeavour to seem what we are not, spoils everything in the world; and it is this alone which renders insufferable a great many people who would be very amiable if they would only be content to be themselves. And this is true not only of persons but also of whole societies and peoples. I know several cultivated and flourishing country towns which would be very pleasant places to live in but for a disgusting imitation of what is done in the capitals—that is, an attempt to be, in so far as they can, capital cities rather than provincial ones.

CII. The years of childhood are, in the memory of every man, the fabulous years of his life; as, in a nation's memories, the fabulous years are those of that nation's youth.

CV. Cunning, which appertains to the intellect, is often used to make up for a certain lack of that quality, or to defeat greater intellectual powers in others.

CVIII. While men are still immature, they try hard to appear mature, and when they have become so, to seem still green. Oliver Goldsmith, the author of *The Vicar of Wakefield*, cast off the title of doctor when he reached the age of forty, for this token of importance had become distasteful to him, after being so dear to him in his early years.

CX. It is curious to observe that almost all men of real worth have simple manners; and that yet almost always simple manners are considered a sign of little worth.

O

11. The Last Years: Florence and Naples 1830–7

Scende la luna; e si scolora il mondo.[1]

I

After his return to Florence in 1830, Leopardi announced the publication of a new edition of his Canti, *which was to include the poems he had recently written in Pisa and Recanati. It appeared in the spring of 1831, and quoted on the title-page two lines of Petrarch's:*

Accomplished is the end of my brief fable,
Half-way through life, I know my time is spent.

The tragic letter of dedication, 'To my Friends in Tuscany', reveals how little hope he had of regaining his health, or of ever being able to work again.

Dear Friends of mine, Let this book be dedicated to you in which I have attempted, as one often does in poetry, to sublimate my grief—a book with which (I cannot say it without tears) I bid farewell to letters and to my studies. I had hoped that these beloved studies would sustain my old age, I believed that with the loss of all other pleasures, all the joys of childhood and of youth, I had yet acquired one treasure which no power, no misfortune could steal away. But I had not yet reached my twentieth year when more than half of that single blessing was snatched away from me by an infirmity of nerves and health which, while it destroyed the value of life for me, yet offered no hope of death; and two years before I was thirty, this work of

[1] 'The moon descends, and all the world grows dim.'

destruction was completed; and, as I now believe, for ever. You are well aware that I have not even been able to read these pages, and that to correct them, I have had to make use of the eyes and hand of others.

I will complain no more, my dear friends: my conscious-ness of the extent of my grief is not compatible with lamen-tation. I have lost everything: I am only a useless block that feels and suffers. Yet now, even now, my friends, I have acquired your friendship and your company; they take the place of my studies, of every hope and delight, and would almost make up for my troubles, if these ailments of mine allowed me to enjoy them as much as I desire, and if I did not know that Fate will soon deprive me of these too, obliging me to wear out the years that may still be left to me, without any civilized comfort, in a place where the dead are happier than the living. But your love will remain with me, and will endure even when my body, which has already ceased to live, has turned to ashes. Farewell. Your Leopardi.[1]

This letter betrays Leopardi's greatest fear: that, when his Florentine friends realized that he was no longer able to work, they would cut off his allowance (as indeed they did), and he would be obliged to return to Recanati. It was this fear that he confided one evening to a new friend: a handsome, romantic, amorous, enthusiastic young Neapolitan, who had been exiled from the kingdom of Naples on account of his Liberal opinions—Antonio Ranieri.

'That evening'—the account is Ranieri's own—'by the faint light of his shaded lamp, I saw that he was weeping, and, indescribably moved by those words and tears, I said what a man would only say at the age that I was then: "Leopardi, you shall not return to Recanati! The little that I have will suffice for two as well as for one. . . . Never shall we be parted!"'

The closeness of his association with Ranieri, and, later on, their three-cornered relationship, which has already been described, with Fanny Targioni, did not fail to awaken some malicious comment in the small world of Florence—but I do not think that we should

[1] *Epistolario*, VI, 15 December 1830.

*conclude that Leopardi's and Ranieri's relationship was homosexual.
Though some of Ranieri's papers do imply that the young Neapolitan
was ambivalent, Leopardi's own views about homosexuality—in
spite of his cult of 'the ancients'—were quite uncompromising, and
besides, it is necessary to remember the extreme romanticism of expression that convention then permitted to friends of the same sex.
(A similar tone may be found, for instance, in many of Foscolo's
letters.) Moreover, one should remember the circumstances under
which this friendship began: Leopardi's extreme poverty and
anxiety about his future, his loneliness in Florence, his semi-blindness
and ever-increasing physical dependence, and his long-suppressed
craving for companionship and affection. When Ranieri, after spending two years with him, returned to his own family in Naples, his
words to his sister were quite literally true: 'I have left in Florence
an immortal man, but a mortal invalid, for the protraction of whose
life my brotherly care is an absolute necessity.' And it was this
invalid who, during the following months of separation—deserted by
Fanny, cut off from most of his Florentine friends, and living all day
alone in a dark room, during an acute attack of ophthalmia—sent
off to Naples, day after day, the series of brief, despairing notes
which at last brought Ranieri back to Florence.*

My Ranieri, you will never desert me, never cool in your
love. I do not want you to sacrifice yourself for me; on the
contrary, I ardently wish you to consider, first and foremost,
what is best for you. But whatever you may decide, you will
arrange matters in such a way that we can live for each
other, or at least that I can live for you, my last and only
hope. Good-bye, my soul. I strain you close to my heart,
which in every possible and impossible event will remain
yours eternally.

*For weeks the correspondence continued in this tone, Ranieri still
lingering in Naples, and Leopardi preparing to join him there.*

If you cannot get away, shall I not come to you? Shall we
not be united all the same, and soon? I am threatened with

the loss of my sight and cannot write; but listen, Ranieri, in memory of all the time we have spent together, remember that, by God, I must embrace you before I die.

As the months passed, the notes became little more than a cry of pain.

My Ranieri, I long for you as for the Messiah. Whether I can do without you or not, you well know.

Believe me, my Ranieri, this scrap of paper represents the most that I can manage. My father and brother write complaining that they receive no answers to their letters, that they have had no news of me for three months, and I do not even finish reading their letters. All day I cry out for you.

At last Ranieri set off, but when he got to Rome, he found another note waiting for him.

God grant that I may see you before I die; it now seems to me hardly likely, although certainly not through your fault. Farewell, ὦ πολὺ ἐπικαλούμενε, farewell with all my heart.[1]

As soon as Ranieri got back to Florence, Leopardi's health temporarily improved, but it was not until four months later, in September 1833, that the two friends set off—in a tightly-sealed carriage—for Naples, where they had decided to make their home, together with Ranieri's sister, Paolina. Their first summer at Capodimonte was probably the happiest period of Leopardi's four years in Naples, the last years of his life. His health was better; he was able to enjoy the milder climate and a few new friends (among them the young German poet, August von Platen); he went to the theatre; he sat for long hours outside Vito's famous café in the Largo della Carità, eating ices and watching the tumult and gaiety of

[1] *Epist.* VI, pp. 239–49, 10 January–13 April [1833].

*Neapolitan street-life. He even used to wander down to the quay by
the water's edge, at S. Lucia, where the fishermen drew up their nets
(sometimes flinging a portion of their rich haul into the open sacks of
the mendicant friars), and the fishwives screamed and tore out each
other's hair. But most of all he enjoyed listening, in the evenings,
spell-bound among listeners no less enthralled, no less swiftly moved
to tears and laughter than those who once followed the battles of the
Iliad, to the* cantastorie *who told for the thousandth time the epic
tales of Tasso or Ariosto.*

The crowd take sides [he wrote] with the heroes with such
ardour that after the recital, as they talk it over with each
other, they argue and come to blows, and sometimes even
kill each other. Very late at night two of them who had
been disputing heatedly, went to wake up the famous
Genovesi to ask him whether it was Rinaldo or Gernando[1]
who was in the right. . . . It is thus that a poem may truly be
said to have been brought before the public![2]

*It is not difficult to understand the fascination that such scenes as
these held for Leopardi. 'A stranger here'—not only in Naples, but
in life itself—he watched this apotheosis of human vigour with the
peculiarly sharp vision that usually is only granted to a foreigner.
Anonymous, unnoticed, one more little hunchback in the crowd, he
could enjoy a vicarious sense of colour and of life. But there were
also other, less happy, sides to his life in Naples. The Neapolitan
intellectuals, with a few exceptions, did not like him, nor he them; he
was as little in sympathy with their proselytizing Catholicism as he
had been with the humanitarian Liberalism of the Florentines;
while they, on their side, disapproved of his philosophy and did not
care much for his verse. And above all, his friendship with Ranieri
was often clouded by mutual irritation and misunderstandings.*

*Poverty and constant ill-health—both extending indefinitely into
the future, without any reasonable hope of relief—these are trials
which, at extremely close quarters, may put any friendship to the*

[1] In Tasso's *Gerusalemme Liberata*.
[2] *Zibaldone*, II, pp. 1207–8.

test. 'Nothing is rarer,' as Leopardi himself wrote, 'than a person whom one can bear with all the time.' Moreover, there was also between the two men not only a clash of individual temperaments, but of irreconcilable differences in manners and habits as between the North and the South. Ranieri was effusive, emotional, gregarious, emphatic; Leopardi, reserved, gentle, melancholy, mistrustful. In spite of his failing sight, he was desperately attempting (though seldom successfully) to earn a little money, but was obliged to dictate most of his letters, as well as his literary work, to Ranieri or Paolina, who also took it in turns to read aloud to him, sometimes all through the night—until, Ranieri wrote, they were reminded of the torture by which certain Eastern peoples destroyed their prisoners: captivos insomnis occidebant.[1] *Certainly Leopardi was neither a considerate guest nor an easy patient: when the doctor ordered him to give up all sweet food and especially ices, he would sugar his coffee and lemonade till they became like a syrup, and steal out of the house, like a schoolboy, alone, to eat more ices at Vito's. He would alternate between pitch darkness and dazzling light, between eating too much meat and a completely vegetarian diet, and would declare that, in the whole of Naples, the bread of only one baker was edible. And sometimes, too, he plainly said how much he disliked Naples and the Neapolitans, complaining of the noise, the dust, the dishonesty, of 'this half-barbarian and half-African place'. On the other hand, Ranieri seems to have been intensely and possessively jealous, extremely touchy, and wholly incapable of understanding any desire for quiet or privacy—and he finally set down his grievances (when he was over eighty), in a highly rhetorical and inaccurate book,* Seven Years of Companionship with Giacomo Leopardi, *which has given rise to much unpleasant controversy.*

But when all this has been said, it must also be remembered that for nearly seven years Ranieri was Leopardi's constant amanuensis, nurse, and companion, that his admiration for him as a great poet never failed, and that he stayed with him and cared for him until the end. Whatever mixture of truth and falsehood there may have been in his senile outpourings, one can hardly deny respect to such a friendship, nor something of the quality which Leopardi, three

---

[1] 'They killed their prisoners by depriving them of sleep.'

*years before his first meeting with Ranieri, had himself described
in the last lines of his* Dialogue between Plotinus and Porphyry:

Let us live, my Porphyry, and comfort each other; let us
not refuse to bear the part that destiny has allotted to us of
the evils of our kind. Let us give each other companionship
and encouragement, each bringing help and succour to the
other, so that we may accomplish as best we can this labour
of our life, which doubtless will be brief. Neither when
death comes shall we lament, nor in our last hour shall
friends and companions fail us, but cheer shall be in the
thought that, when we are no more, they will remember us
often, and love us still.[1]

II

*We have now come to the last two years of Leopardi's life. At the
end of 1835 he wrote a letter to his sister Paolina, in which he
promised to pay his family a visit, as soon as his health and the
weather permitted.*

Dear Pilla, I am overcome with melancholy, when I think
what a long time I have spent without seeing you all. . . .
This time, when we are together again, I shall have no
lack of stories and tales to keep you happy for many
evenings.[2]

*But when the spring came, he went instead with Ranieri to a little
villa above Torre del Greco, on the slopes of Vesuvius, and there
they remained for nearly three months. The little white villa where
they lived—surrounded by vineyards and orchards, but very close to
the barren hillside where a river of lava had poured down from the
volcano, destroying all vegetation but a sea of golden broom—is still
called, from the title of the great poem he wrote there,* la villa della
ginestra. *Here, we may hope, Leopardi found some peace. But*

---

[1] *Poesie e Prose*, I, p. 1016: *Dialogue between Plotinus and Porphyry*.
[2] *Epist.* VI, 4 December 1835.

*when, in the following winter, he and Ranieri went back there—
driven away from Naples by an outbreak of cholera—he found the
little house both cold and damp, and his ill-health continued to
increase: he suffered from chronic bronchitis, from a swelling of the
legs which his doctor called dropsy, from insomnia, colitis, and
asthma, and above all from the increasing constriction caused by the
pressure of his deformed thorax on both his lungs and heart, which
eventually brought about his death.*

*The extent of his weariness, as well as of his cumulative sense of
failure, can be measured in a letter to a young French philologist,
Charles Lebreton, who had written to him saying, 'You are the poet
of all men of feeling.'*

If I wished for praise, yours would not be at all indifferent
to me: it is for spirits like yours, for tender and sensitive
hearts, that poets write—and that I, too, would write, if I
were a poet. My good friend De Sinner has depicted me to
you in too favourable a light. . . . Pray tell him that, in
spite of the fine title of *Opere* that my bookseller has chosen
to give to my collection, I have never accomplished any real
work. I have only made attempts, always believing them to
be preludes—but my career has gone no further.[1]

*Yet still he went on working. It was at this time that he produced
the two greatest poems of his later years,* The Broom *and* The
Setting of the Moon, *of which the last lines were written only a
few hours before his death.*

*The story of his last days is very poignant. He had returned with
Ranieri to Naples, but hardly had they got there than a fresh
epidemic of cholera broke out, bringing panic with it. Long pro-
cessions of penitents carried holy images through the streets; the
schools were shut, the shops deserted. Whole areas in the slums were
closed, being marked at each end with a Cross, and a 'Lord, have
mercy upon us'. Even the masked members of the* Misericordia,
*who came to take away the corpses, dared not enter there, but stood
outside, crying, 'Bring out your dead!'*

[1] *Epist.* VI, enclosed in a letter to De Sinner, dated 6 April 1836.

Leopardi, too, was deeply infected by the prevailing terror, and only his increasing weakness prevented him and Ranieri from hurrying off again to Torre del Greco. 'Do you know', he said one day to Paolina Ranieri, 'that something very strange is happening to me? . . . When I think of my approaching destruction, I seem to see myself lying in a ditch, with a crowd of ribald fools dancing on my belly.'[1]

He now well knew that death could not be far off. On 27 May 1837 he wrote to his father:

I have been attacked for the first time by a real asthma, which prevents me from walking, lying down, or sleeping. . . . If I escape the cholera, I shall make every effort, as soon as my health permits, in any weather or season, to see you again, for now I too am in a hurry, being convinced . . . that the end of my life, which God has ordained, is not far off. My daily and incurable physical sufferings have at length reached such a pitch, that further they cannot go. I hope that when at last the feeble resistance offered to them by my dying body has been overcome, they will lead me to the eternal rest I call upon unceasingly—not from courage, but from the intensity of my pain. I thank you and my mother for the ten *scudi*, I kiss the hands of both of you, I embrace my brothers, and I beg you all to commend me to God, so that, after having seen you once again, a quick death may bring an end to my physical sufferings, for which there is no other cure. Your most loving son, Giacomo.[2]

His death came eighteen days later. On 13 June, the day before his death, a German friend who had gone to see him described him as being extraordinarily serene and gentle, with something childlike and candid in his expression; as if, he wrote, some dim reflection of the dawn of his childhood were mingling with another approaching dawn. The next day was the one on which they intended to move back to the country. Leopardi woke up feeling well, and, after

[1] A. Brofferio, *I miei tempi*, p. 81.
[2] *Epist.* VI, 27 May 1837.

drinking a large cup of sweet chocolate, dictated to Ranieri, in a voice so faint that it could hardly be heard, the last six lines of The Setting of the Moon.

An account of his last hours was set down by Ranieri. By midday the carriage was already at the door, but Leopardi said that he felt his asthma growing worse and would like to see the doctor. Ranieri replied that he would fetch him. 'I believe that, in spite of all my efforts, some small part of my deep emotion must have shown in my expression, for, getting up, Leopardi made fun of it, and reminded me of the long life enjoyed by all asthmatics.'

Ranieri soon brought the doctor to the house. 'But now everything was changed. Accustomed, by long and painful habit, to frequent warnings of death, our beloved patient could no longer distinguish the true from the false. . . . He was cheered by our arrival and smiled at us, and argued gently with Mannella (the doctor), although with a voice fainter than usual, about his nervous disease, his certainty of diminishing it with food, his distaste for ass's milk. . . . But Mannella, skilfully taking me aside, told me to send for a priest at once, since there was no time for anything else. . . .

'In the meantime we all of us remained beside Leopardi, Paolina supporting his head and drying the sweat that ran down from that wide forehead of his, while I, seeing him overtaken by an evil and dark stupor, strove to arouse him as usual with smelling salts of various kinds. He opened his eyes wider than usual and looked straighter than ever into mine, then: "I can't see you any more," he said, and ceased to breathe. His pulse and heart were no longer beating and at that moment Padre Felice of Sant'Agostino, a barefoot friar, came into the room, while I, beside myself, was calling in a loud voice to him who had been my father, my brother, and my friend, and who—although he still seemed to see me—did not answer.'

The relentless ill-fortune that attended Leopardi throughout his life was no kinder in the disposal of his bones. After various macabre incidents, what was left of them was first buried at Pozzuoli, then in the church's sacristy and later on in its porch—while finally, in 1939, the casket containing them was transferred to the side of the great cliff of Mergellina, above a little circular structure *of Roman masonry popularly known as Virgil's tomb, which looks out across the bay towards the slopes of Vesuvius. The stone which covers them bears a somewhat flowery inscription composed by Giordani. But it is open to wonder whether Leopardi would not have preferred the bare, bleak truth of the epitaph which he himself had written for the subject of the most autobiographical of his* Operette, The Memorable Sayings of Filippo Ottonieri:

Bones
Of Filippo Ottonieri
Born to Noble Deeds
And Glory
Lived Idle and Useless
And Died without Renown
Not Unaware of his Nature
Nor of his Fate.

II. *Poetry*

Translated by John Heath-Stubbs

NOTE ON THE PRESENT TRANSLATIONS FROM THE *CANTI*

With the exception of my version of the 'Bruto Minore', which is here printed for the first time, these translations were originally undertaken some twenty years ago, in a spirit of youthful enthusiasm for the poet, coupled with, I am afraid, a less than perfect knowledge of his language. They have now been thoroughly revised from the first edition. I have very much welcomed the opportunity of doing this, and would like to express my gratitude to the Marchesa Iris Origo for many very helpful suggestions. I have attempted to follow the verse forms of the poet as closely as English will permit. Leopardi's poems fall for the most part into two groups: those written in *endecasillabi sciolti* and those written in the *canzone libera*. The former metre, which is the equivalent of English blank verse (which in fact, in the sixteenth century, historically derived from it), should offer no difficulty to the English translator. The latter form, as its name denotes, is an extension of the classical Italian *canzoni*, as developed by the poets of the Middle Ages and the Renaissance. Leopardi took it over from the dramatic choruses of Tasso and his followers, and made it his most characteristic vehicle. As Professor F. T. Prince has pointed out, it had also had its impact on English versification in Milton, notably in 'Lycidas'. One might add the Songs of William Drummond, in the same period, from which the odes of Patmore's 'Unknown Eros' derived. The form consists in an irregular alternation of eleven-syllable and seven-syllable lines, partly rhymed and partly unrhymed. In my translations I have followed exactly Leopardi's arrangement of long and short lines which give their basic architectonic structure to the poems. But I have taken the liberty of very much reducing or altogether omitting the rhymes. This inevitably leads to some loss in the musical quality of the poetry, but it is perhaps justified in a language where rhyme comes to hand less easily than in Italian. It

209

permits a closer adherence to the sense than would otherwise be possible.

Leopardi's language is highly literary and allusive. His poems contain many echoes of the Greek and Latin classics, and turns of phrase inherited from the Arcadians of the late seventeenth and eighteenth centuries in Italy. Nevertheless he sought to restore to the Italian of his day a greater purity of diction than was commonly practised. He found his model for this in Petrarch, and also, we are told, was accustomed to wander about the streets of Recanati listening to the speech of the common people. This possessed a greater strength than the language of the would-be cultivated circles into which he was born (who often thought it more refined to speak French rather than their native tongue). His reform of language, then, would appear to present rather close analogies to that undertaken by the contemporary English Romantics. The latter likewise looked back beyond the stylizations of Augustan diction to the purity of Elizabethan English, while at the same time postulating 'a selection of the real language of men'. In these translations I have therefore attempted a middle style, with the language of the English Romantics, especially Wordsworth, in mind. An historical pastiche of early nineteenth-century diction would not, however, be in place, and sometimes the nature of Leopardi's thought seemed to call for a more modern turn of phrase.

One important poem of Leopardi's, 'Il Risorgimento', I have been unable to translate because it is written in a metre derived from Metastasio which would appear to have no possible equivalent in English.

JOHN HEATH-STUBBS

XXXIII.

Il tramonto della luna.

Quale in notte solinga,
Sovra campagne inargentate ed acqua,
Là 've zefiro aleggia,
E mille vaghi aspetti
E ingannevoli obbietti
Fingon l'ombre lontane
Infra l'onde tranquille
E rami e siepi e collinette e ville;
Giunta al confin del cielo,
Dietro Apennino od Alpe, o del Tirreno
Nell'infinito seno
Scende la luna; e si scolora il mondo;
Spariscon l'ombre, ed una

First Lines of Leopardi's Last Poem
in His Own Hand

P

L'Infinito

Sempre caro mi fu quest'ermo colle,
E questa siepe, che da tanta parte
Dell'ultimo orizzonte il guardo esclude.
Ma sedendo e mirando, interminati
Spazi di là da quella, e sovrumani
Silenzi, e profondissima quiete
Io nel pensier mi fingo; ove per poco
Il cor non si spaura. E come il vento
Odo stormir tra queste piante, io quello
Infinito silenzio a questa voce
Vo comparando: e mi sovvien l'eterno,
E le morte stagioni, e la presente
E viva, e il suon di lei. Così tra questa
Immensità s'annega il pensier mio:
E il naufragar m'è dolce in questo mare.

The Infinite

This lonely hill was always dear to me,
And this hedgerow, that hides so large a part
Of the far sky-line from my view. Sitting and gazing,
I fashion in my mind what lie beyond—
Unearthly silences, and endless space,
And very deepest quiet; then for a while
The heart is not afraid. And when I hear
The wind come blustering among the trees
I set that voice against this infinite silence:
And then I call to mind Eternity,
The ages that are dead, and the living present
And all the noise of it. And thus it is
In that immensity my thought is drowned:
And sweet to me the foundering in that sea.

1819

La sera del dì di festa

Dolce e chiara è la notte e senza vento,
E queta sovra i tetti e in mezzo agli orti
Posa la luna, e di lontan rivela
Serena ogni montagna. O donna mia,
Già tace ogni sentiero, e pei balconi
Rara traluce la notturna lampa:
Tu dormi, che t'accolse agevol sonno
Nelle tue chete stanze; e non ti morde
Cura nessuna; e già non sai nè pensi
Quanta piaga m'apristi in mezzo al petto.
Tu dormi: io questo ciel, che sì benigno
Appare in vista, a salutar m'affaccio,
E l'antica natura onnipossente,
Che mi fece all'affanno. A te la speme
Nego, mi disse, anche la speme; e d'altro
Non brillin gli occhi tuoi se non di pianto.
Questo dì fu solenne: or da' trastulli
Prendi riposo; e forse ti rimembra
In sogno a quanti oggi piacesti, a quanti
Piacquero a te: non io, non già, ch'io speri,
Al pensier ti ricorro. Intanto io chieggo
Quanto a viver mi resti, e qui per terra
Mi getto, e grido, e fremo. Oh giorni orrendi
In così verde etate! Ahi, per la via
Odo non lunge il solitario canto
Dell'artigian, che riede a tarda notte,
Dopo i sollazzi, al suo povero ostello;
E fieramente mi si stringe il core,
A pensar come tutto al mondo passa,
E quasi orma non lascia. Ecco è fuggito
Il dì festivo, ed al festivo il giorno
Volgar succede, e se ne porta il tempo

The Evening after the Holy Day

The night is soft and clear, and no wind blows;
The quiet moon stands over roofs and orchards
Revealing from afar each peaceful hill.
Beloved, now every alley way is silent;
At intervals along the balconies
The night-long lantern gleams; you are asleep,
And gentle slumber now gathers about
Your quiet chamber, and no single care
Gnaws at your heart; you do not know at all,
Nor think that you have opened in my breast
A very grievous wound. You are asleep:
And I have come abroad now to salute
This sky whose aspect seems to be so gentle,
And ancient Nature powerful over all,
Who has fashioned me for trouble. 'I deny
All hope to you,' she has said, 'yea, even hope;
Your eyes shall not be bright for any cause,
Except with weeping.' This was a festal day:
And you are resting after its delights;
And maybe in your dreams you still remember
How many eyes took pleasure in your beauty,
How many, too, pleased you: I find no place—
Not that I hoped it now—among your thoughts.
Meantime I ask how many years of life
Remain to me, and therefore here I cast
Myself upon the ground, and cry, and rage.
Oh terrible days, even of our green youth!
Alas, I hear not far along the road
The lonely singing of a workman, coming
Back to his poor home so late at night,
After the sports; and fiercely my heart aches
Thinking how all this world passes away

Ogni umano accidente. Or dov'è il suono
Di que' popoli antichi? or dov'è il grido
De' nostri avi famosi, e il grande impero
Di quella Roma, e l'armi, e il fragorio
Che n'andò per la terra e l'oceano?
Tutto è pace e silenzio, e tutto posa
Il mondo, e più di lor non si ragiona.
Nella mia prima età, quando s'aspetta
Bramosamente il dì festivo, or poscia
Ch'egli era spento, io doloroso, in veglia,
Premea le piume; ed alla tarda notte
Un canto che s'udia per li sentieri
Lontanando morire a poco a poco,
Già similmente mi stringeva il core.

And leaves no trace. For look, the festival
Is over now, an ordinary day
Succeeds tomorrow; all things our race has known
Time likewise bears away. Where now is the voice
Of the ancient peoples, the clamour of our ancestors
Who were renowned, and that great Empire of Rome,
The arms, and the clash they made by land and sea?
All is silence and peace; the world is still;
There are no tidings now remain of them.
Once in my boyhood, when so eagerly
We would look forward to the holiday,
Finding it over, I lay upon my bed,
Wakeful and very unhappy; late at night
A singing heard along the alley ways
Little by little dying into the distance,
Even as this does now, gripped at my heart.

1819

Alla luna

O graziosa luna, io mi rammento
Che, or volge l'anno, sovra questo colle
Io venia pien d'angoscia a rimirarti:
E tu pendevi allor su quella selva
Siccome or fai, che tutta la rischiari.
Ma nebuloso e tremulo dal pianto
Che mi sorgea sul ciglio, alle mie luci
Il tuo volto apparia, che travagliosa
Era mia vita: ed è, né cangia stile,
O mia diletta luna. E pur mi giova
La ricordanza, e il noverar l'etate
Del mio dolore. Oh come grato occorre
Nel tempo giovanil, quando ancor lungo
La speme e breve ha la memoria il corso,
Il rimembrar delle passate cose,
Ancor che triste, e che l'affanno duri!

To the Moon

O gracious Moon, I call to mind again
It was a year ago I climbed this hill
To gaze upon you in my agony;
And you were hanging then above that wood,
Filling it all with light, as you do now.
But dim and tremulous your face appeared,
Seen through the tears that rose beneath my eyelids,
My life being full of travail; as it is still—
It does not change, O my sweet Moon. And yet
Remembrance helps, and reckoning up
The cycles of my sorrow. How sweet the thought
That brings to mind things past, when we are young—
When long's the road for Hope, for Memory brief—
Though they were sad, and though our pain endures.

1819

Il sogno

Frammento

ALCETA

Odi, Melisso: io vo' contarti un sogno
Di questa notte, che mi torna a mente
In riveder la luna. Io me ne stava
Alla finestra che risponde al prato,
Guardando in alto: ed ecco all'improvviso
Distaccasi la luna; e mi parea
Che quanto nel cader s'approssimava,
Tanto crescesse al guardo; infin che venne
A dar di colpo in mezzo al prato; ed era
Grande quanto una secchia, e di scintille
Vomitava una nebbia, che stridea
Sì forte come quando un carbon vivo
Nell'acqua immergi e spegni. Anzi a quel modo
La luna, come ho detto, in mezzo al prato
Si spegneva annerando a poco a poco,
E ne fumavan l'erbe intorno intorno.
Allor mirando in ciel, vidi rimaso
Come un barlume, o un'orma, anzi una nicchia,
Ond'ella fosse svelta; in cotal guisa,
Ch'io n'agghiacciava; e ancor non m'assicuro.

MELISSO

E ben hai che temer, che agevol cosa
Fora cader la luna in sul tuo campo.

ALCETA

Chi sa? non veggiam noi spesso di state
Cader le stelle?

The Dream

A Fragment

ALCETAS

Hear me, Melissus; I will tell you a dream
I had last night, which comes to mind again,
Now that I see the moon. I stood at the window
Which looks out on the field, and turned my eyes
Up to the sky; and then, all of a sudden,
The moon was loosened; and it seemed to me
That coming nearer and nearer as it fell down,
The bigger it appeared, until it tumbled
In the middle of the field, with a crash, and was
As big as a bucket is; and it spewed forth
A cloud of sparks, which spluttered, just as loud
As when you put a live coal under water
Till it goes out. For it was in that way
The moon, I'm telling you, in the middle of the field,
Went out, and little by little it all turned black.
And round about the grass went up in smoke.
And then, looking up at the sky, I saw was left
A kind of glimmer, or mark, or rather a socket,
From which it had been torn, and at that sight
I froze with terror; and don't feel easy yet.

MELISSUS

And well you might, indeed; for sure enough,
The moon *might* tumble down into your field.

ALCETAS

Who knows? For don't we often see in summer
Stars falling?

MELISSO

Egli ci ha tante stelle,
Che picciol danno è cader l'una o l'altra
Di lor, e mille rimaner. Ma sola
Ha questa luna in ciel, che da nessuno
Cader fu vista mai se non in sogno.

But then, there are so many stars:
And little harm if one or other of them
Do fall—there's thousands left. But there is only
This one moon in the sky, and nobody
Has ever seen it fall, except in dreams. . . .

1819

Bruto Minore

Poi che divelta, nella tracia polve
Giacque ruina immensa
L'italica virtute, onde alle valli
D'Esperia verde, e al tiberino lido,
Il calpestio de' barbari cavalli
Prepara il fato, e dalle selve ignude
Cui l'Orsa algida preme,
A spezzar le romane inclite mura
Chiama i gotici brandi;
Sudato, e molle di fraterno sangue,
Bruto per l'atra notte in erma sede,
Fermo già di morir, gl'inesorandi
Numi e l'averno accusa,
E di feroci note
Invan la sonnolenta aura percote.

Stolta virtù, le cave nebbie, i campi
Dell'inquiete larve
Son le tue scole, a ti si volge a tergo
Il pentimento. A voi, marmorei numi,
(Se numi avete in Flegetonte albergo
O su le nubi) a voi ludibrio e scherno
È la prole infelice
A cui templi chiedeste, e frodolenta
Legge al mortale insulta.
Dunque tanto i celesti odii commove
La terrena pietà? dunque degli empi
Siedi, Giove, a tutela? e quando esulta
Per l'aere il nembo, e quando
Il tuon rapido spingi,
Ne' giusti e pii la sacra fiamma stringi?

The Younger Brutus

What time uprooted in the Thracian dust
Lay, an immense ruin
Italy's virtue, from whence the Fates prepared
For green Hesperia's vales and Tiber's banks
Tramp of barbarian horse, and from stark forests,
Oppressed by the frozen Bear,
To the destruction of Rome's famous walls,
Called forth the Gothic swords;
Worn out and dripping with his kindred's blood
Brutus, in blackest night seated alone,
Resolute now on his own death, accused
Avernus and the inexorable Powers, and thus with
    savage accents,
Vainly made tremulous the drowsy air.

'Stupid Virtue, the hollow clouds, the fields
Haunted by unquiet ghosts—
These are your schools, and at your back comes round
Bitter remorse. To you, marmoreal Powers,
(If Powers there be in hold of Phlegethon
Or here beneath the clouds), a laughing-stock
And scorn is our sad race
From whom you beg temples and with fraudulent
    laws
Insult mortality.
Is Heaven's hatred then so much provoked
By earthly piety? Do you, Jove, sit
Impiety's protector? And when exults
The cloudburst through the air, and when
Hurtles the rapid thunder,
Whelm on the good and just your sacred fires?

Preme il destino invitto e la ferrata
Necessità gl'infermi
Schiavi di morte: e se a cessar non vale
Gli oltraggi lor, de' necessarii danni
Si consola il plebeo. Men duro è il male
Che riparo non ha? dolor non sente
Chi di speranza è nudo?
Guerra mortale, eterna, o fato indegno,
Teco il prode guerreggia,
Di cedere inesperto; e la tiranna
Tua destra, allor che vincitrice il grava,
Indomito scrollando si pompeggia,
Quando nell'alto lato
L'amaro ferro intride,
E maligno alle nere ombre sorride.

Spiace agli Dei chi violento irrompe
Nel Tartaro. Non fora
Tanto valor ne' molli eterni petti.
Forse i travagli nostri, e forse il cielo
I casi acerbi e gl'infelici affetti
Giocondo agli ozi suoi spettacol pose?
None fra sciagure e colpe,
Ma libera ne' boschi e pura etade
Natura a noi prescrisse,
Reina un tempo e Diva. Or poi ch'a terra
Sparse i regni beati empio costume,
E il viver macro ad altre leggi addisse;
Quando gl'infausti giorni
Virile alma ricusa,
Riede natura, e il non suo dardo accusa?

Di colpa ignare e de' lor proprii danni
Le fortunate belve
Serena adduce al non previsto passo
La tarda età. Ma se spezzar la fronte

Unconquerable Fate and iron
Necessity bear down
Upon the sickly slaves of Death; no intermission
Availing for his outrage, the common man
Consoles himself that ills are necessary.
Is the irreparable less harsh? Is grief unfelt
By him who's stripped of hope?
War to the death, eternal, the brave soldier
Wages with you, base Fate,
Not schooled to yield; and with the tyrannous grip
Of your right hand, victorious on him laid,
Shrugs it off unsubdued, with a last gesture
When in his own proud flank
The bitter steel makes entry,
And grimly smiles towards the blackening shades.

Displeasing to the gods, who violent, storms
The underworld: such valour
Is not for their feeble, eternal breasts.
The Heavens perhaps devised our sufferings,
Our bitter lot and our tormented passions,
As a mere spectacle to please their sight.
Calamities nor crimes,
But free, unsullied ages in the woods,
Nature ordained for us,
Our queen and goddess once. Now when on earth
Impious custom wrecks her hallowed reign,
Our meagre life kept back by other laws,
When one of manly soul
Rejects the ill-omened days,
Will Nature blame his dart as not her own?

They know no guilt, nor their own suffering,
The fortunate wild herds;
Calmly, their latter age leads on apace
Without foreknowledge. But if distress should urge
   them

Ne' rudi tronchi, o da montano sasso
Dare al vento precipiti le membra,
Lor suadesse affanno;
Al misero desio nulla contesa
Legge arcana farebbe
O tenebroso ingegno. A voi, fra quante
Stirpi il cielo avvivò, soli fra tutte,
Figli di Prometeo, la vita increbbe;
A voi le morte ripe,
Se il fato ignavo pende,
Soli, o miseri, a voi Giove contende.

E tu dal mar cui nostro sangue irriga,
Candida luna, sorgi,
E l'inquieta notte e la funesta
All'ausonio valor campagna esplori.
Cognati petti il vincitor calpesta,
Fremono i poggi, dalle somme vette
Roma antica ruina;
Tu sì placida sei? Tu la nascente
Lavinia prole, e gli anni
Lieti vedesti, e i memorandi allori;
E tu su l'alpe l'immutato raggio
Tacita verserai quando ne' danni
Del servo italo nome,
Sotto barbaro piede
Rintronerà quella solinga sede.

Ecco tra nudi sassi o in verde ramo
E la fera e l'augello,
Del consueto obblio gravido il petto,
L'alta ruina ignora e le mutate
Sorti del mondo: e come prima il tetto
Rosseggerà del villanello industre,
Al mattutino canto
Quel desterà le valli, e per le balze
Quella l'inferma plebe

To dash their heads on the rough trunks, or to
    consign
From mountain rocks their bodies headlong down
Into the wind, no arcane law
Nor dark conceit stands to contend against
Their wretched longings. You, among so many
Stocks Heaven vivifies, for you alone,
Sons of Prometheus, life is a torment;
And Jove to you alone
Forbids, O wretched men,
If tardy Fate delays, the shores of death.

And you, pale moon, rising out of the sea
Our blood incarnadines,
Survey the unquiet night, and these sad plains,
Ill-fated for the might of Italy.
The victor tramples on his kinsmen's hearts;
The hills are loud, from topmost summits ruins
Rome's antique glory down;
And do you watch so calmly, you who saw
The Latin nation's birth, the joyful years
And all its memorable laurels won?
And you, silent above the Alps shall shed
Your still unaltering beams, when mid the wrongs
Of Italy's servile name
That solitary seat
Is deafened by the tramp of barbarous feet.

Among the naked rocks, on the green bough,
The beast and wild bird
In customary oblivion of sleep
Know not the deep ruin nor the changed
State of the world; and when the labouring peasant's
Rooftop is touched by crimson of the dawn,
With morning canticles
The one will wake the valleys, and the other
From the high cliffs

Agiterà delle minori belve.
Oh casi! oh gener vano! abbietta parte
Siam delle cose; e non le tinte glebe,
Non gli ululati spechi
Turbò nostra sciagura,
Nè scolorò le stelle umana cura.

Non io d'Olimpo o di Cocito i sordi
Regi, o la terra indegna,
E non la notte moribondo appello;
Non te, dell'atra morte ultimo raggio,
Conscia futura età. Sdegnoso avello
Placàr singulti, ornàr parole e doni
Di vil caterva? In peggio
Precipitano i tempi; e mal s'affida
A putridi nepoti
L'onor d'egregie menti e la suprema
De' miseri vendetta. A me dintorno
Le penne il bruno augello avido roti;
Prema la fera, e il nembo
Tratti l'ignota spoglia;
E l'aura il nome e la memoria accoglia.

Startle the weaker droves of lesser animals.
Condition vain, vain race of man, we are
The abject part of things! Neither the bloodstained
    soil
Nor the rebellowing caves
Has our disaster troubled,
Nor does human anguish dim the stars.

Neither to you, Olympus, nor the deaf
Lords of Cocytus, nor to unworthy Earth,
Nor, dying, to the night, do I appeal;
Nor you, the last beam gleaming through black death,
Conscious posterity. Shall the vile crowd's
Sobs placate my arrogant tomb, their words
And offerings deck it out? From bad to worse
The times rush on; not well it is we assign
To our corrupt descendants
The honour of outstanding minds, their woes'
Ultimate vindication. Let the dark bird,
Whose pinions are about me, greedily tear;
Let the beast prey, and the rain cloud
Draw up the unnoted spoils,
The wind receive my name and memory.

December 1821

Alla primavera

o delle favole antiche

Perchè i celesti danni
Ristori il sole, e perchè l'aure inferme
Zefiro avvivi, onde fugata e sparta
Delle nubi la grave ombra s'avvalla;
Credano il petto inerme
Gli augelli al vento, e la diurna luce
Novo d'amor desio, nova speranza
Ne' penetrati boschi e fra le sciolte
Pruine induca alle commosse belve;
Forse alle stanche e nel dolor sepolte
Umane menti riede
La bella età, cui la sciagura e l'atra
Face del ver consunse
Innanzi tempo? Ottenebrati e spenti
Di febo i raggi al misero non sono
In sempiterno? ed anco,
Primavera odorata, inspiri e tenti
Questo gelido cor, questo ch'amara
Nel fior degli anni suoi vecchiezza impara?

Vivi tu, vivi, o santa
Natura? vivi e il dissueto orecchio
Della materna voce il suono accoglie?
Già di candide ninfe i rivi albergo,
Placido albergo e specchio
Furo i liquidi fonti. Arcane danze
D'immortal piede i ruinosi gioghi
Scossero e l'ardue selve (oggi romito
Nido de' venti): e il pastorel ch'all'ombre

To Spring

or, Concerning the Ancient Myths

Even though the sun repair
The ruin of the sky, the western breeze
Quicken the sickly air, from whence is fled,
Scattered, the heavy shadow of the clouds,
And though the birds confide
Their undefended bodies to the winds,
The light of day, piercing among the coverts
And loosening the hoar-frost, breed new hope,
Fresh amorous desire among the beasts;
Yet may a thought revisit the tired mind
Of Man, by grief entombed,
Of that fair former age, which all too soon
The obscure splendour of truth
And time's disasters utterly consumed?
For him, must Phoebus' beams be dark, and
  quenched
For all eternity?
And fragrant Spring, shall you not touch once more
And breathe upon this frozen heart; which age
Embitters in the flowering time of life?

And are you living yet,
O sacred Nature? May our human ears,
So long unused, catch that maternal voice?
The brooks were once a home for the white nymphs,
Their shelter and their glass
The liquid springs; and the high mountain ridges
To secret dancing of immortal feet
Trembled, and the deep forests (now
The lonely haunt of winds). The shepherd-boy

Meridiane incerte ed al fiorito
Margo adducea de' fiumi
Le sitibonde agnelle, arguto carme
Sonar d'agresti Pani
Udì lungo le ripe; e tremar l'onda
Vide, e stupì, che non palese al guardo
La faretrata Diva
Scendea ne' caldi flutti, e dall'immonda
Polve tergea della sanguigna caccia
Il niveo lato e le verginee braccia.

Vissero i fiori e l'erbe,
Vissero i boschi un dì. Conscie le molli
Aure, le nubi e la titania lampa
Fur dell'umana gente, allor che ignuda
Te per le piagge e i colli,
Ciprigna luce, alla deserta notte
Con gli occhi intenti il viator seguendo,
Te compagna alla via, te de' mortali
Pensosa imaginò. Che se gl'impuri
Cittadini consorzi e le fatali
Ire fuggendo e l'onte,
Gl'ispidi tronchi al petto altri nell'ime
Selve remoto accolse,
Viva fiamma agitar l'esangui vene,
Spirar le foglie, e palpitar segreta
Nel doloroso amplesso
Dafne o la mesta Filli, o di Climene
Pianger credè la sconsolata prole
Quel che sommerse in Eridano il sole.

Nè dell'umano affanno,
Rigide balze, i luttuosi accenti
Voi negletti ferìr mentre le vostre
Paurose latebre Eco solinga,
Non vano error de' venti,

Who sought at noon-tide the uncertain shade
And led his thirsty lambs
Down to the flowery river's brink, might hear
Sounding along those banks
The rustic Pan's shrill song or, struck with wonder,
Gaze on the rippling waters, for unrevealed
The quiver-bearing goddess
Went down to the warm flood, to cleanse away,
After the bloodstained hunt, immodest dust
From off her snowy flank and virgin arms.

The very grass and flowers
And every thicket lived, in former days!
The gentle airs, the clouds, and Titan's lamp
Were mindful of the race of Man, and then,
O Cyprian star of Venus,
The traveller going through the lonely night
Followed your naked beauty with fixed eyes
Over the hills and shores, and made of you
Companion on his way, and fancied, too,
You cared for mortal men. Others, who fled
The tainted intercourse
Of towns, their shame and tumult, deep in woods
Clasping the rough-boled trees,
Believed that in their bloodless veins there surged
The vital flame, while the leaves breathed, and
    trembled,
Hid in that sad embrace,
Daphne, or mournful Phyllis, or unconsoled,
Some child of Clymene weeping for him
Who plunged the bright sun in Eridanus.

Nor, you harsh cliffs, on you
Could beat unheeded then the sorrowing voice
Of our distress, while lonely Echo haunted
Your fearful hiding-places: not the wind's
Empty illusion then—

Ma di ninfa abitò misero spirto,
Cui grave amor, cui duro fato escluse
Delle tenere membra. Ella per grotte,
Per nudi scogli e desolati alberghi,
Le non ignote ambasce e l'alte e rotte
Nostre querele al curvo
Etra insegnava. E te d'umani eventi
Disse la fama esperto,
Musico augel che tra chiomato bosco
Or vieni il rinascente anno cantando,
E lamentar nell'alto
Ozio de' campi, all'aer muto e fosco,
Antichi danni e scellerato scorno,
E d'ira e di pietà pallido il giorno.

    Ma non cognato al nostro
Il gener tuo; quelle tue varie note
Dolor non forma, e te di colpa ignudo,
Men caro assai la bruna valle asconde.
Ahi ahi, poscia che vote
Son le stanze d'Olimpo, e cieco il tuono
Per l'atre nubi e le montagne errando,
Gl'iniqui petti e gl'innocenti a paro
In freddo orror dissolve; e poi ch'estrano
Il suol nativo, e di sua prole ignaro
Le meste anime educa;
Tu le cure infelici e i fati indegni
Tu de' mortali ascolta,
Vaga natura, e la favilla antica
Rendi allo spirto mio; se tu pur vivi,
E se de' nostri affanni
Cosa veruna in ciel, se nell'aprica
Terra s'alberga o nell'equoreo seno,
Pietosa no, ma spettatrice almeno.

A nymph's unhappy ghost had dwelling there,
Whom grievous love and fate too harsh had parted
From her soft limbs. And she from the bare shelves,
The caves and desolate places, would proclaim
The not unnoted grief, to the hollow sky
Hurling the broken words
Of our complaint. And legend told of you,
Musical bird, well-versed
In human deeds, amid the leafy coverts
Singing now Spring is born again, you mourned
To the dark silent air,
In stillness of the fields, your ancient wrongs,
And all the dreadful tale of your revenge
In that wan day when wrath and pity met.

But we can claim no kindred
Now with your race; nor human grief informs
Your varied notes; darkling the valley hides you,
Free from all guilt—the less belov'd for that.
Alas, alas, for empty
Stand the Olympian halls, and the blind thunder
Wandering among the hills and the black clouds
Indifferently dissolves with a cold horror
Guilty or guiltless breast; strange is become
The soil that bore us, and knowing not her offspring
Is nurse to the sad soul.
But, O fair Nature, heed our griefs, and this
Destiny undeserved,
And touch my spirit once more with the ancient fire;
This, if indeed you be a living power,
Or if there be in heaven,
One earth beneath the sun, or the sea's bosom,
One Being, conscious there of our distress,
Spectator of our pain, though pitiless.

January 1822

Ultimo canto di Saffo

Placida notte, e verecondo raggio
Della cadente luna; e tu che spunti
Fra la tacita selva in su la rupe,
Nunzio del giorno; oh dilettose e care
Mentre ignote mi fur l'erinni e il fato,
Sembianze agli occhi miei; già non arride
Spettacol molle ai disperati affetti.
Noi l'insueto allor gaudio ravviva
Quando per l'etra liquido si volve
E per li campi trepidanti il flutto
Polveroso de' Noti, e quando il carro,
Grave carro di Giove a noi sul capo,
Tonando, il tenebroso aere divide.
Noi per le balze e le profonde valli
Natar giova tra' nembi, e noi la vasta
Fuga de' greggi sbigottiti, o d'alto
Fiume alla dubbia sponda
Il suono e la vittrice ira dell'onda.

Bello il tuo manto, o divo cielo, e bella
Sei tu, rorida terra. Ahi di cotesta
Infinita beltà parte nessuna
Alla misera Saffo i numi e l'empia
Sorte non fenno. A' tuoi superbi regni
Vile, o natura, e grave ospite addetta,
E dispregiata amante, alle vezzose
Tue forme il core e le pupille invano
Supplichevole intendo. A me non ride
L'aprico margo, e dall'eterea porta
Il mattutino albor; me non il canto

Sappho's Last Song

O tranquil night, and you, O modest beams
Of the setting moon, and you, whose light has
  pierced
Among the voiceless woods above this rock,
Day's messenger—sights that were dear to me,
Delightful to my eyes in former times,
Still ignorant of Fate and the cruel Fury;
These mild scenes please my despair no more.
But even now for such as I there lives
An unaccustomed joy, when the dusty winds
Turn from the south, and sweep the trembling plain
And liquid fields of ether, and the car,
Jove's heavy chariot, is overhead,
Thundering, and cleaving through the darkening sky;
Fitting it were to plunge among the clouds,
Up on the cliff-tops and high mountain vales,
Those terror-driven flocks' tremendous flight,
Or in the deep flood's tumult, as it breaks
Upon the treacherous shore—
Anger of waves, triumphant as they roar!

How beautiful your mantle is, O sky:
And you are fair, O dewy earth. Alas,
The hostile Powers to wretched Sappho gave
No part at all in all this infinite beauty!
In vain, O Nature, vanquished at your throne,
I turn my eyes and suppliant heart towards
This haunting loveliness—of no account,
Rejected lover, and unwelcome guest.
Never again the sunny river-banks
Shall smile for me, nor the ethereal gate
Of earliest dawn; no more shall greet my ears

De' colorati augelli, e non de' faggi
Il murmure saluta: e dove all'ombra
Degl'inchinati salici dispiega
Candido rivo il puro seno, al mio
Lubrico piè le flessuose linfe
Disdegnando sottragge,
E preme in fuga l'odorate spiagge.

Qual fallo mai, qual sì nefando eccesso
Macchiommi anzi il natale, onde sì torvo
Il ciel mi fosse e di fortuna il volto?
In che peccai bambina, allor che ignara
Di misfatto è la vita, onde poi scemo
Di giovanezza, e disfiorato, al fuso
Dell'indomita Parca si volvesse
Il ferrigno mio stame? Incaute voci
Spande il tuo labbro: i destinati eventi
Move arcano consiglio. Arcano è tutto,
Fuor che il nostro dolor. Negletta prole
Nascemmo al pianto, e la ragione in grembo
De' celesti si posa. Oh cure, oh speme
De' più verd'anni! Alle sembianze il Padre,
Alle amene sembianze eterno regno
Diè nelle genti; e per virili imprese,
Per dotta lira o canto,
Virtù non luce in disadorno ammanto.

Morremo. Il velo indegno a terra sparto,
Rifuggirà l'ignudo animo a Dite,
E il crudo fallo emenderà del cieco
Dispensator de' casi. E tu cui lungo
Amore indarno, e lunga fede, e vano
D'implacato desio furor mi strinse,
Vivi felice, se felice in terra
Visse nato mortal. Me non asperse
Del soave licor del doglio avaro

The carolling of many-coloured birds;
Nor shall I hear the murmur of the beech-trees;
And nevermore under the leaning willows,
Where the bright stream lays its pure bosom bare,
The gentle waters turn themselves aside,
Disdain my unlovely feet,
And hurrying press to where the banks lie sweet.

But how have I offended, and what crime
Did I commit before my birth, that Heaven
Should be so grim, and Fortune's face averted?
In childhood did I sin—the time of life
Which knows not of misdoing—that the harsh thread
Winds from the spindle of implacable Fate,
My youth cut short and withered? Upon your lips
Breathed then imprudent words; for things ordained
Work by their own dark council. All is dark,
Except our pain. We are neglected children,
And only born to weep; the cause remains
Upon the laps of the Celestial Ones.
Oh cares and hopes, even of our greenest years!
To form alone, to pleasing outward form,
The Father grants always to bear the rule
With men; through worthier powers, through song,
Or the lyre's skilfulness,
No virtue shines in an unlovely dress.

We die; this worthless veil scattered in earth,
The naked spirit fleeing to Dis, amends
The harsh fault of the blind disposing Power.
And you, for whom vain love and lasting faith
Have held me, and the empty fury of
Unsatisfied desire—live happy, if indeed
Such in this world be any mortal's lot.
But Jupiter, for me, out of the urn
Whence flows the pleasant wine of happiness,
Dealt with no generous hand, since perished all

Giove, poi che perìr gl'inganni e il sogno
Della mia fanciullezza. Ogni più lieto
Giorno di nostra età primo s'invola.
Sottentra il morbo, e la vecchiezza, e l'ombra
Della gelida morte. Ecco di tante
Sperate palme e dilettosi errori,
Il Tartaro m'avanza; e il prode ingegno
Han la tenaria Diva,
E l'atra notte, e la silente riva.

The dear illusions and the dreams of youth.
For the most full of joy of all our days
Are first to fly away, and then creep in
Disease, old age, the shade of frigid death.
Behold, for all the palms I might have won,
And sweet deceiving hopes, Tartarus waits;
And the aspiring mind must Proserpine
Possess for evermore,
The sable night, and quiet Stygian shore.

May 1822

A Silvia

Silvia, rimembri ancora
Quel tempo della tua vita mortale,
Quando beltà splendea
Negli occhi tuoi ridenti e fuggitivi,
E tu, lieta e pensosa, il limitare
Di gioventù salivi?

Sonavan le quiete
Stanze, e le vie dintorno,
Al tuo perpetuo canto,
Allor che all'opre femminili intenta
Sedevi, assai contenta
Di quel vago avvenir che in mente avevi.
Era il maggio odoroso: e tu solevi
Così menare il giorno.

Io gli studi leggiadri
Talor lasciando e le sudate carte,
Ove il tempo mio primo
E di me si spendea la miglior parte,
D'in su i veroni del paterno ostello
Porgea gli orecchi al suon della tua voce,
Ed alla man veloce
Che percorrea la faticosa tela.
Mirava il ciel sereno,
Le vie dorate e gli orti,
E quinci il mar da lungi, e quindi il monte.
Lingua mortal non dice
Quel ch'io sentiva in seno.

Che pensieri soavi,
Che speranze, che cori, o Silvia mia!

To Sylvia

Sylvia, do you remember yet
The season of your mortal lifetime here,
When beauty shone indeed
In the elusive laughter of your eyes,
And full of joy and wonder you approached
The threshold of your years?

The quiet chambers rang,
And all the ways around,
With your continual song;
When you were sitting at your woman's work,
Intent, happy enough
With what bright future occupied your mind.
It was the fragrant May-time; even so
You used to pass the day.

I, at my easy task,
Sometimes laying aside the well-thumbed page,
Which had consumed away
My better parts and my first youthful age,
High on the terrace of my father's house,
Pricked up my ears at music of your voice,
And at your hand which sped
About your labours as you wove your web.
I gazed on the clear skies,
Gardens, and golden ways,
And there the far-off sea, and here the mountains.
No mortal tongue can say
What were my feelings then.

What dreams, what pleasing thoughts,
What stirrings of the heart, my Sylvia!

Quale allor ci apparia
La vita umana e il fato!
Quando sovviemmi di cotanta speme,
Un affetto mi preme
Acerbo e sconsolato,
E tornami a doler di mia sventura.
O natura, o natura,
Perchè non rendi poi
Quel che prometti allor? perchè di tanto
Inganni i figli tuoi?

Tu pria che l'erbe inaridisse il verno,
Da chiuso morbo combattuta e vinta,
Perivi, o tenerella. E non vedevi
Il fior degli anni tuoi;
Non ti molceva il core
La dolce lode or delle negre chiome,
Or degli sguardi innamorati e schivi;
Nè teco le compagne ai dì festivi
Ragionavan d'amore.

Anche peria fra poco
La speranza mia dolce: agli anni miei
Anche negaro i fati
La giovanezza. Ahi come,
Come passata sei,
Cara compagna dell'età mia nova,
Mia lacrimata speme!
Questo è quel mondo? questi
I diletti, l'amor, l'opre, gli eventi
Onde cotanto ragionammo insieme?
Questa la sorte dell'umane genti?
All'apparir del vero
Tu, misera, cadesti: e con la mano
La fredda morte ed una tomba ignuda
Mostravi di lontano.

How fair the life of man
And destiny appeared!
When I remember now how much I hoped for,
A passion falls upon me,
Bitter, disconsolate;
I turn again to mourn my evil fate.
O Nature, Nature, why,
Why do you not give now
The things you promised then, why so deceive
Your children, mortal men?

Before the winter's cold withered the grass,
Assailed and conquered by a hid disease
You died, poor gentle child; and never saw
The flowering of your years;
Nor was your heart to melt,
Hearing soft flattery of your dark hair,
Or when they praised your shy enamoured glances;
Nor girl-companions on a holiday
Had talked with you of love.

And even so with me,
All my fond dreams lie dead; for youth itself
The Destinies withheld
From my first years. Alas,
How you are fled, are fled,
Dearest companion of my earliest age,
My Hope, for whom these tears are shed!
Is this that world? And those
Delights, and love, labours, and happenings,
Of which so often we discoursed together?
Is this the lot then of the race of Man?
For when the truth appeared,
Poor thing, you fell away; and from afar
Showed with your hand the cold image of death
And a bare sepulchre.

19–20 April 1828

Il passero solitario

D'in su la vetta della torre antica,
Passero solitario, alla campagna
Cantando vai finchè non more il giorno;
Ed erra l'armonia per questa valle.
Primavera dintorno
Brilla nell'aria, e per li campi esulta,
Sì ch'a mirarla intenerisce il core.
Odi greggi belar, muggire armenti;
Gli altri augelli contenti, a gara insieme
Per lo libero ciel fan mille giri,
Pur festeggiando il lor tempo migliore:
Tu pensoso in disparte il tutto miri;
Non compagni, non voli,
Non ti cal d'allegria, schivi gli spassi;
Canti, e così trapassi
Dell'anno e di tua vita il più bel fiore.

Oimè, quanto somiglia
Al tuo costume il mio! Sollazzo e riso,
Della novella età dolce famiglia,
E te german di giovinezza, amore,
Sospiro acerbo de' provetti giorni,
Non curo, io non so come; anzi da loro
Quasi fuggo lontano;
Quasi romito, e strano
Al mio loco natio;
Passo del viver mio la primavera.
Questo giorno ch'omai cede alla sera,
Festeggiar si costuma al nostro borgo.
Odi per lo sereno un suon di squilla,
Odi spesso un tonar di ferree canne,

The Solitary Thrush

From the high summit of this ancient tower,
O solitary bird, you still sing on
To the wide countryside, while daylight dies;
And down the valley strays your harmony.
Now all around the spring
Shines in the air and triumphs through the fields,
And hearts grow tender but to gaze on it.
Hark to the bleating flocks, the lowing herds,
The other happy birds that chirp together
Or take their wheeling flights through the free heavens,
Thus welcoming the season of their joy.
But pensive and apart you view it all;
You choose no mates, nor fly,
Care not for pleasure, and avoid their play;
But seem to waste in song
The flower of all your lifetime and the year.

Alas, how like indeed
Your way of life and mine! Pleasure and laughter,
Those sweet companions of our youthful age,
And sharp regret of all our later days,
And you, O Love, so near akin to Youth—
I do not care for these, I know not why,
But rather fly from them;
Almost a hermit, strange
Even to my native ground,
I pass the springtide of my life away.
This day, which now already yields to evening,
Our little town keeps as a festival:
Hark to the sound of bells through the clear sky!
And often, too, rattle of distant guns

Che rimbomba lontan di villa in villa.
Tutta vestita a festa
La gioventù del loco
Lascia le case, e per le vie si spande;
E mira ed è mirata, e in cor s'allegra.
Io solitario in questa
Rimota parte alla campagna uscendo,
Ogni diletto e gioco
Indugio in altro tempo: e intanto il guardo
Steso nell'aria aprica
Mi fere il Sol che tra lontani monti,
Dopo il giorno sereno,
Cadendo si dilegua, e par che dica
Che la beata gioventù vien meno.

Tu, solingo augellin, venuto a sera
Del viver che daranno a te le stelle,
Certo del tuo costume
Non ti dorrai; che di natura è frutto
Ogni vostra vaghezza.
A me, se di vecchiezza
La detestata soglia
Evitar non impetro,
Quando muti questi occhi all'altrui core,
E lor fia vòto il mondo, e il dì futuro
Del dì presente più noioso e tetro,
Che parrà di tal voglia?
Che di quest'anni miei? che di me stesso?
Ahi pentirommi, e spesso,
Ma sconsolato, volgerommi indietro.

Reverberating back from farm to farm;
In holiday attire,
The young folk of the place
Have left their homes and spread about the roads
To see and to be seen, the light of heart.
Lonely, I take my way
To this remote part of the countryside,
And leave all sports aside
Until some other time; meanwhile I catch,
Athwart the still, bright air,
The sun's glance, which behind the distant hills,
As ends this clear, calm day,
Sinks down and vanishes, and seems to tell
How youth's blest season, too, dwindles away.

You, lonely little bird, when comes the evening
Of that brief life the stars have measured for you,
Surely will not repine
The use you made of it; for all your longings
Were planted there by Nature.
For me, if I must pass
The hateful gate of age,
When these eyes shall become
Mute for all other hearts, and the whole world
Empty for them, and each succeeding day
More sad and tedious than the last—how then
Shall my desires appear,
And these my early years, and I myself?
Alas, I shall repent, and many times
Look back at them, and not be comforted.

c. 1828?

Le ricordanze

Vaghe stelle dell'Orsa, io non credea
Tornare ancor per uso a contemplarvi
Sul paterno giardino scintillanti,
E ragionar con voi dalle finestre
Di questo albergo ove abitai fanciullo,
E delle gioie mie vidi la fine.
Quante immagini un tempo, e quante fole
Creommi nel pensier l'aspetto vostro
E delle luci a voi compagne! allora
Che, tacito, seduto in verde zolla,
Delle sere io solea passar gran parte
Mirando il cielo, ed ascoltando il canto
Della rana rimota alla campagna!
E la lucciola errava appo le siepi
E in su l'aiuole, susurrando al vento
I viali odorati, ed i cipressi
Là nella selva; e sotto al patrio tetto
Sonavan voci alterne, e le tranquille
Opre de' servi. E che pensieri immensi,
Che dolci sogni mi spirò la vista
Di quel lontano mar, quei monti azzurri,
Che di qua scopro, e che varcare un giorno
Io mi pensava, arcani mondi, arcana
Felicità fingendo al viver mio!
Ignaro del mio fato, e quante volte
Questa mia vita dolorosa e nuda
Volentier con la morte avrei cangiato.

Nè mi diceva il cor che l'età verde
Sarei dannato a consumare in questo
Natio borgo selvaggio, intra una gente
Zotica, vil; cui nomi strani, e spesso

Memories

O you bright stars of the Bear, I did not think
That I should come once more, as was my custom,
To gaze upon you glittering above
My father's garden, or converse with you
From the windows of this house, where as a boy
I lived, and saw the end of happiness.
Time was, how many mad imaginings
I fashioned in the thought of your bright aspect,
And your companion stars. For then I used
To pass away the most part of the evening
Quietly sitting on the green turf, watching
The sky, and listening to the frogs that sang
Far-off upon the plain. The fire-fly wandered
About the hedgerows and above the flower-beds,
And the wind sighed among the fragrant alleys
And through the cypress-trees there in the wood;
While sounded from the house at intervals
Voices of servants at their ordered tasks.
But what vast thoughts and what sweet visions then
That distant sea called forth, and those blue mountains
Discerned from far away!—which then I thought
To cross some day, inventing for myself
An unknown world, and unknown happiness
To suit my life to come—not knowing my fate,
Nor, willingly, how many times I would
Have changed that bare and sorry life for death.

For my heart never told me my green age
Was doomed to waste here, in this barbarous town
Where I was born, with a cheap boorish people,
Who hold in no repute learning or knowledge

Argomento di riso e di trastullo,
Son dottrina e saper; che m'odia e fugge,
Per invidia non già, che non mi tiene
Maggior di se, ma perchè tale estima
Ch'io mi tenga in cor mio, sebben di fuori
A persona giammai non ne fo segno.
Qui passo gli anni, abbandonato, occulto,
Senz'amor, senza vita; ed aspro a forza
Tra lo stuol de' malevoli divengo:
Qui di pietà mi spoglio e di virtudi,
E sprezzator degli uomini mi rendo,
Per la greggia ch'ho appresso: e intanto vola
Il caro tempo giovanil; più caro
Che la fama e l'allor, più che la pura
Luce del giorno, e lo spirar: ti perdo
Senza un diletto, inutilmente, in questo
Soggiorno disumano, intra gli affanni,
O dell'arida vita unico fiore.

Viene il vento recando il suon dell'ora
Dalla torre del borgo. Era conforto
Questo suon, mi rimembra, alle mie notti,
Quando fanciullo, nella buia stanza,
Per assidui terrori io vigilava,
Sospirando il mattin. Qui non è cosa
Ch'io vegga o senta, onde un'immagin dentro
Non torni, e un dolce rimembrar non sorga.
Dolce per se; ma con dolor sottentra
Il pensier del presente, un van desio
Del passato, ancor tristo, e il dire: io fui.
Quella loggia colà, volta agli estremi
Raggi del dì; queste dipinte mura,
Quei figurati armenti, e il Sol che nasce
Su romita campagna, agli ozi miei
Porser mille diletti allor che al fianco
M'era, parlando, il mio possente errore
Sempre, ov'io fossi. In queste sale antiche,

(Often indeed their jest, a thing to laugh at),
A folk who hate and shun me, not from envy—
They do not judge me better than themselves—
But they suppose that in my heart I think so,
Although I never showed it any man.
And so I pass the years, alone, obscure,
Loveless, and lifeless; and I am forced to grow
Bitter myself, with this malignant crowd,
And putting off my pity and my manhood,
I make myself despise the human race,
Even as this herd has taught me; and, meanwhile,
The dear season of youth is passing—dearer
Than laurelled fame, or the clear light of day,
Than breath itself—and so it is I lose you,
Having reaped not one delight, and all things wasted,
In this inhuman spot, among afflictions,
O solitary flower of barren life!

The tolling of the hour comes on the wind
From the town-belfry. A sound which was my comfort,
As I remember, in those fearful nights
Of boyhood, when I lay in my dark room,
Beset by terrors, longing for the dawn.
There is no object here which meets my sense
Which does not bring some image back again,
Or raise some sweet remembrance—sweet in itself,
But then creeps in, with pain, thought of the present,
And so, an empty longing for the past,
Though it was sad, and these words: 'I have been.'
That gallery I knew, facing the last
Gleams of the daylight, and those painted walls—
Figures of flocks, the sun rising above
A lonely plain—these in my idle times
Proffered so much delight, when still remained
The strong illusion at my side, which spoke
To me at all hours, in whatever place.

Al chiaror delle nevi, intorno a queste
Ampie finestre sibilando il vento,
Rimbombaro i sollazzi e le festose
Mie voci al tempo che l'acerbo, indegno
Mistero delle cose a noi si mostra
Pien di dolcezza; indelibata, intera
Il garzoncel, come inesperto amante,
La sua vita ingannevole vagheggia,
E celeste beltà fingendo ammira.

O speranze, speranze; ameni inganni
Della mia prima età! sempre, parlando,
Ritorno a voi; che per andar di tempo,
Per variar d'affetti e di pensieri,
Obbliarvi non so. Fantasmi, intendo,
Son la gloria e l'onor; diletti e beni
Mero desio; non ha la vita un frutto,
Inutile miseria. E sebben vóti
Son gli anni miei, sebben deserto, oscuro
Il mio stato mortal, poco mi toglie
La fortuna, ben veggo. Ahi, ma qualvolta
A voi ripenso, o mie speranze antiche,
Ed a quel caro immaginar mio primo;
Indi riguardo il viver mio sì vile
E sì dolente, e che la morte è quello
Che di cotanta speme oggi m'avanza;
Sento serrarmi il cor, sento ch'al tutto
Consolarmi non so del mio destino.
E quando pur questa invocata morte
Sarammi allato, e sarà giunto il fine
Della sventura mia; quando la terra
Mi fia straniera valle, e dal mio sguardo
Fuggirà l'avvenir; di voi per certo
Risovverammi; e quell'imago ancora
Sospirar mi farà, farammi acerbo
L'esser vissuto indarno, e la dolcezza
Del dì fatal tempererà d'affanno.

In these old rooms, while the snow gleamed outside,
And the wind whistled round the ample windows,
My voice re-echoed, gay and full of pleasure
Then, in that season when the harsh unkind
Mystery of things still seems to us to be
So full of sweetness. Like an untried lover,
The boy, deluded still, gazes on life,
Which is untouched and virgin, fashioning
A beauty from the skies to wonder at.

O dreams, O dreams, O you the dear illusions
Of my young years, always I turn again
To you, in musing; though time goes, and though
Our thoughts and passions change, forget you not.
Phantoms—I know it now—are glory and honour;
All good and all delight are mere desire;
The waste and misery of life bear at the last
No single fruit. And though my years are empty,
And this, my life's condition, desert and dark,
Fortune has taken little—too well I see it.
But oh, as often as I think of you,
My early hopes, the dear imaginings
I once possessed, then look, and see how vile
And sorry my life is, and death alone,
Of all I ever hoped for, now remaining,
I feel my heart turn cold, and then I know
Nothing can recompense me for my fate.
When death, invoked so often, stands before me,
And I have reached the end of my misfortunes,
When earth seems a strange valley, and when the future
Eludes my gaze, I know for sure that I
Shall still remember you, my dreams; that image
Shall make me grieve once more, with bitterness
That I have lived in vain, and with distress
Mingle the sweetness of my dying day.

E già nel primo giovanil tumulto
Di contenti, d'angosce e di desio,
Morte chiamai più volte, e lungamente
Mi sedetti colà su la fontana
Pensoso di cessar dentro quell'acque
La speme e il dolor mio. Poscia, per cieco
Malor, condotto della vita in forse,
Piansi la bella giovanezza, e il fiore
De' miei poveri dì, che sì per tempo
Cadeva: e spesso all'ore tarde, assiso
Sul conscio letto, dolorosamente
Alla fioca lucerna poetando,
Lamentai co' silenzi e con la notte
Il fuggitivo spirto, ed a me stesso
In sul languir cantai funereo canto.

Chi rimembrar vi può senza sospiri,
O primo entrar di giovinezza, o giorni
Vezzosi, inenarrabili, allor quando
Al rapito mortal primieramente
Sorridon le donzelle; a gara intorno
Ogni cosa sorride; invidia tace,
Non desta ancora ovver benigna; e quasi
(Inusitata maraviglia!) il mondo
La destra soccorrevole gli porge,
Scusa gli errori suoi, festeggia il novo
Suo venir nella vita, ed inchinando
Mostra che per signor l'accolga e chiami?
Fugaci giorni! a somigliar d'un lampo
Son dileguati. E qual mortale ignaro
Di sventura esser può, se a lui già scorsa
Quella vaga stagion, se il suo buon tempo,
Se giovanezza, ahi giovanezza, è spenta?

O Nerina! e di te forse non odo
Questi luoghi parlar? caduta forse
Dal mio pensier sei tu? Dove sei gita,

Even in that first youthful tumult of
Delight, anguish, desire, I called on death
Time upon time, and seated for long hours
Beside the fountain, thought of ending there
Beneath those waters all my hope and pain;
Then, brought in peril of life by blind disease,
Mourned for the fair season of youth, the flower
Of my impoverished days untimely fallen;
And often, late at night, seated upon
My bed, the only witness of my sorrow,
Playing the poet by the uncertain lamp,
Lamented with long stillness of the night
The passing of my spirit, and to myself
Chanted a death-song for my failing life.

Who can remember you without a sigh,
Our opening time of youth?—Oh indescribable
And lovely days!—When first on the rapt mortal
Young girls begin to smile, and all things vie
To give him pleasure; Envy holds her peace,
Unwaked as yet, or kindly; and the world
(Unprecedented wonder) seems to hold forth
A hand to help him, and forgives his errors,
Makes holiday to greet the new-comer
Who enters thus on life, and bowing down,
Acclaims and owns him lord of all existence.
Fugitive days!—for like a flash of lightning
They are gone away. Is that man ignorant
Then, of misfortune, if this fairest season
Has fled from him, and the best years of life
In youth, ah youth, are all wasted away?

But O Nerina, does not this place speak
Of you, and can it be that you indeed
Are faded from my thoughts? Where are you gone?

S

Che qui sola di te la ricordanza
Trovo, dolcezza mia? Più non ti vede
Questa Terra natal: quella finestra,
Ond'eri usata favellarmi, ed onde
Mesto riluce delle stelle il raggio,
È deserta. Ove sei, che più non odo
La tua voce sonar, siccome un giorno,
Quando soleva ogni lontano accento
Del labbro tuo, ch'a me giungesse, il volto
Scolorarmi? Altro tempo. I giorni tuoi
Furo, mio dolce amor. Passasti. Ad altri
Il passar per la terra oggi è sortito,
E l'abitar questi odorati colli.
Ma rapida passasti; e come un sogno
Fu la tua vita. Ivi danzando; in fronte
La gioia ti splendea, splendea negli occhi
Quel confidente immaginar, quel lume
Di gioventù, quando spegneali il fato,
E giacevi. Ahi Nerina! In cor mi regna
L'antico amor. Se a feste anco talvolta,
Se a radunanze io movo, infra me stesso
Dico: o Nerina, a radunanze, a feste
Tu non ti acconci più, tu più non movi.
Se torna maggio, e ramoscelli e suoni
Van gli amanti recando alle fanciulle,
Dico: Nerina mia, per te non torna
Primavera giammai, non torna amore.
Ogni giorno sereno, ogni fiorita
Piaggia ch'io miro, ogni goder ch'io sento,
Dico: Nerina or più non gode; i campi,
L'aria non mira. Ahi tu passasti, eterno
Sospiro mio: passasti: e fia compagna
D'ogni mio vago immaginar, di tutti
I miei teneri sensi, i tristi e cari
Moti del cor, la rimembranza acerba.

For memories, O sweetness of my life,
Are all I find of you. This countryside
Where you were born knows you no more. That window
Where once you used to talk with me is empty,
Reflecting the sad glitter of the stars.
Where are you? For the echo of your voice
Is heard no more—whose distant accents once
Falling upon my ears, made me turn pale.
That was another time. Your days are over,
My sweet beloved. You have passed. To others
Is given now to go about the land
And find a dwelling in these fragrant hills.
But swiftly you passed by, and all your life
Was like a dream. For you went dancing forth,
And joy shone on your brows, and in your eyes
The sure imaginings and light of youth,
And then Fate struck you down, and you lay still.
Alas, Nerina! for the old love yet
Reigns in my heart. And if at any time
I take my way on days of festival
Or go to watch the dancing, to myself
I say: 'Nerina, now you deck yourself
No more, nor go to dance or festival.'
When May returns, and lovers greet their girls
With carolling and gifts of flowering branches,
I say: 'Nerina, never more for you
Returns the spring; and love returns no more.'
Every fine day, and every blossoming bank
I look upon, feeling my heart rejoice,
I say: 'Nerina now feels joy no more,
Nor looks upon the fields or on the sky.'
For you have passed away, my everlasting
Sorrow—have passed, and made companion
Of all my fair imaginings, and all
My tenderest feelings, in the sad and dear
Moods of the heart, a bitter memory.

26 August–12 September 1829

La quiete dopo la tempesta

Passata è la tempesta:
Odo augelli far festa, e la gallina,
Tornata in su la via,
Che ripete il suo verso. Ecco il sereno
Rompe là da ponente, alla montagna;
Sgombrasi la campagna,
E chiaro nella valle il fiume appare.
Ogni cor si rallegra, in ogni lato
Risorge il romorio
Torna il lavoro usato.
L'artigiano a mirar l'umido cielo,
Con l'opra in man, cantando,
Fassi in su l'uscio; a prova
Vien fuor la femminetta a còr dell'acqua
Della novella piova;
E l'erbaiuol rinnova
Di sentiero in sentiero
Il grido giornaliero.
Ecco il Sol che ritorna, ecco sorride
Per li poggi e le ville. Apre i balconi,
Apre terrazzi e logge la famiglia:
E, dalla via corrente, odi lontano
Tintinnio di sonagli; il carro stride
Del passeggier che il suo cammin ripiglia.

Si rallegra ogni core.
Sì dolce, sì gradita
Quand'è, com'or, la vita?
Quando con tanto amore
L'uomo a' suoi studi intende?
O torna all'opre? o cosa nova imprende?
Quando de' mali suoi men si ricorda?

The Calm after the Storm

The storm has passed away;
I hear the birds rejoice, the barn-door hen,
Gone back into the lane,
Reiterate her call. Look, the clear sky
Breaks through there in the west, above the mountain;
The plains cast off their gloom;
And the bright stream appears down in the valley.
All hearts are glad once more; on every side
Begins the noise and stir
Of labour, as before.
The craftsman, with his work in hand, goes singing,
To view the rain-swept sky
Outside his door; a woman
Comes running out, to be the first to fill
Her pail with fresh rain-water;
The herb-seller again,
Going from lane to lane,
Takes up his daily cry.
Look now, the sun returns, and smiles down
On hillsides and on houses. And now the household
Throws open windows, balconies, and rooms;
And mark, upon the high-street, some way off,
Jingle of harness-bells, the creaking cart,
As now the traveller renews his journey.

So every heart is glad.
And when, but now, is life
So gracious and so sweet?
When else with so much liking
Does man resume his labours,
Turn to his wonted work, or start some new one?
And when is he less conscious of his ills?

Piacer figlio d'affanno;
Gioia vana, ch'è frutto
Del passato timore, onde si scosse
E paventò la morte
Chi la vita abborria;
Onde in lungo tormento,
Fredde, tacite, smorte,
Sudàr le genti e palpitàr, vedendo
Mossi alle nostre offese
Folgori, nembi e vento.

   O natura cortese,
Son questi i doni tuoi,
Questi i diletti sono
Che tu porgi ai mortali. Uscir di pena
È diletto fra noi.
Pene tu spargi a larga mano; il duolo
Spontaneo sorge: e di piacer, quel tanto
Che per mostro e miracolo talvolta
Nasce d'affanno, è gran guadagno. Umana
Prole cara agli eterni! assai felice
Se respirar ti lice
D'alcun dolor: beata
Se te d'ogni dolor morte risana.

Pleasure is trouble's child;
And empty joy, the fruit
Of terror overpast, makes even the man
Who learned to loathe his life
Tremble with fear at death;
And thus, in long-drawn torment,
Men, cold, and pale, and silent,
Shudder and sweat, the while they see above,
Against them gathering round,
Lightning, and clouds, and wind.

O bounteous Nature, these
Are then your gifts, and this
The happiness you offer
Us mortal men! The issue out of pain
Is happiness enough;
And pains you scatter with a generous hand,
While sorrow springs even of its own accord;
And what of pleasure by some miracle
Is born from trouble, is great gain. O human kind,
Dear to the eternal powers, happy indeed
If granted pause for breath
After each grief; most blest
If even these are cured at last by death.

17–20 September 1829

Il sabato del villaggio

La donzelletta vien dalla campagna,
In sul calar del sole,
Col suo fascio dell'erba; e reca in mano
Un mazzolin di rose e di viole,
Onde, siccome suole,
Ornare ella si appresta
Dimani, al dì di festa, il petto e il crine.
Siede con le vicine
Su la scala a filar la vecchierella,
Incontro là dove si perde il giorno;
E novellando vien del suo buon tempo,
Quando ai dì della festa ella si ornava,
Ed ancor sana e snella
Solea danzar la sera intra di quei
Ch'ebbe compagni dell'età più bella.
Già tutta l'aria imbruna,
Torna azzurro il sereno, e tornan l'ombre
Giù da' colli e da' tetti,
Al biancheggiar della recente luna.
Or la squilla dà segno
Della festa che viene;
Ed a quel suon diresti
Che il cor si riconforta.
I fanciulli gridando
Su la piazzuola in frotta,
E qua e là saltando,
Fanno un lieto romore:
E intanto riede alla sua parca mensa,
Fischiando, il zappatore,
E seco pensa al dì del suo riposo.

Saturday Evening in the Village

The young girl now comes back from the open fields,
About the set of sun,
Bearing her swathe of grass, and in her hand
A bunch of roses and of violets,
As is her custom, for
Tomorrow's holiday,
To make more beautiful her breast and hair.
And the old woman sits
Upon the steps among her neighbours, spinning.
Turning herself to where the day goes down,
And telling tales how she, in better times,
Decked herself out against the holiday,
And graceful still, and fresh,
Would dance the evening through among the rest,
Who were companions of her lovely prime.
Darkens the air, the sky
Takes on a deeper blue, and shadows fall
Cast by the roofs and hills
Beneath the whiteness of the rising moon.
And now the bell proclaims
The holy day's approach,
And at that sound, it seems,
Each heart is cheered once more.
The small boys shouting in troops
About the village square
Go leaping hither and thither
And make a cheerful noise;
Meanwhile the labourer goes whistling home,
Back to his frugal meal,
And thinks about the coming day of rest.

Poi quando intorno è spenta ogni altra face,
E tutto l'altro tace,
Odi il martel picchiare, odi la sega
Del legnaiuol, che veglia
Nella chiusa bottega alla lucerna,
E s'affretta, e s'adopra
Di fornir l'opra anzi il chiarir dell'alba.

Questo di sette è il più gradito giorno,
Pien di speme e di gioia:
Diman tristezza e noia
Recheran l'ore, ed al travaglio usato
Ciascuno in suo pensier farà ritorno.

Garzoncello scherzoso,
Cotesta età fiorita
È come un giorno d'allegrezza pieno,
Giorno chiaro, sereno,
Che precorre alla festa di tua vita.
Godi, fanciullo mio; stato soave,
Stagion lieta è cotesta.
Altro dirti non vo'; ma la tua festa
Ch'anco tardi a venir non ti sia grave.

When every other light around is out,
All other sound is mute,
Hark to the hammer knocking, and the saw—
The carpenter is up,
Working by lamplight in his shuttered shop,
And labours on, in haste
To get all finished before morning comes.

This is the best-loved day of all the week,
Most full of hope and joy;
The morrow will bring back
Sadness and tedium, and each within his thought
Returns once more to find his usual labour.

You little playful boy,
Even this your flowering time
Is like a day filled up with grace and joy—
A clear, calm day that comes
As a precursor to life's festival.
Be happy, little boy;
A joyful time is this.
More I'd not tell you; but if your holiday
Seem somewhat tardy yet, let not that grieve you.

28 September 1829

Canto notturno di un pastore errante dell'Asia

Che fai tu, luna, in ciel? dimmi, che fai,
Silenziosa luna?
Sorgi la sera, e vai,
Contemplando i deserti; indi ti posi.
Ancor non sei tu paga
Di riandare i sempiterni calli?
Ancor non prendi a schivo, ancor sei vaga
Di mirar queste valli?
Somiglia alla tua vita
La vita del pastore.
Sorge in sul primo albore;
Move la greggia oltre pel campo, e vede
Greggi, fontane ed erbe;
Poi stanco si riposa in su la sera:
Altro mai non ispera.
Dimmi, o luna: a che vale
Al pastor la sua vita,
La vostra vita a voi? dimmi: ove tende
Questo vagar mio breve,
Il tuo corso immortale?

Vecchierel bianco, infermo,
Mezzo vestito e scalzo,
Con gravissimo fascio in su le spalle,
Per montagna e per valle,
Per sassi acuti, ed alta rena, e fratte,
Al vento, alla tempesta, e quando avvampa
L'ora, e quando poi gela,
Corre via, corre, anela,
Varca torrenti e stagni,

Night Song of a Nomadic Shepherd in Asia

What are you doing in Heaven? O Moon, tell me,
What, O you silent Moon?
You rise at eve, and go
Gazing upon the deserts, and then set.
Are you not weary yet,
Traversing still that everlasting round?
Are you not tired of it, and still desire
To look upon these valleys?
Much like that life of yours
The shepherd's life appears:
Rising at earliest dawn
He moves his flock across the plains, and sees
The herds, and wells, and grass,
And wearied out, rests in the evening's shade;
He hopes for nothing more.
Tell me, O Moon, what worth
The shepherd's life to him,
And yours to you? Tell me, and whither tending
This my brief pilgrimage,
And your undying course?

A weak, white-haired old man,
Half-naked, with bare feet,
A very heavy burden on his shoulders,
Over the hills and valleys,
Over sharp-pointed rocks, deep sands, and thickets,
Through wind, through storm, under the scorching day
And cold that follows it,
Runs on, eager, runs on,
Traversing pools and torrents,

Cade, risorge, e più e più s'affretta,
Senza posa o ristoro,
Lacero, sanguinoso; infin ch'arriva
Colà dove la via
E dove il tanto affaticar fu volto:
Abisso orrido, immenso,
Ov'ei precipitando, il tutto obblia,
Vergine luna, tale
È la vita mortale.

　　Nasce l'uomo a fatica,
Ed è rischio di morte il nascimento.
Prova pena e tormento
Per prima cosa: e in sul principio stesso
La madre e il genitore
Il prende a consolar dell'esser nato.
Poi che crescendo viene,
L'uno e l'altro il sostiene, e via pur sempre
Con atti e con parole
Studiasi fargli core,
E consolarlo dell'umano stato:
Altro ufficio più grato
Non si fa da parenti alla lor prole.
Ma perchè dare al sole,
Perchè reggere in vita
Chi poi di quella consolar convenga?
Se la vita è sventura,
Perchè da noi si dura?
Intatta luna, tale
È lo stato mortale.
Ma tu mortal non sei,
E forse del mio dir poco ti cale.

　　Pur tu, solinga, eterna peregrina,
Che sì pensosa sei, tu forse intendi,
Questo viver terreno,
Il patir nostro, il sospirar, che sia;

Falls down, rises again, still hastening onward,
Taking no pause nor rest,
Bloodstained and torn, until at last he finds
The end of his long road,
Which he has reached with so much weariness—
A ghastly, huge abyss:
And there he casts him in, all things forgetting.
Such, O you virgin Moon,
Such is the life of man!

Man is brought forth in labour;
There is the risk of death in being born,
And so he learns to know of pain and torment
Even in that first thing. From the beginning
His mother and his father
Seek to console their offspring for his birth,
And as he lives and grows
Strive to encourage him, endeavouring,
By every deed and word,
To keep him in good heart,
To comfort him for this his human station;
No duty is more kindly
That parents may accomplish for their children;
Yet why bring forth to light,
Why, living, still maintain
The child, if such must be his consolation?
If life is our misfortune
Why must we still endure?
Such, O unblemished Moon,
The mortal life of man;
But you, immortal, care,
As it may be, but little for my words.

For you, eternal, lonely wanderer,
Seeming so full of thought, must understand
What is this life below,
And all our sighings and our sufferings;

Che sia questo morir, questo supremo
Scolorar del sembiante,
E perir dalla terra, e venir meno
Ad ogni usata, amante compagnia.
E tu certo comprendi
Il perchè delle cose, e vedi il frutto
Del mattin, della sera,
Del tacito, infinito andar del tempo.
Tu sai, tu certo, a qual suo dolce amore
Rida la primavera,
A chi giovi l'ardore, e che procacci
Il verno co' suoi ghiacci.
Mille cose sai tu, mille discopri,
Che son celate al semplice pastore.
Spesso quand'io ti miro
Star così muta in sul deserto piano,
Che, in suo giro lontano, al ciel confina;
Ovver con la mia greggia
Seguirmi viaggiando a mano a mano;
E quando miro in cielo arder le stelle;
Dico fra me pensando:
A che tante facelle?
Che fa l'aria infinita, e quel profondo
Infinito seren? che vuol dir questa
Solitudine immensa? ed io che sono?
Così meco ragiono: e della stanza
Smisurata e superba,
E dell'innumerabile famiglia;
Poi di tanto adoprar, di tanti moti
D'ogni celeste, ogni terrena cosa,
Girando senza posa,
Per tornar sempre là donde son mosse;
Uso alcuno, alcun frutto
Indovinar non so. Ma tu per certo,
Giovinetta immortal, conosci il tutto.
Questo io conosco e sento,
Che degli eterni giri,

And what is death, and the last fading out
Of colour from the cheeks,
The vanishing from earth, till we are lost
To all familiar, loving fellowship.
Surely you understand
The reason of it all, and see the fruit
Of evening and of morning,
And of the endless, silent pace of time.
You know, you surely know, for whom spring smiles,
And for what tender love;
Who profits by the heat, what is procured
By winter with its frosts.
You know and search out many thousand things
Which still are hidden from a simple shepherd.
And when I gaze upon you,
Who mutely stand above the desert plains
Which heaven with its far circle but confines,
Or often, when I see you
Following step by step my flock and me,
Or watch the stars that shine there in the sky,
Musing, I say within me:
'Wherefore those many lights,
That boundless atmosphere,
And infinite calm sky? And what the meaning
Of this vast solitude? And what am I?'
Thus reasoning with myself, and of that splendid
Immeasurable hall
And numberless tribe of stars,
The motions and the workings
Of every thing on earth or in the sky,
Circling unendingly,
Returning still from whence their course began,
I can divine no plan
Nor guess the purpose there; but surely, you,
Undying maiden, understand it all.
Yet this I know and feel:
The everlasting round,

Che dell'esser mio frale,
Qualche bene o contento
Avrà fors'altri; a me la vita è male.

  O greggia mia che posi, oh te beata,
Che la miseria tua, credo, non sai!
Quanta invidia ti porto!
Non sol perchè d'affanno
Quasi libera vai;
Ch'ogni stento, ogni danno,
Ogni estremo timor subito scordi;
Ma più perchè giammai tedio non provi.
Quando tu siedi all'ombra, sovra l'erbe,
Tu se' queta e contenta;
E gran parte dell'anno
Senza noia consumi in quello stato.
Ed io pur seggo sovra l'erbe, all'ombra,
E un fastidio m'ingombra
La mente, ed uno spron quasi mi punge
Sì che, sedendo, più che mai son lunge
Da trovar pace o loco.
E pur nulla non bramo,
E non ho fino a qui cagion di pianto.
Quel che tu goda o quanto,
Non so già dir; ma fortunata sei.
Ed io godo ancor poco,
O greggia mia, nè di ciò sol mi lagno.
Se tu parlar sapessi, io chiederei:
Dimmi: perchè giacendo
A bell'agio, ozioso,
S'appaga ogni animale;
Me, s'io giaccio in riposo, il tedio assale?

  Forse s'avess'io l'ale
Da volar su le nubi,
E noverar le stelle ad una ad una,
O come il tuono errar di giogo in giogo,

And my own feeble being,
May be a source of pleasure and of good
To others, but for me this life is bad.

And you, my flock, who take your ease—Oh happy,
Not knowing, as I believe, your wretchedness!
How do I envy you!
Not only that you seem
Made free of all distress,
All harm and all privation
And each inordinate terror soon forgetting;
But more, because you know no tedium.
For, resting in the shade, upon the grass,
Content you are and quiet,
Without repining pass
In this calm manner the year's greater part.
But when, beneath the shade, and on the grass,
I sit, disgust of life
Cumbers my mind, and a goad drives me on,
And sitting there, still am I far removed
From peace or from repose;
And yet I nothing want,
Nor hitherto found cause for my complaint.
I cannot comprehend
The source of all your joy; yet you are bless'd;
My flock, I joy but little,
And yet not only therefore do I mourn;
This I would ask you, had you power to speak:
'Tell me, why every beast
Lying at his fair ease
Is well contented in his idleness;
But if I lie at rest, spleen seizes on me?'

If I, maybe, had wings
To fly above the clouds,
To number one by one the very stars,
Or wander with the storm from peak to peak,

Più felice sarei, dolce mia greggia,
Più felice sarei, candida luna.
O forse erra dal vero,
Mirando all'altrui sorte, il mio pensiero:
Forse in qual forma, in quale
Stato che sia, dentro covile o cuna,
È funesto a chi nasce il dì natale.

Should I be happier then, my gentle flock?
Should I be happier, O you pale Moon?
Or are my thoughts astray,
Thus contemplating alien destinies?
Perhaps whatever rank or form we take,
In the child's cradle or beast's couching-place,
The day of birth, for each that's born, is dark.

Between 22 October 1829 and 9 April 1830

A se stesso

Or poserai per sempre,
Stanco mio cor. Perì l'inganno estremo,
Ch'eterno io mi credei. Perì. Ben sento,
In noi di cari inganni,
Non che la speme, il desiderio è spento.
Posa per sempre. Assai
Palpitasti. Non val cosa nessuna
I moti tuoi, nè di sospiri è degna
La terra. Amaro e noia
La vita, altro mai nulla; e fango è il mondo.
T'acqueta omai. Dispera
L'ultima volta. Al gener nostro il fato
Non donò che il morire. Omai disprezza
Te, la natura, il brutto
Poter che, ascoso, a comun danno impera,
E l'infinita vanità del tutto.

To Himself

Now be for ever still,
Weary my heart. For the last cheat is dead,
I thought eternal. Dead. For us, I know
Not only the dear hope
Of being deluded gone, but the desire.
Rest still for ever. You
Have beaten long enough. And to no purpose
Were all your stirrings; earth not worth your sighs.
Boredom and bitterness
Is life; and the rest, nothing; the world is dirt.
Lie quiet now. Despair
For the last time. Fate granted to our kind
Only to die. And now you may despise
Yourself, nature, the brute
Power which, hidden, ordains the common doom,
And all the immeasurable emptiness of things.

Early 1833

Sopra il ritratto di una bella donna

scolpito nel monumento sepolcrale della medesima

Tal fosti: or qui sotterra
Polve e scheletro sei. Su l'ossa e il fango
Immobilmente collocato invano,
Muto, mirando dell'etadi il volo,
Sta, di memoria solo
E di dolor custode, il simulacro
Della scorsa beltà. Quel dolce sguardo,
Che tremar fe, se, come or sembra, immoto
In altrui s'affisò; quel labbro, ond'alto
Par, come d'urna piena,
Traboccare il piacer; quel collo, cinto
Già di desio; quell'amorosa mano,
Che spesso, ove fu porta,
Sentì gelida far la man che strinse;
E il seno, onde la gente
Visibilmente di pallor si tinse,
Furo alcun tempo: or fango
Ed ossa sei: la vista
Vituperosa e trista un sasso asconde.

Così riduce il fato
Qual sembianza fra noi parve più viva
Immagine del ciel. Misterio eterno
Dell'esser nostro. Oggi d'eccelsi, immensi
Pensieri e sensi inenarrabil fonte,
Beltà grandeggia, e pare,
Quale splendor vibrato
Da natura immortal su queste arene,

On the Portrait of a Beautiful Lady

Carved on her Sepulchral Monument

Even so you must have been;
Who now are only dust and skeleton
Under the ground, while motionless, above
The bones and dirt, is set this empty image
Of all your ravished beauty—
Sole warden now of grief and memory—
That dumbly gazes on the flying years.
The look which made men tremble, being fixed
Upon them steadfastly (as now it seems);
The curving lip, that was
A vessel flowing over with delight;
The throat girt round about once with desire;
The hand, which felt turn cold,
So often, that which it reached forth to hold;
The breast which visibly
Made men turn pale—all these things once were here;
But now you are no more than dirt and bones,
And now a thing of stone
Must hide the sad, malignant spectacle.

And thus does Fate subdue
The likeness which among us seems to be
The heavens' liveliest image. Everlasting
Mystery of our being. Today, on high,
Spring of unerring feelings and vast thoughts,
Beauty mounts up, and seems
A fitful splendour cast
Upon these sands from an undying nature,

Di sovrumani fati,
Di fortunati regni e d'aurei mondi
Segno e sicura spene
Dare al mortale stato:
Diman, per lieve forza,
Sozzo a vedere, abominoso, abbietto
Divien quel che fu dianzi
Quasi angelico aspetto,
E dalle menti insieme
Quel che da lui moveva
Ammirabil concetto, si dilegua.

Desiderii infiniti
E visioni altere
Crea nel vago pensiere,
Per natural virtù, dotto concento;
Onde per mar delizioso, arcano
Erra lo spirto umano,
Quasi come a diporto
Ardito notator per l'Oceano:
Ma se un discorde accento
Fere l'orecchio, in nulla
Torna quel paradiso in un momento.

Natura umana, or come,
Se frale in tutto e vile,
Se polve ed ombra sei, tant'alto senti?
Se in parte anco gentile,
Come i più degni tuoi moti e pensieri
Son così di leggeri
Da sì basse cagioni e desti e spenti?

Giving our mortal state
Earnest of more than human destinies,
And of the fortunate realms
And golden worlds beyond;
Tomorrow, at a touch,
Is all cast down, abominable, and foul
To look upon, what once
Possessed an angel's brightness,
And that which in our minds
Had moved us on to frame
Such wonderful conceits, dissolved away.

Learnèd consort of sounds,
By virtue of their being,
Creates for truant thought
High visions and desirings infinite;
Mysterious, the spirit of man may thus
Wander delightful seas,
As a keen swimmer goes
Among the ocean waves in his disport;
But let one false note strike
Upon the listening ear—
That moment, Paradise is turned to naught.

If, Human Nature, then,
In all things fallible
You are but dust and shade, whence these high feel-
    ings?
In any part if noble,
How is it that your worthiest thoughts and passions
Can be so lightly stirred
And roused and quenched even by such base occasions?

Between autumn 1833 and summer 1835

La ginestra

o il fiori del deserto

Καὶ ἠγάπησαν οἱ ἄνθρωποι μᾶλλον τὸ σκότος ἢ τὸ φῶς.
E gli uomini vollero piuttosto le tenebre che la luce.

GIOVANNI, III, 19

Qui su l'arida schiena
Del formidabil monte
Sterminator Vesevo,
La qual null'altro allegra arbor nè fiore,
Tuoi cespi solitari intorno spargi,
Odorata ginestra,
Contenta dei deserti. Anco ti vidi
De' tuoi steli abbellir l'erme contrade
Che cingon la cittade
La qual fu donna de' mortali un tempo,
E del perduto impero
Par che col grave e taciturno aspetto
Faccian fede a ricordo al passeggero.
Or ti riveggo in questo suol, di tristi
Lochi e dal mondo abbandonati amante,
E d'afflitte fortune ognor compagna.
Questi campi cosparsi
Di ceneri infeconde, e ricoperti
Dell'impietrata lava,
Che sotto i passi al peregrin risona;
Dove s'annida e si contorce al sole
La serpe, e dove al noto
Cavernoso covil torna il coniglio;
Fur liete ville e colti,
E biondeggiàr di spiche, e risonaro
Di muggito d'armenti;
Fur giardini e palagi,

The Broom

or, the Flower of the Desert

Καὶ ἠγάπησαν οἱ ἄνθρωποι μᾶλλον τὸ σκότος ἢ τὸ φῶς.
And men loved darkness rather than light—

John iii. 19

Upon the arid shoulder
Of this most terrible mountain,
Vesuvius the destroyer,
Graced by no other tree or flowering plant,
You scatter here your solitary shrubs,
O fragrant-blossoming broom,
Contented with the deserts. So have I seen
Your shoots make beautiful that lonely land
Which girds about the city
Who once had been the mistress of the world,
And to the wayfarer,
Even by her grave and ever-silent aspect,
Gives testimony of an empire lost.
I meet you here once more, O you the lover
Of all sad places and deserted worlds,
The constant comrade of afflicted fortune.
Among these fields, now strewn
With barren cinders only, covered up
By lava turned to stone
That rings beneath the passing traveller's feet;
Where the snake nestles, coiled in the hot sun,
Or under the south wind
The rabbit seeks again his scooped-out burrow,
Were farmsteads and tilled glebe,
And yellowing blades of wheat, and here the sound
Of lowing herds of cattle,
Gardens and palaces,

Agli ozi de' potenti
Gradito ospizio; e fur città famose
Che coi torrenti suoi l'altero monte
Dall'ignea bocca fulminando oppresse
Con gli abitanti insieme. Or tutto intorno
Una ruina involve,
Dove tu siedi, o fior gentile, e quasi
I danni altrui commiserando, al cielo
Di dolcissimo odor mandi un profumo,
Che il deserto consola. A queste piagge
Venga colui che d'esaltar con lode
Il nostro stato ha in uso, e vegga quanto
È il gener nostro in cura
All'amante natura. E la possanza
Qui con giusta misura
Anco estimar potrà dell'uman seme,
Cui la dura nutrice, ov'ei men teme,
Con lieve moto in un momento annulla
In parte, e può con moti
Poco men lievi ancor subitamente
Annichilare in tutto.
Dipinte in queste rive
Son dell'umana gente
Le magnifiche sorti e progressive.

Qui mira e qui ti specchia,
Secol superbo e sciocco,
Che il calle insino allora
Dal risorto pensier segnato innanti
Abbandonasti, e volti addietro i passi,
Del ritornar ti vanti,
E procedere il chiami.
Al tuo pargoleggiar gl'ingegni tutti,
Di cui lor sorte rea padre ti fece,
Vanno adulando, ancora
Ch'a ludibrio talora
T'abbian fra se. Non io

Pleasant retreats for leisure
Of great patricians, and here were famous cities
Which the huge mountain, from its fiery mouth
Pouring forth streams of flame, has overwhelmed
With those that dwelt in them. Now all around,
One single ruin spreads,
Wherein you take your root, O courteous flower,
As if in pity of the doom of others,
And cast a pleasant fragrance to the skies,
Making the desert glad. Now let him come
And view these slopes, whose wont it is to flatter
Our mortal state; here he may gaze and see
How loving Nature cares
For our poor human race, and learn to value
At a just estimate the strength of man,
Whom the harsh Nurse, even when he fears it least,
With a slight motion can in part destroy,
And may, with one no less
Slight than the last, even now and with no warning
Wholly annihilate.
Graven upon these cliffs
Is that *magnificent*
Progressive destiny of Humankind.

Here gaze, and see your image,
O proud and foolish century,
You who have gone astray
And left the path by reawakening thought
Marked out for you till now, and turning back,
Even of your regress boast,
Proclaiming it advance.
All those fine wits their evil fate has made
You father forth, with flattery receive
Your childish words, although
Deep in their hearts at times
They mock at you. But I

Con tal vergogna scenderò sotterra;
Ma il disprezzo piuttosto che si serra
Di te nel petto mio,
Mostrato avrò quanto si possa aperto:
Ben ch'io sappia che obblio
Preme chi troppo all'età propria increbbe.
Di questo mal, che teco
Mi fia comune, assai finor mi rido.
Libertà vai sognando, e servo a un tempo
Vuoi di novo il pensiero,
Sol per cui risorgemmo
Della barbarie in parte, e per cui solo
Si cresce in civiltà, che sola in meglio
Guida i pubblici fati.
Così ti spiacque il vero
Dell'aspra sorte e del depresso loco
Che natura ci diè. Per questo il tergo
Vigliaccamente rivolgesti al lume
Che il fe palese: e, fuggitivo, appeli
Vil chi lui segue, e solo
Magnanimo colui
Che se schernendo o gli altri, astuto o folle,
Fin sopra gli astri il mortal grado estolle.

Uom di povero stato e membra inferme
Che sia dell'alma generoso ed alto,
Non chiama se nè stima
Ricco d'or nè gagliardo,
E di splendida vita o di valente
Persona infra la gente
Non fa risibil mostra;
Ma se di forza e di tesor mendico
Lascia parer senza vergogna, e noma
Parlando, apertamente, e di sue cose
Fa stima al vero uguale.
Magnanimo animale
Non credo io già, ma stolto,

Would not go to the grave bearing such shame,
Though easily I might
Vie with the rest to imitate their ravings
And make my song acceptable to you;
Rather would I reveal the deep contempt
That lies locked in my breast,
And show it openly, while still I may;
Although I know oblivion
Lies heavy on whom displeases his own age.
But I have learned to laugh
At that bad fate we both will share together.
You dream of liberty, the while you forge
New bonds for thought—through which
Alone man rose, in part,
From barbarism, whence only civil life
Has grown, and we may guide the common-wealth
To better things. And thus
The truth displeased you, telling
Of that low station and harsh destiny
Nature has given us. So, like a coward
You turned your back upon the light, which showed
This truth to you, and fleeing it, called base
Those who still followed it; and he
Alone was great of soul who, knave or madman,
Could fool himself or others, and would raise
The state of mortal men above the stars.

A man of poor estate, and weak in body,
Being of a high nobility of soul,
Supposes not, nor claims
That he is rich or handsome,
Nor makes himself a laughing-stock for men
By show of splendid living,
Or valour in his person;
But without shame allows it to appear
In strength and wealth he is a beggar still,

Quel che nato a perir, nutrito in pene,
Dice, a goder son fatto,
E di fetido orgoglio
Empie le carte, eccelsi fati e nove
Felicità, quali il ciel tutto ignora,
Non pur quest'orbe, promettendo in terra
A popoli che un'onda
Di mar commosso, un fiato
D'aura maligna, un sotterraneo crollo
Distrugge sì, che avanza
A gran pena di lor la rimembranza.
Nobil natura è quella
Che a sollevar s'ardisce
Gli occhi mortali incontra
Al comun fato, e che con franca lingua,
Nulla al ver detraendo,
Confessa il mal che ci fu dato in sorte,
E il basso stato e frale;
Quella che grande e forte
Mostra se nel soffrir, nè gli odii e l'ire
Fraterne, ancor più gravi
D'ogni altro danno, accresce
Alle miserie sue, l'uomo incolpando
Del suo dolor, ma dà la colpa a quella
Che veramente è rea, che de' mortali
Madre è di parto e di voler matrigna.
Costei chiama inimica; e incontro a questa
Congiunta esser pensando,
Siccome è il vero, ed ordinata in pria
L'umana compagnia,
Tutti fra se confederati estima
Gli uomini, e tutti abbraccia
Con vero amor, porgendo
Valida e pronta ed aspettando aita
Negli alterni perigli e nelle angosce

Speaks openly of this, rates his condition
According to the truth.
Nor do I think that creature
Of a high mind, but foolish,
Who, born to perish, and reared up in pain,
Says: 'I was made for joy',
And with his festering pride
Covers whole pages, promising on earth
High destinies and new felicity
Which Heaven knows nothing of, much less this earth,
To a people whom one wave
From a troubled sea, one breath
Of poisoned air, one tremor underground
Might utterly destroy
That scarce the memory remained of them.
But noble of soul is he
Who burns to lift his eyes
Against the common doom,
And with free tongue, not docking any truth,
Admits the weak, low state,
The evil lot assigned to us by fate;
He who in suffering,
Shows himself great and strong
And will not add fraternal wrath and hatred—
The worst of ills—to all
His other miseries
By blaming man for his unhappiness,
But lays the fault on her who is indeed
The guilty one, the Power who is our mother
In that she brought us forth, step-mother in will.
He calls her enemy, and thus, believing—
As is indeed the truth—
The human race was from the first conjoined
And ranked against the foe,
He takes all men as his confederates,
Embraces all men with a general love

Della guerra comune. Ed alle offese
Dell'uomo armar la destra, e laccio porre
Al vicino ed inciampo,
Stolto crede così qual fora in campo
Cinto d'oste contraria, in sul più vivo
Incalzar degli assalti,
Gl'inimici obbliando, acerbe gare
Imprender con gli amici,
E sparger fuga e fulminar col brando
Infra i propri guerrieri.
Così fatti pensieri
Quando fien, come fur, palesi al volgo,
E quell'orror che primo
Contra l'empia natura
Strinse i mortali in social catena,
Fia ricondotto in parte
Da verace saper, l'onesto e il retto
Conversar cittadino,
E giustizia e pietade, altra radice
Avranno allor che non superbe fole,
Ove fondata probità del volgo
Così star suole in piede
Quale star può quel ch'ha in error la sede.

   Sovente in queste rive,
Che, desolate, a bruno
Veste il flutto indurato, e par che ondeggi,
Seggo la notte; e su la mesta landa
In purissimo azzurro
Veggo dall'alto fiammeggiar le stelle,
Cui di lontan fa specchio
Il mare, e tutto di scintille in giro
Per lo vòto seren brillare il mondo.
E poi che gli occhi a quelle luci appunto,
Ch'a lor sembrano un punto,

Which is sincere; he offers,
And looks for prompt and valiant aid from them
Amid the anguish and recurring dangers
Of this their common war. But against man
To take up arms, or seek to lay a snare
To cause his neighbour stumble,
Seems mad to him, as if one in the camp
Hemmed in by enemies, beneath the threat
Of their most keen assault,
Forgot the foe, and stirred up bitter strife
Among the allied ranks,
And scattered flight and tumult with his sword
Through his own warriors.
When thoughts like these again
Shall be revealed, as once, unto the crowd,
That horror, which at first
Bound men in fellowship,
Together linked against an evil Nature,
Shall be in part restored
By knowledge of the truth; honour, right-dealing
In civil intercourse,
Justice and piety shall find a different soil
Than those proud follies, founded upon which
The probity of the mob
Stands firm as all things else rooted in error.

By these deserted banks,
On which the hardened flood
Casts a dark cloak, and still seems moving waves,
Often I sit by night and mark on high
In heaven's purest blue,
The stars burning above this mournful plain,
And where the far-off sea
Becomes their mirror, and the whole world ablaze
With glittering sparks circling the empty sky.
And when I fix my eyes upon those lights,
Which seem to them mere points,

E sono immense, in guisa
Che un punto a petto a lor son terra e mare
Veracemente; a cui
L'uomo non pur, ma questo
Globo ove l'uomo è nulla,
Sconosciuto è del tutto; e quando miro
Quegli ancor più senz'alcun fin remoti
Nodi quasi di stelle,
Ch'a noi paion qual nebbia, a cui non l'uomo
E non la terra sol, ma tutte in uno,
Del numero infinite e della mole,
Con l'aureo sole insiem, le nostre stelle
O sono ignote, o così paion come
Essi alla terra, un punto
Di luce nebulosa; al pensier mio
Che sembri allora, o prole
Dell'uomo? E rimenbrando
Il tuo stato quaggiù, di cui fa segno
Il suol ch'io premo; e poi dall'altra parte,
Che te signora e fine
Credi tu data al Tutto, e quante volte
Favoleggiar ti piacque, in questo oscuro
Granel di sabbia, il qual di terra ha nome,
Per tua cagion, dell'universe cose
Scender gli autori, e conversar sovente
Co' tuoi piacevolmente, e che i derisi
Sogni rinnovellando, ai saggi insulta
Fin la presente età, che in conoscenza
Ed in civil costume
Sembra tutte avanzar; qual moto allora,
Mortal prole infelice, o qual pensiero
Verso te finalmente il cor m'assale?
Non so se il riso o la pietà prevale.

Come d'arbor cadendo un picciol pomo,
Cui là nel tardo autunno
Maturità senz'altra forza atterra,

Yet are so vast that all
The earth and sea compared with them are truly
Only a point; to which
Not only man, but this
Globe, wherein man is nothing,
Is utterly unknown; and when I see—
Beyond them infinitely more remote—
Those clustering knots of stars
Which look to us like clouds, where are unknown
Not only man and earth, but all together,
So infinite in number and in mass,
The golden sun among the rest, our stars,
Or seeming even as themselves appear
To us on earth—a point
Of nebulous light; then to my questing thought
What is it you appear
O son of man? Remembering
Your state below, of which the soil I tread
Bears testimony still, and yet that you
Think lordship and a purpose
Assigned you by the Whole; how many times
You have been pleased to say on this obscure
Grainlet of sand, which bears the name of earth,
The authors of the universal cause
Came down, on your account, often conversing
At pleasure with your race, and how this age,
Which seems in knowledge and in civil arts
The most advanced, heaps insult on the wise,
Renewing once again
These long-derided dreams; what feeling then,
Unhappy children of mortality,
What thought of you at last my heart assails?
I cannot say if pity or scorn prevails.

As a small apple falling from the tree,
Which late in autumn-time
Its ripeness and no other force impels,

D'un popol di formiche i dolci alberghi,
Cavati in molle gleba
Con gran lavoro, e l'opre
E le ricchezze che adunate a prova
Con lungo affaticar l'assidua gente
Avea provvidamente al tempo estivo,
Schiaccia, diserta e copre
In un punto; così d'alto piombando,
Dall'utero tonante
Scagliata al ciel profondo,
Di ceneri e di pomici e di sassi
Notte e ruina, infusa
Di bollenti ruscelli,
O pel montano fianco
Furiosa tra l'erba
Di liquefatti massi
E di metalli e d'infocata arena
Scendendo immensa piena,
Le cittadi che il mar là su l'estremo
Lido aspergea, confuse
E infranse e ricoperse
In pochi istanti: onde su quelle or pasce
La capra, e città nove
Sorgon dall'altra banda, a cui sgabello
Son le sepolte, e le prostrate mura
L'arduo monte al suo piè quasi calpesta.
Non ha natura al seme
Dell'uom più stima o cura
Che alla formica: e se più rara in quello
Che nell'altra è la strage,
Non avvien ciò d'altronde
Fuor che l'uom sue prosapie ha men feconde.

Ben mille ed ottocento
Anni varcàr poi che spariro, oppressi
Dall'ignea forza, i popolati seggi,
E il villanello intento

Crushes the loved homes of a tribe of ants,
Tunnelled in the soft loam
With infinite toil, their works,
And all their wealth, which, jealously collecting,
That busy race had garnered with long care
And patient forethought through the summer season—
Burying and laying waste,
All in a moment; so, falling from on high,
Hurled through the utmost heaven,
A cloud of cinders, pumice-stone, and rocks,
Darkness and ruin, mingled
With boiling streams of lava,
Or down the mountain side,
Raging across the fields,
All in a molten mass
Of red-hot sand and metals mixed together,
A mighty flood swept down,
And overwhelmed, destroyed, and covered up
Those cities which the sea
Washed on the farther shore,
In a few moments; whence above them now
Browses the goat, new towns
Rise in their stead, whose seat is still upon
The sepulchres of those, while the steep mountain
Seems spurning with its foot their prostrate walls.
Nature has no more care
Or value for man's need
Than for the ant's; and if disaster falls
More rarely on the former
No other cause can be
Than when he breeds, man's less fertility.

Full eighteen hundred years
Have passed away, since vanished, overwhelmed
By the force of fire, these peopled seats of men:
And the poor husbandman

Ai vigneti, che a stento in questi campi
Nutre la morta zolla e incenerita,
Ancor leva lo sguardo
Sospettoso alla vetta
Fatal, che nulla mai fatta più mite
Ancor siede tremenda, ancor minaccia
A lui strage ed ai figli ed agli averi
Lor poverelli. E spesso
Il meschino in sul tetto
Dell'ostel villereccio, alla vagante
Aura giacendo tutta notte insonne
E balzando più volte, esplora il corso
Del temuto bollor, che si riversa
Dall'inesausto grembo
Su l'arenoso dorso, a cui riluce
Di Capri la marina
E di Napoli il porto e Mergellina.
E se appressar lo vede, o se nel cupo
Del domestico pozzo ode mai l'acqua
Fervendo gorgogliar, desta i figliuoli,
Desta la moglie in fretta, e via, con quanto
Di lor cose rapir posson, fuggendo,
Vede lontan l'usato
Suo nido, e il picciol campo,
Che gli fu dalla fame unico schermo,
Preda al flutto rovente,
Che crepitando giunge, e inesorato
Durabilmente sovra quei si spiega.
Torna al celeste raggio
Dopo l'antica obblivion l'estinta
Pompei, come sepolto
Scheletro, cui di terra
Avarizia o pietà rende all'aperto;
E dal deserto foro
Diritto infra le file
Dei mozzi colonnati il peregrino
Lunge contempla il bipartito giogo

Tending his vines, whom scarce the scorched, dead soil
Upon these plains affords a livelihood,
Lifts yet suspicious glances
Towards the fatal summit,
Which, now become no milder than before,
Still full of terror stands, still threatening
Disaster for himself, his sons, and their
Impoverished fields. And often
The wretch, upon the roof
Of his poor cottage, lying
Sleepless all night beneath the wandering air,
Time upon time starts up, to mark the flow
Of that dread simmering, which still pours out
From the unexhausted womb
Over the sandy ridge, and shines upon
The shores about Capri,
And Mergellina, and the Bay of Naples.
And if he sees it coming near, or deep
In his domestic well he hears the water
Gurgling and boiling, he awakes his children,
In haste awakes his wife, and snatching up
Whatever they can seize, they go, and fleeing,
See, far behind, their home,
Their little field, which was
The sole protection they possessed from famine,
Prey to the burning flood,
Which hissing, overtakes it, then unappeased,
Spreads ever-during over all they had.
Returns to light of day,
Which old oblivion had quenched for her,
Pompeii, a skeleton,
Out of the grave by greed or piety
Dragged forth into the open;
From her deserted forum
Upright among the ranks
Of broken colonnades, the traveller
May gaze long on the forked peak of the mountain,

E la cresta fumante,
Che alla sparsa ruina ancor minaccia.
E nell'orror della secreta notte
Per li vacui teatri,
Per li templi deformi e per le rotte
Case, ove i parti il pipistrello asconde,
Come sinistra face
Che per vòti palagi atra s'aggiri,
Corre il baglior della funerea lava,
Che di lontan per l'ombre
Rosseggia e i lochi intorno intorno tinge.
Così, dell'uomo ignara e dell'etadi
Ch'ei chiama antiche, e del seguir che fanno
Dopo gli avi i nepoti,
Sta natura ognor verde, anzi procede
Per sì lungo cammino
Che sembra star. Caggiono i regni intanto,
Passan genti e linguaggi: ella nol vede:
E l'uom d'eternità s'arroga il vanto.

E tu, lenta ginestra,
Che di selve odorate
Queste campagne dispogliate adorni,
Anche tu presto alla crudel possanza
Soccomberai del sotterraneo foco,
Che ritornando al loco
Già noto, stenderà l'avaro lembo
Su tue molli foreste. E piegherai
Sotto il fascio mortal non renitente
Il tuo capo innocente:
Ma non piegato insino allora indarno
Codardamente supplicando innanzi
Al futuro oppressor; ma non eretto
Con forsennato orgoglio inver le stelle,
Nè sul deserto, dove
E la sede e i natali
Non per voler ma per fortuna avesti;

And on its smoking crest,
Which threatens still the ruins scattered round,
And in the horror of the secret night,
Among the empty theatres,
Temples defaced, and shattered dwelling-houses,
Where now the bat conceals its progeny,
Like an ill-omened torch
Which darkly flickers through deserted halls,
Still runs the glimmer of the deadly lava,
Which far-off through the shadows
Glows red, and tinges everything around.
Even so, knowing naught of man, or of the ages
Which he calls ancient, or the long succession
Of various generations,
Nature stays ever fresh, or rather she
Travels so long a course,
That still she seems to stay. While empires fall,
While tongues and peoples pass, nothing she sees;
And man presumes to boast eternity.

And you, O gentle broom,
Who with your fragrant thickets
Make beautiful this spoiled and wasted land,
You, too, must shortly fall beneath the cruel
Force of the subterranean fire, returning
To this, its wonted place,
Which soon shall stretch its greedy fringe above
Your tender shrubs. You then
Will bend your harmless head, not obstinate
Beneath the rod of fate;
Nor yet till then in vain and cowardly fashion
Bow down to the oppressor still to come;
Nor upright in mad pride against the stars;
Amid the desert, where
You find your home and birthplace,
Allotted you by fortune, not your will;

Ma più saggia, ma tanto
Meno inferma dell'uom, quanto le frali
Tue stirpi non credesti
O dal fato o da te fatte immortali.

But wiser still, and less
Infirm in this than man, you do not think
Your feeble stock immortal,
Made so by destiny or by yourself.

After April 1836

Il tramonto della luna

Quale in notte solinga,
Sovra campagne inargentate ed acque,
Là 've zefiro aleggia,
E mille vaghi aspetti
E ingannevoli obbietti
Fingon l'ombre lontane
Infra l'onde tranquille
E rami e siepi e collinette e ville;
Giunta al confin del cielo,
Dietro Apennino od Alpe, o del Tirreno
Nell'infinito seno
Scende la luna; e si scolora il mondo;
Spariscon l'ombre, ed una
Oscurità la valle e il monte imbruna;
Orba la notte resta,
E cantando, con mesta melodia,
L'estremo albor della fuggente luce,
Che dianzi gli fu duce,
Saluta il carrettier dalla sua via;

Tal si dilegua, e tale
Lascia l'età mortale
La giovinezza. In fuga
Van l'ombre e le sembianze
Dei dilettosi inganni; e vengon meno
Le lontane speranze,
Ove s'appoggia la mortal natura.
Abbandonata, oscura
Resta la vita. In lei porgendo il guardo,
Cerca il confuso viatore invano
Del cammin lungo che avanzar si sente
Meta o ragione; e vede
Che a se l'umana sede,
Esso a lei veramente è fatto estrano.

The Setting of the Moon

As in the lonely night,
Above the waters and the silvered plains,
Where fluttering breezes move,
And distant shadows feign
A thousand images,
Illusory and fair,
Among the quiet waves,
Hedgerows, and trees, and hills, and villages—
Having reached the sky's confine,
Past Apennine, or Alp, or in the Tyrrhene
Sea's unsounded bosom,
The moon descends, and all the world grows dim,
The shadows disappear,
And one same darkness blots out vale and mountain.
While night remains, bereaved,
And singing, with a mournful melody,
The wagoner hails the last gleam of that light
Which now is vanishing
And on his journey still had been his guide;

Thus disappears, even so
From human life must go,
The season of youth. Away
Depart the shadowy forms
And beautiful illusions; less now seem
Those far-off hopes on which
Our suffering mortal nature learned to lean.
Desolate, full of darkness,
Our life remains. And gazing round on it,
Bewildered, vainly would the traveller trace
On the long road which lies before him yet
Reason or bourn; he finds
That he has now become
A stranger here where dwells the human race.

Troppo felice e lieta
Nostra misera sorte
Parve lassù, se il giovanile stato,
Dove ogni ben di mille pene è frutto,
Durasse tutto della vita il corso.
Troppo mite decreto
Quel che sentenzia ogni animale a morte,
S'anco mezza la via
Lor non si desse in pria
Della terribil morte assai più dura.
D'intelletti immortali
Degno trovato, estremo
Di tutti i mali, ritrovàr gli eterni
La vecchiezza, ove fosse
Incolume il desio, la speme estinta,
Secche le fonti del piacer, le pene
Maggiori sempre, e non più dato il bene.

Voi, collinette e piagge,
Caduto lo splendor che all'occidente
Inargentava della notte il velo,
Orfane ancor gran tempo
Non resterete; che dall'altra parte
Tosto vedrete il cielo
Imbiancar novamente, e sorger l'alba:
Alla qual poscia seguitando il sole,
E folgorando intorno
Con sue fiamme possenti,
Di lucidi torrenti
Inonderà con voi gli eterei campi.
Ma la vita mortal, poi che la bella
Giovinezza sparì, non si colora
D'altra luce giammai, nè d'altra aurora.
Vedova è insino al fine; ed alla notte
Che l'altre etadi oscura,
Segno poser gli Dei la sepoltura.

Too sweet, too full of joy,
Had seemed our mortal state
To those above, if our first youthful time,
Whose every good is bred from thousand pains,
Had lasted out the whole course of our life.
Too mild were that decree
Which sentences to death each living thing,
Did not the path to it,
Though half completed yet,
First show itself more harsh than terrible death.
The Eternal Ones devised
The last of all our ills,
Worthy invention of immortal minds—
Old age, where still desire
Survives, with hope extinct,
When pleasure's founts run dry, and every pain
Grows more and more, while good comes not again.

You, banks and little hills,
Though hidden be the light which from the west
Had silvered all the mantle of the night,
Orphaned you shall not long
Remain, for very soon you may discern
Once more the eastern skies
Grow pale with morning, till the dawn arise,
Whom the sun follows after, and comes forth,
Blazing and bright again,
And with his ardent beams,
His shining streams of light,
Floods all your summits and the ethereal plain.
But mortal life, when the fair time of youth
Has vanished, never then grows bright again
With any radiance more, or second dawn.
Widowed until the end; and in the night,
Where through the dark we come,
The gods have set a sign for us, the tomb.

Completed 14 June 1837

309

SELECT BIBLIOGRAPHY

The volumes listed below are only a very small selection of indispensable works. For a full bibliography, both of Leopardi's own works (in manuscript and print) and of all that has been written about him, the reader is referred to:

Bibliografia Leopardiana

> Vol. I (up to 1898) by G. Mazzatinti and M. Menghini. Florence, 1898.
>
> Vol. II (1898–1930) by Giulio Natali. Florence, Olschki, 1932.
>
> Vol. III (1931–51) by Giulio Natali and C. Musumarra. Florence, Olschki, 1953.
>
> Vol. IV (1952–60) by A. Tortoreto. Florence, Olschki, 1963.

The texts translated in this volume are those in Francesco Flora's editions of Leopardi's *Poesie e Prose* and of the *Zibaldone*, and in Francesco Moroncini's edition of the *Epistolario* (Florence, Le Monnier, 1934–49).

I. WORKS OF LEOPARDI

Le Poesie e le Prose, edited by Francesco Flora, Milan, Mondadori, 1940 (7th ed., 1962). (Vol. I: *Canti, Poesie Varie, Memorie e Disegni letterari*, and *Operette Morali*, with a long and illuminating Introduction and Chronology by Prof. Flora; Vol. II: *Pensieri, Volgarizzamenti, Saggi e Discorsi*, and *Varia*.)

Zibaldone di Pensieri, edited by Francesco Flora. Milan, Mondadori, 1937 (6th ed., 1961) With a full analytical index.

Opere di G.L., edited by Giuseppe De Robertis, Milan–Rome, Rizzoli, 1937–8.

> Vol. I: *Canti, Operette Morali, Pensieri*, etc.
>
> Vol. II: *Scritti vari, Lettere* (selected).
>
> Vol. III: *Zibaldone* (selected).

Epistolario di G.L., edited by Francesco Moroncini, complete edition in 6 vols. with notes and letters from L.'s correspondents, and a 7th vol. (after Prof. Moroncini's death) edited by G. Ferretti. Florence, Le Monnier, 1934–49.

Opere di G.L., critical edition by Francesco Moroncini. A full
critical edition, containing variants to the texts, and
reproductions of Leopardi's autographs, with his own cor-
rections.
Vols. I and II: *I Canti*. Bologna, Capelli, 1927.
Vols. III and IV: *Operette Morali*. Bologna, Capelli, 1928.
Vols. V and VI: *Opere Minori*. Bologna, Capelli, 1931.
Operette Morali di G.L., with Preface and Notes by Giovanni Gentile. Bologna, Zanichelli, 1918.

II. CRITICAL WORKS

Francesco De Sanctis, 'Giacomo Leopardi' in *La Letteratura
Italiana nel Secolo XIX* edited by W. Binni, Bari, Laterza, 1953.
Francesco De Sanctis, *Nuovi Saggi Critici* edited by Luigi Russo.
Bari, Laterza, 1957. (These two volumes contain, between
them, all De Sanctis' most important essays on Leopardi.)
Giosuè Carducci, 'Degli Spiriti e delle Forme nella Poesia di
G.L.' and 'Le Tre Canzoni Patriotiche di G.L. (1898)' in
Opere, Vol. XVI, *Poesia e Storia*. Bologna, Zanichelli, 1903.
Giuseppe De Robertis, *Saggio su Leopardi*. Florence, Vallecchi,
1944.
Benedetto Croce, 'G.L.' in *Poesia e Non-Poesia*. Bari, Laterza,
1942.
Attilio Momigliano, 'Il Carteggio di Leopardi' in *Cinque Saggi*.
Florence, Sansoni, 1945.
Karl Vossler, *Leopardi*, Munich, Musarius Verlag, 1923. (Italian
translation by T. Gnoli: Naples, 1925.)

III. BIOGRAPHIES

G. Chiarini, *Vita di G. Leopardi*. Florence, Barbera, 1905.
G. A. Levi, *Leopardi*. Massa, Principato, 1931.
Giovanni Ferretti, *Vita di G.L.* Bologna, Zanichelli, 1940.
Michele Saponaro, *Leopardi*. Milan, Garzanti, 1941.
A. Zottoli, *Storia di un'anima*. Bari, Laterza, 1927.
Autobiografia di Monaldo Leopardi (the poet's father), ed. by A.
Avoli. Recanati, 1891.

IV. TRANSLATIONS AND CRITICAL WORKS IN FRENCH AND ENGLISH

A. French

Œuvres de Giacomo Leopardi in 'Collection Unesco d'Œuvres Représentatives'. Paris, Del Duca, 1964. This is a complete translation of Leopardi's *Canti*, *Operette Morali*, and *Pensieri*, and a selection from the *Zibaldone* (prose translated by Juliette Bertrand, poems by F. A. Alard, P. H. Jaccottet and G. Nicole), with an Introduction by Giuseppe Ungaretti and a reprint of Sainte-Beuve's essay on Leopardi.

A. Bouché-Lecrecq: *Leopardi, sa vie et ses œuvres*, Paris, 1874.

I. O.

B. English

The early translations from Leopardi's verse, such as those of Frederick Townsend (*Poems of Giacomo Leopardi*, New York and London, 1888), Francis H. Cliffe (*The Poems of Leopardi*, London, 1893), and J. M. Morrison (*The Poems ('Canti') of Leopardi*, London, 1900) unfortunately cannot be recommended either on the score of accuracy or poetic merit. G. L. Bickersteth's edition of *The Poems of Leopardi* (Cambridge, 1923) contains a complete verse translation in the metres of the original, together with very full notes and commentary to which I must express my debt. The translations, however, employ an elaborate poetic diction which seems to me to veil rather than to reveal the poetic qualities of the original. R. C. Trevelyan's *Translations From Leopardi* (Cambridge, 1944) are reliable, but seem to me to be metrically too free and to err on the side of the prosaic. The versions of Robert Lowell in *Imitations* (1962) are poetic re-creations rather than accurate versions, and the same must be said of Ezra Pound's *Her Monument, The Image Cut Thereon* in *Personae*.

The *Operette Morali* have been translated by James Thomson, *Essays, Dialogues and Thoughts of Giac. Leopardi* (London, 1905), Charles Edwardes, *Essays and Dialogues of Giacomo Leopardi* (London, 1882), and Major-General Patrick Maxwell, *Essays, Dialogues and Thoughts of Count Giac. Leopardi* (Glasgow, 1905). The first of these is the most noteworthy.

The fullest biographical and critical studies are those of Iris Origo, *Leopardi: a Study in Solitude* (London, 1953) and J. H. Whitfield, *Giacomo Leopardi* (Oxford, 1954).

J. H.-S.